THE COMPANION GUIDE TO

*South-West France*

*Bordeaux and the Dordogne*

# THE COMPANION GUIDES

GENERAL EDITOR: VINCENT CRONIN

*It is the aim of these guides to provide a Companion,
in the person of the author, who knows intimately
the places and people of whom he writes, and is able to
communicate this knowledge and affection to his readers.
It is hoped that the text and pictures will aid them
in their preparations and in their travels, and will
help them to remember on their return.*

THE GREEK ISLANDS · SOUTHERN GREECE · PARIS
THE SOUTH OF FRANCE · ROME · VENICE · LONDON
FLORENCE · JUGOSLAVIA
THE WEST HIGHLANDS OF SCOTLAND · UMBRIA
SOUTHERN ITALY · TUSCANY · EAST ANGLIA
THE SOUTH OF SPAIN · MADRID AND CENTRAL SPAIN
IRELAND · KENT AND SUSSEX · NORTH WALES · BURGUNDY
THE COAST OF NORTH-EAST ENGLAND
THE COAST OF SOUTH-WEST ENGLAND
THE COAST OF SOUTH-EAST ENGLAND
NORTHUMBRIA · DEVON AND CORNWALL

*In Preparation*

MAINLAND GREECE · THE ÎLE DE FRANCE
EDINBURGH AND THE BORDER COUNTRY · SOUTH WALES
TURKEY · THE WELSH MARCHES

Guides to Rome, Venice, Paris, Florence, London, the South of
France and the West Highlands of Scotland are available in
paperback in the Fontana edition

THE COMPANION GUIDE TO

# South-West France

## Bordeaux and the Dordogne

❧

Richard Barber

COLLINS

ST JAMES'S PLACE, LONDON

1977

William Collins Sons & Co Ltd
London · Glasgow · Sydney · Auckland
Toronto · Johannesburg

First published 1977
© Richard Barber 1977

Hardback ISBN 0 00 211149 7
Limpback ISBN 0 00 216773 5

Maps by Constance Deare
Set in Monotype Times
Made and Printed in Great Britain by
William Collins Sons & Co Ltd, Glasgow

# Contents

✤

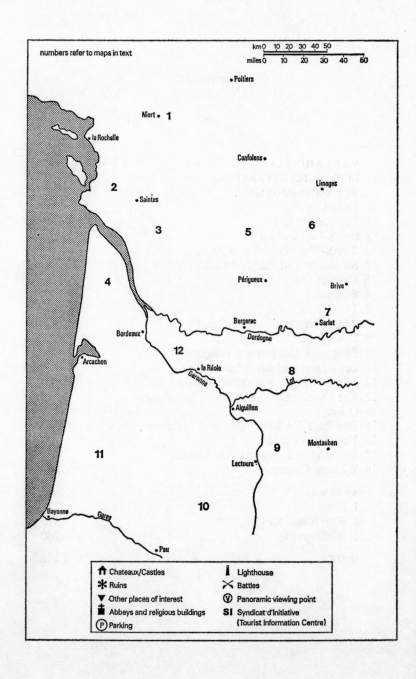

numbers refer to maps in text

| km | 0 | 10 | 20 | 30 | 40 | 50 | |
| miles | 0 | | 10 | 20 | 30 | 40 | 50 |

- Poitiers

Niort • **1**

• la Rochelle

Confolens •

**2**

• Saintes

Limoges •

**3**          **5**          **6**

Périgueux •          Brive •

**7**

Bergerac          • Sarlat

Bordeaux •          Dordogne

**12**

• la Réole          **8**

Garonne          Lot

Arcachon •

Aiguillon •

**9**          Montauban •

**11**          Lectoure •

**10**

Bayonne •          Gaves

• Pau

| ♠ Chateaux/Castles | ⚓ Lighthouse |
| ✳ Ruins | ✕ Battles |
| ▼ Other places of interest | Ⓥ Panoramic viewing point |
| ⛪ Abbeys and religious buildings | **SI** Syndicat d'Initiative |
| Ⓟ Parking | (Tourist Information Centre) |

# Maps and Plans

❧

# Illustrations

.ᴖ

# Acknowledgements

❧

So many people have contributed in various ways
to the making of this guide that it seems invidious
to single out particular names. I should, however,
like to mention Eric Elstob, who first introduced
me to the area; the librarian of the Centre d'Études
Supérieures de Civilisation Mediévale at Poitiers,
M. Georges Pon, who gave me access to the in-
valuable collection of local history material there;
and Norman Scarfe, who most kindly read and
criticised several chapters of the present work in
manuscript during his travels in the area.

I would also like to acknowledge the valuable
help of the map designers, Brian and Constance
Deare; Mrs L. Merrifield, who compiled the index;
Sonia Cole, who corrected the diagram on p. 170
and Pru Harrison, who turned a very difficult
manuscript into an excellent typescript. Finally, for
permission to include three poems from *Medieval
Latin Lyrics* by Helen Waddell my thanks are due
to Constable & Co. Ltd; permission for the
inclusion of the quotation from *Arthur and His
Times* by Jack Lindsay was kindly given by
Frederick Muller Ltd; and the quotation from
'When You are Old' by W. B. Yeats is included by
kind permission of Miss Anne Yeats and The
Macmillan Company of London and Basingstoke.

# Preface

The south-west of France offers as much variety as any ordinary traveller could wish for; its monuments and remains range from darkest pre-history at Les Eyzies to post-war architecture at Royan, its landscapes from the smiling green of the Dordogne valley to the empty expanses of the Landes coast, its cooking from the seafood of the Atlantic to the country produce of the Périgord. But certain characteristics predominate – the countryside and country towns, the castles and churches. The seeker after the baroque or after fashionable cities or resorts must go elsewhere. South-west France has changed relatively little since the end of the Middle Ages: a static population, no great industrial revolution, a pattern of farming that has remained much the same. Even now there is no proper motorway in the area, and only one city of major importance.

Many visitors will be content to enjoy the *douceur de vivre*, the good food and the pleasures of the countryside, without going to a single castle or church. But there is a great deal more. For the English traveller who is interested in the past this is a very special terrain indeed: much of England's history between 1154 and 1453 was determined by what happened in Aquitaine, in the long drawn-out struggle for the remains of the Continental empire created by Henry II. This is the land of Eleanor of Aquitaine, the scene of Richard I's death, of the Black Prince's triumphs and disasters. It is also the landscape in which some of the greatest medieval poetry and architecture was created. Here many of the troubadours lived, and here still stand Romanesque churches with luxuriant carved doorways or simple elegant lines. Like the landscape itself, the art of the region is intimate rather than grandiose, and speaks to us all the more directly for its lack of rhetoric.

These characteristics – medieval history and architecture – are my own particular interests, and I make no apology for including a good deal of medieval history: this is a region where the Middle Ages are still very much in evidence, and the why and wherefore of such things as *bastides* takes us back, if we are to begin to under-

13

stand what we are looking at, straight to the fourteenth century. Beyond the Middle Ages the region has less to offer, but I hope that I have done it justice. Of all the French provinces those of the south-west suffered most from the religious wars of the sixteenth century and from the predominance of Paris from the seventeeth century on. Bordeaux in the late eighteenth century recaptured something of its old prestige and splendour, but otherwise there is little to show. Only a handful of great figures stand out, but as isolated, individual geniuses – Montaigne, La Rochefoucauld, Montesquieu; and in the nineteenth century the *somnolences aquitaines* take over. Only in the past two decades has the economic and social life of the region regained its vigour.

Beyond the history and the monuments, I have tried to outline briefly something of the scenery, which is one of the glories of the region; but I make no pretence to be a word-painter, and scenery is best experienced rather than described. Nor is it the kind of scenery that lends itself easily to photography; so the reader must trust to my signposts and explore for himself.

It is always difficult to set limits for a regional guidebook, and south-west France is no exception: what looks like a neat division on the map always has its flaws in practice. For better or worse, the definition that has emerged takes us from Poitiers to the edge of the Pyrenees (but not into the distinctive Basque country) and from the Atlantic coast to the western edge of the Massif Central, stopping at the foothills of the latter. As to the arrangement of the book, each chapter broadly represents a region with a distinctive character. The chapters are not in any way related to a specific scale of time or distance, if only because I personally find estimates of how long a visit or a journey will take to be misleading; too much depends on the individual and on circumstance. So I have left the traveller to plan his own day's journey, though it may help to point out that each chapter is arranged as a continuous line of travel rather than excursions from one centre. However, as most chapters have one particular town as their central feature, it should not be too difficult to use them as the basis for a series of explorations from a single base. In places, cross-references are given to avoid repeating matters of substance which have been described elsewhere.

As to practical matters, this is not an area easily explored by public transport, unless you have a good deal of time at your disposal. Only the major towns are served by rail and although there are relatively good rural bus services it is a slow way of covering the considerable distances involved. So the traveller is likely to be car-borne, and the following Michelin maps in the yellow 1:200 000 series are therefore essential: 68 (Niort-Chateauroux); 71 (La Rochelle-Bordeaux); 72 (Angoulême-Limoges); 75 (Bordeaux-Tulle); 78 (Bordeaux-Biarritz); 79 (Bordeaux-Montauban); 82 (Pau-Toulouse).

These are vital for navigating country byroads, and also contain a good deal of useful information. Parking in towns is rarely a problem: local tourist offices will explain the 'disque' system, though I have found that foreign numberplates are usually adequate! Roads are generally good, though byroads may have very rough surfaces, and can be steep. If you are going to explore extensively on such roads it is a good idea to have your brake-pads checked before leaving, as such driving conditions soon wear them out. Petrol pumps can be infrequent in remoter parts, such as the Landes and Gers, and a spare can is advisable, as well as the usual kit of touring spares. One other item, if you are going to look at architectural details, is a pair of binoculars: many fine capitals are high up and difficult to make out. Opening hours do change from year to year, and although those given are as accurate as possible, they cannot be guaranteed exact. Churches are often shut from 12.00 until 14.00; out-of-the-way churches may be locked, but I have tried to give directions for finding the key wherever possible.

Hotels and guides to hotels are dealt with in Appendix 2: the red Michelin guide is still probably the best, but I have also suggested some alternatives, depending on your style of travel. France is expensive and a minimum of £10 per head per day should be allowed for two people staying in modest hotels. If single bedrooms or more luxurious accommodation is wanted this should be increased to £15-20.

Finally, when is the best time to visit south-west France? It is difficult to make a definite recommendation. May is ideal in many ways; the weather is often perfect and the countryside at its freshest; but many places, particularly the smaller châteaux, are only open from July to September. July and August are the peak holiday months in France, to an even greater extent than in England: the exodus from the towns begins on 14 July and lasts until the first week of September. The middle to the end of September is perhaps the best moment of all, given good weather; more places are open than in May, and most of the landscape is glorious to look at on a fine early autumn day. That is my own preference – with the trees on the road from Limoges to Périgueux just turning golden in the hazy sunlight, and the mist still lingering by a château-crowned cliff.

# Chapter 1

# Poitiers

꘎

A fourteenth-century Englishman travelling to Aquitaine, whether
as merchant, soldier or royal official, would have gone by sea, at
best a voyage of ten days or so, at worst a nightmare of weeks in
Atlantic storms. Many of the travellers went ashore at the first
piece of land in the Gironde estuary rather than make up-river for
Bordeaux itself: and here at the church of Notre Dame de Fin des
Terres (Our Lady of Land's End) at Soulac, they would give thanks
for their safe arrival. Here too English pilgrims to St James's shrine
at Santiago de Compostela would gather before setting out south
to Spain. But most pilgrims – unlike the traders and royal servants –
would come down the roads of France after the short Channel
crossing, through the French territories where Englishmen could not
normally go (for pilgrims had a kind of diplomatic immunity) and
then into Aquitaine.

Today there is no regular passenger service to Bordeaux by sea,
but it is the main airport of the region, and a convenient point of
arrival if you come by train. The traveller by car will probably find
himself on one of the old pilgrim roads, or their modern equivalents.
From the south of England the easiest route across is by the
Southampton–Cherbourg ferry, and then through Brittany via
Nantes to La Rochelle. From London there is a choice of crossings,
but whether you go by Dover, Folkestone or Newhaven there are
two possible ways south on reaching the French coast. For those
who do not mind heavy traffic on good roads, the choice will be the
A 1 leading into the Paris ring-motorway (the *périphèrique*) and then
south on the A 10 to Tours, a road which will be completed in 1976
and will reach Poitiers in 1977. The more attractive route is the
slower road to Rouen, which then swings in a wide circle down to
Alençon and Le Mans, and so to Tours. From Tours the N 10 goes
straight and level to Poitiers. By either route it is a good day's drive
from the French side of the Channel to Poitiers; and there is much
to tempt the less energetic traveller to linger on the way. An overnight stop will probably be needed, and it is undoubtedly cheaper to

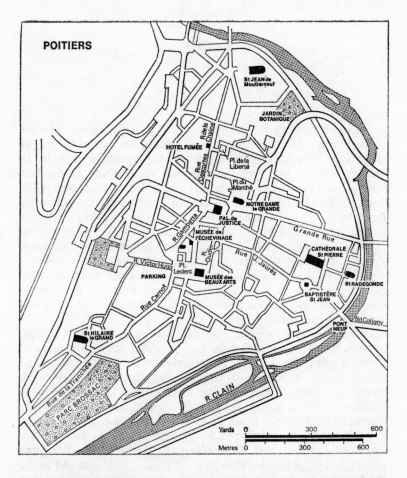

POITIERS

St JEAN de
Moutierneuf

JARDIN
BOTANIQUE

R de la
Chaine

HOTEL FUMÉE

Rue
Descartes

Pl. de la
Liberté

Pl. du
Marché

NOTRE DAME
le GRANDE

PAL. de
JUSTICE

R. Gambetta

MUSÉE de
l'ÉCHEVINAGE

Grande Rue

R. Oudin

Rue J. Jaurès

CATHÉDRALE
St PIERRE

R. Victor Hugo

Pl.
Leclerc

PARKING

MUSÉE des
BEAUX ARTS

BAPTISTÈRE
St JEAN

St RADEGONDE

Rue Carnot

Bd Coligny

PONT
NEUF

St HILAIRE
le GRAND

Rue de la Tranchée

PARC BROSSAC

R. CLAIN

Yards 0     300     600

Metres 0     300     600

stay outside the Paris region, say at least seventy kilometres from Paris, and both cheaper and quieter to turn off the main roads, to find a small country town.

The first route, being largely motorway, avoids the historic centres of Orléans and Tours, and offers only the faceless engineering of the road with occasional glimpses of countryside. The slower route maps out much of the history of English involvement in France. **Rouen** was the ancient capital of Normandy and its dukes: here William the Conqueror planned his invasion of England, and here his

successors ruled until 1204. It was retaken in 1419 by Henry V
after a bitter siege lasting five and a half months, and remained in
English hands for three decades. Here Joan of Arc was burnt in
1431. The road south of Rouen follows the Seine valley and there
is an alternative route, attractive but often very slow, which avoids
Rouen and passes through Les Andelys, a strategic border crossing-
point during the struggle between the Plantagenets and the Capetian
kings of France in the years leading to 1204. Above the town rise
the ruins of Richard I's famous Château Gaillard, the almost impregnable castle which he built to defy all comers, and which was
taken only four years after his death by his enemy Philip Augustus.

Le Mans, with a fine Romanesque and Gothic cathedral, was the
birthplace of Henry II. At the height of his power Henry claimed
overlordship from Scotland almost to the Mediterranean, and he
ruled in Aquitaine in the name of his wife, Eleanor of Aquitaine.
But his last days were overshadowed by the rebellion of Richard the
Lionheart, who with Philip Augustus's help defeated him and forced
him to burn Le Mans to cover his retreat. Henry is said to have cursed
God for the loss of 'the city I loved best in all the world' and to have
threatened to keep his soul from him in revenge. In the museum is a
magnificent twelfth-century enamel plaque of Henry's father,
Geoffrey, who was Count of Anjou and Maine and married Matilda
of England. Even more Angevin history can be included by a detour
to Angers, returning to the main road by Saumur and Chinon, where
Henry II died.

Tours has a fine Gothic cathedral – almost the last outpost of this
style before we enter Romanesque country. During the thirteenth and
fourteenth centuries Northern France was relatively wealthy and
could afford to rebuild its churches in the latest style. The south had
been rich in the eleventh and twelfth centuries but its subsequent
poverty prevented such rebuilding and so preserved many earlier
churches. Equally, the wealthy lords of the fifteenth century built their
châteaux on the Loire, within easy reach of Paris, and the south has
relatively few great châteaux; but it has a host of survivals from the
Middle Ages.

Between Tours and Poitiers stretches a flat plain which gives way,
a few miles north of Poitiers, to the rolling hills which are typical of
Poitou. It was somewhere along this road, the N 10, perhaps near
Moussais-la-Bâtaille, on the left of the road just south of Châtellerault, that two great battles of French history were fought. Somewhere around 'the tenth milestone north of Poitiers' (it may have
been at Vouillé, north-west of Poitiers; there is doubt about the

exact site) the armies of the Frankish ruler Clovis and the Visigoth ruler Alaric fought on 25 June 507. The Franks held north-western France, while the Visigoths ruled most of Spain and the larger part of France south of the Loire. Clovis took advantage of religious divisions in Alaric's domains to launch an attack on him. Alaric was a member of the Arian sect of Christianity while most of his subjects were, like the newly converted Clovis, Catholics. Legend relates how Clovis saw a divine signal, a fiery light in the distance above the church of St Hilaire at Poitiers, and carried the day, killing Alaric with his own hand.

The second battle was also a conflict between north and south. Charles Martel met the Saracen armies on 17 October 733. In the battle which followed (variously called the battle of Tours or Poitiers) the Frankish troops stood 'firm as a wall, inflexible as a block of ice', and the Saracen light cavalry under Abd-er-Rahman were unable to break their line. The fighting lasted some days, and ended only when the Saracen leader was killed. This was the furthest north that the Arabs ever penetrated into Europe, and although it was a daring raid rather than the tide of conquest that Charles Martel turned back, it remains one of the most famous battles of history. It reminds us of the dim but haunting possibility of a Moslem empire in eighth-century France, and of the reality of the Spanish *reconquista*, which was only to achieve its task of driving the Arabs from Europe seven hundred years later. Both battles remind us that Aquitaine was part of the Mediterranean world until the end of the Middle Ages, looking south to Italy and Spain, and that only in the sixteenth century did Paris establish its ascendancy over French cultural life.

Poitiers is an uneasy mixture of the very old and very new France. It could have been a superb example of how to preserve a medieval town and yet provide for modern needs, re-exploring the natural advantages of its island site sloping down to the river Clain which its medieval builders had chosen. Instead, there has been some good preservation work, but alas! as we approach on the N 10, bearing left away from the motorway bypass, there are hideous approaches, a faceless international motel, and a rash of suburbs: even the cliffs to the south of the town are crowned by a ring of modern skyscrapers.

Yet the ancient centre remains relatively unspoilt. From neolithic times there has been a settlement here; and Poitiers first appears in history soon after Caesar's first invasion of Britain, because it was surrendered to him by a friendly chieftain, Duratius, in 51 BC. Its ancient name, Limonum, was changed in the third century to

Pictavis, the name of the tribe who inhabited Poitou before the Roman conquest. Under the Romans it remained a local capital, dominated by Bordeaux. Little is left of the Roman town; some of the results of excavations are collected in the little **Musée de l'Échevinage** (p. 28), though the finest pieces are in the **Musée des Beaux Arts**, housed on the ground floor of the nineteenth-century town hall, which dominates the central square. There is a convenient car park just to the west, so this is a good place to start our visit. The building itself is a not unpleasing piece of nineteenth-century Renaissance, with two massive historical canvases on the main staircase by the Symbolist painter Puvis de Chavannes.

The pride of the Roman collection is the Minerva of Poitiers, which later ages have seen in a symbol of Poitiers as a seat of learning, though its intellectual traditions began after the Romans had left. The sculptures in the first room range from Gallic to Romanesque. Note the Celtic preoccupation with heads: these fine portrait heads belong to a head-cult which included nailing the heads of dead enemies outside their hut doors. A square Etruscan funerary urn depicting the fight of Eteocles and Polynices contrasts with a Romanesque capital showing a dispute and a reconciliation. The stone mason himself puts in an appearance on a capital of *circa* 950 from St Porchaire. There is a splendid elephant on a capital from the Church of Moutierneuf (p. 26). The next room leaps forward in time to the Italian and Dutch primitives, a small collection of sixteenth-century Limoges enamels, and Renaissance fragments from the vanished château of Bonnivet. These portray Lodovico Sforza, Duke of Milan, and a profile of Christ. The third room has some dull 'classical' works, but the last room offers bronzes by the *animalier* sculptors and by Maillol, and a select group of canvases. Gustave Moreau's cartoon for a tapestry, 'The Poet and his Muse', is followed by a small group of impressionist paintings, among them works by Bonnard, Sisley and Boudin.

The rue H. Oudin and rue Jean-Jaurès behind the Hôtel de Ville lead to the **Baptistère Saint-Jean**, one of the earliest Christian buildings in France. It was built in the fourth century AD on the foundations of a Roman building destroyed in the Germanic invasion of 276. In the ritual laid down for baptism at the council of Milan in 313 baptism was to be performed by the bishop, in a building near his cathedral designed for the purpose. As the ritual involved total immersion it is easy to understand why a separate building was needed. The original plan of the baptistery was square, with two little sacristies at the west entrance. A foyer led to the central hall, containing an octagonal pool, or piscina, three feet deep. In this the baptism took place: the bishop poured water over the candidate's head and shoulders, repeating the rite three times. The remains of the original piscina have been uncovered by excavations begun in 1958, as has evidence of the building's decay in the fifth century and restoration after Clovis's victory over the Visigoths in the sixth century. Further work was done in the tenth century, which gave the baptistery its present polygonal shape; but the change in the rite of baptism meant that the piscina was no longer needed. It was filled in and replaced by the more familiar fonts. From the twelfth century until the eighteenth the baptistery was used as a parish church, and traces of wall paintings of the twelfth to fourteenth centuries include a Christ in Majesty, peacocks, and a somewhat damaged figure of Constantine, shown on horseback. Constantine was revered as the first Christian emperor, and this image, based on classical statues of emperors on horseback, is one which we shall meet again. Here he is accompanied by three other Christian emperors.

The baptistery is now a museum (open 10–12.30, 14.30–18.00; closed on Wednesdays except in summer) and contains a number of Merovingian stone coffins from the fifth to seventh century. Several of these are finely carved; No 46 in particular has elaborate decoration of a rose pattern, flowers and doves, with a palm-leaf border. At some point it was re-used, since the name originally engraved on it was defaced.

Despite the haphazard appearance of the interior and the wear and tear of a chequered history – it was even a bell foundry in the early nineteenth century – the baptistery retains a striking air of that simplicity and restraint which distinguishes early Christian architecture.

If you return up the rue Jean-Jaurès the first turning on the right leads to the Cathedral, **St Pierre**. The façade has echoes of northern French Gothic about it, particularly its proportions. Above the three doors, which are the original thirteenth-century ones, the tympanums show, on the left, the death and coronation of the Virgin, in the centre, the Last Judgment, and on the right, St Thomas, the apostle who is said to have worked in India, building a miraculous palace for the king of India. The interior contrasts with the façade: instead of the high, narrow nave of a northern French cathedral we have a spacious 'hall-church' with aisles almost as high as the nave. The effect of space is heightened by false perspective, the shortening of the bays and pillar intervals at the east end. The vaulting is in the simple Angevin style of flat curves. The finest examples of this style are to be found on the Loire, for example at Fontevrault, where Henry II himself is buried, and its reappearance here is a reminder that Poitiers became part of the Angevin empire when Henry married Eleanor of Aquitaine in 1155. Eleanor gave money for the building of the cathedral when it was begun in 1162. And, with the aid of binoculars, the figures of Henry and Eleanor and their children can just be discerned at the foot of the great twelfth-century east window showing the Crucifixion. They are shown as donors, holding up a miniature of the window itself, with their children as small figures behind them. This is the earliest of the stained glass, but there are also fine thirteenth-century windows, particularly in the south transept, where the window of the Prodigal Son (right, on end wall) is very rich in colours, and contrasts with the generally blue tone of the other glass. The choir stalls are reputedly the oldest surviving in France, also of the thirteenth century, with small carved details showing figures from biblical history, angels, and the seven deadly sins.

Leaving the cathedral, and turning right down the hill, you come to the east wall of the cathedral, which towers 150 feet above the street. Then, further down the hill, is the church of Ste Radegonde. The tower and the east wall are eleventh-century; the nave was re-built in the thirteenth century. But its history goes back to the sixth century, and to the remarkable figure of its founder and patron, Radegonde. The wife of Clothair I, she fled the licence and dissipation of his court, and came to Poitiers about 560. Here she founded the first nunnery in France, and became one of its two hundred nuns. She refused to be abbess, appointing her friend Agnes instead. In 567 there came to Poitiers the poet Venantius Fortunatus, an Italian by birth, whose travels had taken him to the Frankish court. Radegonde made him welcome and he became her almoner; later he took holy orders and ended his days as bishop of Poitiers. Both he and Radegonde were canonised. Radegonde inspired him to write some of the most enchanting lines in late Latin poetry. He sent her little poems with a bunch of flowers, such as this:

*To the Lady Radegunde, with Violets*

> If 'twere the time of lilies,
>   Or of the crimson rose,
> I'd pluck them in the fields for you,
>   Or my poor garden close:
> Small gift for you so rare.

But I can find no lilies,
    Green herbs are all I bring.
Yet love makes vetches roses,
    And in their shadowing
    Hide violets as fair.
For royal is their purple,
    And fragrant is their breath,
And to one sweet and royal,
    Their fragrance witnesseth
    Beauty abiding there.

Radegonde replied by sending him delicacies which she herself prepared, for Fortunatus was known to be a gourmet. In earlier days he had written to a friend at court:

*To Gogo, that he can eat no more*
Nectar and wine and food and scholar's wit,
    Such is the fashion, Gogo, of thy house.
Cicero art thou, and Apicius too,
    But now I cry you mercy: no more goose!
Where the ox lieth, dare the chickens come?
    Nay, horn and wing unequal warfare keep.
My eyes are closing and my lute is dumb,
    Slower and slower go my songs to sleep.

But as the years drew on he turned to serious things, 'the flowers of Paradise', which Radegonde preferred to his own offerings. When the relic of the True Cross was brought to Poitiers in 568 he wrote the sonorous hymn *'Vexilla regis prodeunt'* ('The royal standard goes before') which was to be the Crusaders' marching song six centuries later. Beside the great classical poets Fortunatus is a lightweight, but he has a warmth that his more formal predecessors lack. Helen Waddell aptly compares him to Robert Herrick, and his poems have the same easy, lyrical grace. As one reads his poems it is not difficult to imagine Radegonde's nunnery as it once was, lying in orchards along the bank of the river Clain.

The church of Radegonde's nunnery was already a place of pilgrimage when she died; but her burial there increased its attraction for the devout. The porch has a flamboyant fifteenth-century Gothic doorway, but on the vault is a fine Romanesque bas-relief which shows Ste Radegonde seated in glory in Paradise, and in the centre of the church is the crypt containing her tomb, an eleventh-century sarcophagus. Fine thirteenth-century glass in the north windows

24

shows the main episodes of her life. Sadly, the wall paintings in the choir were 'restored' in 1849. There are some lively, rustic capitals in the choir, showing the Fall of Man, Daniel and the lions, and monsters and foliage. The enclosed area in front of the church with stone seats was used for sessions of the ecclesiastical courts.

Following the river round to the left, the medieval **Grand Rue** leads back up the hillside to **Notre Dame la Grande,** in the middle of a busy market square. The crowded stalls round this low building give it a homely and modest appearance, but its façade is one of the masterpieces of Poitevin sculpture. Unlike so many façades, which either remain incomplete or are a patchwork of different periods, this was completed in the first half of the twelfth century. Its conical towers, covered with *lauzes* (heavy stone tiles laid in flat layers), and its classical tablature, combined with the rich, almost over-crowded sculpture, earned the church the nickname 'la Byzantine' in the last century. And this is a very formal kind of Romanesque style, with its hierarchy of heaven arranged in order of precedence, working down from Christ in the central mandorla, surrounded by the symbols of the evangelists, through the arcades of apostles,[1] to the lively human details above the deep arches at ground level. These details form a frieze, which reads from left to right: it begins with the Temptation, followed by the prophets; to left and right of the central arch, the Annunciation and Visitation; and, on the right, the Nativity and Baptism of Christ. The figures themselves are still a little stiff and hieratic; the angel of the Annunciation can only kneel half-way to the ground, but this is more than compensated for by the varied relief and surface provided by the arches and arcades, and the different textures of the stonework. It is a façade which changes in every light, though it is best seen in the afternoon or evening, when the light falls across it.

The remainder of the exterior is less distinguished: only the central tower retains its original appearance, and a jumble of fifteenth-century chapels mars the south side. The interior is sombre, its architecture solemn and still compared with the façade. The floor was originally nearly three feet lower than it is now. Victorian wall painting – the French word *badigeon* conveys its horror much more effectively – has destroyed some of the atmosphere; in places it has been removed. Some of the darkness is due to the addition of the side-chapels and organ gallery, so the gloom is not necessarily medieval. The balance of the choir has also been disturbed by the

[1] St Hilaire and St Martin are added to the apostles, so that a visual progression upward can be achieved instead of two equal rows of six.

alterations to the side-chapels, but the original plan is still clear, and the capitals in the ambulatory have some interesting animal and foliage designs. The faded remains of twelfth-century wall paintings can be seen in the choir, but a side staircase leads down to the crypt, where a far better group is preserved, showing four saints (on the walls) and, on the vault, the beasts of the Evangelists.

From the north corner of the **Place du Marché**, the **Place de la Liberté** leads to the **Rue de la Chaine**. On the left, at No 24, is the **Hôtel Berthelot**, a handsome town house built in 1529 by a mayor of Poitiers, with a gateway decorated in the Renaissance style, including busts of the owner and his wife. It now houses the Centre for Studies of Medieval Civilisation of the University of Poitiers, to the work of whose scholars this present book owes a great deal. Further down the rue de la Chaine a number of medieval houses are being restored, under an imaginative scheme covering the whole quarter. (Not without some protest – one splendid graffito declared: *Nous ne voulons pas être un zoo aux touristes!*)

At the foot of the hill the church of **St Jean de Moutierneuf** is all that remains of a Cluniac monastery. Originally entirely Romanesque, the present building has been much rebuilt; the effect of a Gothic choir at the end of a Romanesque choir is unexpectedly pleasing, but the façade has gone and the roof was rebuilt in the seventeenth century. An eleventh-century Latin inscription in the north aisle, near the transept, records the consecration of the church by Urban II in 1096, a few months after he had launched the First Crusade at the Council of Clermont. Restoration work is in progress on the interior. The exterior of the apse can be seen from the boulevards along the river Clain; the apse, with its radiating chapels, form a harmonious group, though the silhouette of the rest of the building is stark.

After climbing back up the rue de la Chaine you will find the **Hôtel Fumée** on the right a few doors after the Hôtel Berthelot, at 8 rue Descartes. This is an early-sixteenth-century house, now occupied by the university, with a 'flamboyant' front and a court-yard with the typical staircase tower and colonnaded gallery of the period. Notice particularly the riot of ornament on the attic windows of the front, the unicorn on the right-hand tower, and the barley-sugar pillars of the courtyard. There is a hint of the medieval past in the battlement over the doorway, but this is decorative rather than a real fortification.

The main university buildings are now entirely outside the old town, on the east bank of the Clain on the road to Limoges. Those parts of it which remain in the town occupy borrowed buildings, because it has a chequered career as an institution. Founded in 1432, it reached its zenith in the sixteenth century, when there were as many as 4,000 students. Only Paris and Lyon outshone it; the chief faculty was that of civil law (not taught at Paris until the 1650s), which about half the students attended. Theology ranked second, and there were thirteen colleges in all. The four 'nations' into which the students were divided show that it was a mainly French university – Aquitaine, Berry, Touraine, Ile de France – though in the early seventeenth century there were also a large community of Germans and an occasional 'red-faced Englishman', including Francis Bacon, later Lord Chancellor, who spent a few months here in 1577–8. The most distinguished of its pupils was Rabelais, who studied here, intermittently, between 1524 and 1527: there are echoes of the theologians of his day in *Gargantua and Pantagruel*. On a later visit to Poitiers Rabelais met the poet Joachim du Bellay; they drank together, and du Bellay told Rabelais about his literary projects, which were to shape the famous poetic group of La Pléiade (The Pleiades). These seven poets, of whom Ronsard (see p. 53) was one, turned their backs on the medieval tradition, and looked to classical literature for their inspiration, while defending the use of French for the highest literary themes. Du Bellay's finest poems are his nostalgic sonnets, but it is only his less eminent fellow-member of the Pléiade and fellow-student, Antoine de Baïf, who alludes to his days at Poitiers in his poems.

After this flowering the seventeenth century saw the gradual decline of the university until the law faculty in 1789 had only fifty pupils, and the other faculties were moribund. The university was not properly revived until the late nineteenth century, by which time its former buildings had passed into other hands or had disappeared.

The **Rue Descartes** opens out into the little **Place Charles VIII**, and then leads into the **Rue des Vieilles Boucheries** (in an English medieval town this would be 'The Shambles'). To the right is a street with the intriguing name **Rue de la Regratterie**. In medieval times 'regrating', or buying food to sell again at a profit, was often regarded as a crime, like usury; but here it was obviously accepted practice. The English word 'huckster' refers to the same practice.

The Rue des Vieilles Boucheries comes out in the Place Lepetit, with the entrance to the **Palais de Justice** on the left. The Renaissance façade is deceptive; behind it lie the great hall of the palace of the Angevin kings, Henry II and Richard I, and the remains of its keep. (To see the outside of the medieval part, go along the **Rue des**

**Cordeliers**.) The great hall, 150 feet by 60 feet, is one of the very few examples of a building of this kind to survive: Westminster Hall is perhaps the nearest parallel. One end was remodelled by Jean, Duc de Berry (a great patron of the arts, whose court was at Poitiers from 1369 to 1416) in the fifteenth century, and given a trio of cavernous chimneypieces in the flamboyant style, whose chimneys curl up the outside wall. Either here, or at the logis de la Rose (53 rue de la Cathédrale) Joan of Arc was examined by a council of theologians appointed by Charles VII and her divine mission to save France was accepted by them. Among the examiners were the Bishop of Poitiers and four members of the theological faculty of the university. From the left-hand corner of the chimney wall a staircase leads up to the roof, with a fine view over the city. The keep, or **Tour Maubergeon**, can be visited on request to the concierge, and contains a fine central hall, with four small rooms at the corners, all rebuilt in the flamboyant style by Jean de Berry.

From the **Place Lepetit** the **Rue Gambetta** leads back to the Hôtel de Ville. On the left a narrow alley leads to the old town hall, or *Échevinage*, which houses a small archaeological museum, a random collection dating from the nineteenth century. Further on the church of **St Porchaire** has a remarkably well-preserved tower of *circa* 1070–80. (St Porchaire was a contemporary of Radegonde and Fortunatus, and abbot of St Hilaire.) It juts out into the busy shopping street incongruously; indeed, it was nearly demolished last century. The capitals on the doorway portray Daniel in the lions' den, with the lions humbly licking his feet; lions, birds and stags decorate the other capitals. The tenth-century sarcophagus of St Porchaire is in the choir; otherwise the interior is sixteenth-century, except for some very early, eighth-century fabric in the west wall.

About a quarter of a mile down the **Rue Carnot** lies the third major church of Poitiers, **St Hilaire-le-Grand**. As a building it is less striking than the cathedral or Notre Dame la Grande, but its historical associations are much greater. It was once the main church of Poitiers: above it Clovis is reputed to have seen a 'fiery light' at the battle of Vouillé in 507 (see p. 20), and until the Revolution the mayor and council celebrated the anniversary of his victory by going in solemn procession to light a lantern at the top of the tower. The best approach to the church is by walking round the outside of the apse and past the bell-tower, set in a little square of trees. For this part is the untouched eleventh-century church, with an orthodox plan of chapels radiating from a choir ambulatory, giving a silhouette, typical of many Poitevin churches, of sloping and curving roofs. On the other hand, the bell-tower is unusual: perhaps its prominence in the external appearance of the church is due to the legend of Clovis's vision, but very few other examples of a bell-tower to the north are known. The rest of the building is plain, because the nave and west end are a nineteenth-century reconstruction.

Despite this rebuilding the interior still looks very like that of the eleventh-century church. The original was carefully copied, though one bay was omitted to make way for a street. Only the obtrusive bands of coloured mortar distract the eye (the whole church would have been painted). Otherwise this is very much the same interior as that finished in 1049 by Walter Coorland, architect to Queen Emma of England. It is clearly a basilica, a church for stately processions and high ceremonies; the tone is set by the altar and crypt, with their theatrical appearance. The original arrangement would have been an altar in front of the archway leading to the crypt. The crypt is now walled off, and the opening would have been much deeper and more dramatic. The raised area of choir and transepts is unchanged in appearance. Unless you happen to arrive during a feast-day service all you will see is the empty stage, through the forest of columns of the aisles and nave, with their interlinking arches.

But who was this dramatic setting designed to honour? St Hilaire is a particularly French saint, and largely honoured in Poitou itself. He was bishop of Poitiers from about 350 to 368, and was one of the earliest of the Fathers of the Western Church. He was the teacher of St Martin of Tours (famous for dividing his cloak with a beggar), but his greatest work was in combating the Arian heresy, which threatened to overwhelm orthodox Catholicism. The idea of heresy is so alien to us now that it is difficult to imagine how ardently the war against it was waged. The Arians regarded the Father as pre-eminent in the Trinity: the Catholics insisted that all persons in the Trinity were equal. It was a complex debate, but it was not resolved by the theologians. When Arianism was rooted out of the Roman Empire some of the Germanic tribes took it up. It was only with their defeat on the battlefield that the Arians lost the argument. So there is a close link between St Hilaire and Clovis's victory over Alaric, because St Hilaire's own triumph had been over Arians within the empire, while Clovis defeated their successors two hundred years later.

During the eleventh century this church must have been a major focal point for pilgrimages. Though there is little written evidence about pilgrims coming to St Hilaire's shrine, the whole design of the church echoes the martyr-churches of the East. Even the cupolas of the roof, added early in the twelfth century, may echo the cupolas which covered such mausoleums. For the cult of relics, long established in the Eastern Church, was relatively new in the West when this church was built. It would be interesting to know more of Queen Emma's involvement in its building. Her husband, Canute, went on pilgrimage to Rome in 1026–7, and if she accompanied him her gifts to St Hilaire probably date from that period, just as Canute endowed the cathedral at Chartres on his journey.

Within the building itself there are a number of carvings, particularly capitals, which are worth seeking out. At the foot of the bell-tower there is a frieze on the north side which includes a dromedary with a palm tree, another echo of the East. In the north transept the pillar nearest the bell-tower has a capital showing the death of St Hilaire, a formal composition completed by two swooping angels bearing off his soul, shown as a naked man. The remaining capitals are mostly monsters or decorative patterns: the pillars in the nave just before the crossing have an extra capital half-way down, lions who guard the altar and crypt. Also in the crossing, but very difficult to see, one of the capitals shows the Flight into Egypt.

With a power and dignity lacking in both the interiors of the cathedral and Notre Dame la Grande, St Hilaire is a setting worthy of great occasions, but it seems to have been overshadowed by the other churches. It was only because the cathedral was being rebuilt that Richard Coeur-de-Lion was invested with the insignia of the counts of Poitou in St Hilaire on 11 June 1172, and once the new cathedral was complete such ceremonies naturally took place there. Even its school, famous in the eleventh century, seems to have sunk into decline in the following years, perhaps because of the growing pre-eminence of Paris; the university was only founded in 1432, and Poitiers had no great tradition of learning in the Middle Ages.

Return to the rue de la Tranchée, and a turning to the left leads to the **Parc de Blossac**, an eighteenth-century park which Arthur Young admired when he visited Poitiers in 1788. (Otherwise he said of the town that it was 'one of the worst built towns I have seen in France, very large and irregular containing scarcely anything worthy of notice'.) Laid out in the 1770s by the local *intendant*, the Comte de Blossac, it was widely praised, and Blossac planned to cut a street through the existing town to the town hall to join up with its central avenue. In the last decade the vista over the river Clain has been spoiled by the ring of new skyscrapers on the far bank. At the end of the park is a stretch of the twelfth-century town ramparts. A short walk along the rue de la Tranchée and the rue Carnot brings us back to our starting point.

The boulevards along the edge of the river down to the Pont Neuf, a neo-classical structure of 1778, bring us across the river, where the Boulevard Coligny leads up to a spur on the cliffs from which there is a fine view over Poitiers, used as an observation post by Admiral Coligny, the Protestant (Huguenot) leader in the wars of religion, when he besieged Poitiers in 1569. Coligny wanted to lead his army north to campaign on the Loire, but the staunchly royalist nobles of Poitou forced him to turn aside and secure Poitiers first. The siege lasted a month and a half, but Coligny was unable to take the town, which was well defended by a garrison not much smaller than his own forces. In later years Poitiers became a stronghold of the fanatical Catholic 'leaguers', who had sworn to eradicate the Huguenots, and had to be subdued in 1593 by Henri IV before peace was possible.

At the top of the Boulevard Coligny the right-hand road leads to the **Hypogée Martyrium**, just off the N 147 to Limoges. The key to the building is at 101 rue Père-de-la-Croix. It is a seventh-century memorial chapel, once thought to have been a memorial to the early Christian martyrs buried in the cemetery in which it was built, but probably a memorial to the abbot Mellebaude. It is the earliest example of a funerary chapel built to echo the Holy Sepulchre in its details and iconography, and is perhaps connected with a special local cult of the True Cross, represented elsewhere in Poitiers by the relic of Ste Radegonde (and Fortunatus's hymn *Vexilla regis*) and the crucifixion window in the cathedral. The building is set in a shady garden of cypresses, which screen it from the nearby houses. Between the trees are a number of sarcophagi and fragments excavated from the cemetery. What remains of the original chapel is below ground level. In a case on the wall is part of the lintel, with an inscription which declares that 'this is the tomb of abbot Mellebaude, here Christ is worshipped'. On the right of the original doorway another inscription repeats this, ending with a curse on anyone who destroys the building. Fragments of the detailed decoration, evoking the Holy Sepulchre by symbols or by inscriptions, survive: the most important, and the key to the significance of the whole monument, is a stone pedestal to the left of the east wall. Comparison with eighth-century miniatures revealed that this was part of a crucifixion group, showing the two crucified thieves. On the walls are fragments of a group of saints, as yet unidentified. Something of the effect of the original chapel survives: a carefully wrought shrine, richly carved and painted, designed for private meditation and prayer by devout pilgrims.

A little further along the road toward Limoges a turning to the left leads to a funerary monument of a different kind, the remains of a large dolmen. The *Pierre Levée* was still standing in Rabelais's time, and was a popular picnic spot for students, who, he says, used to meet there and climb on top 'to banquet with a multitude of flagons, hams and pâtés, and to write their names on it with a knife'. It was broken in the eighteenth century, but engravings record it as thirty-six feet long, twenty-four feet wide, and standing nine feet high.

Six miles south of Poitiers, in the valley of the Clain, stands the **Abbey of Ligugé**, which is reached by a turning to the left off the N 10 to Angoulême. It was here that St Martin lived, as a disciple of St Hilaire, between 361 and 370, before he became bishop of Tours. He had been an officer in the Roman army before his conversion: one day he met a beggar, half-dead with cold, and, cutting his cloak in two, gave him half of it. In a dream he saw Christ wearing half of his cloak, and was baptised.

The first building on the site, now uncovered by excavations, was a Roman villa, in the ruins of which Martin established himself as a hermit. However, he was soon surrounded by a band of disciples, and instead founded a monastery, the earliest in France. The fourth-century sanctuary has been found, as well as the crypt of the seventh-century church, below the nave of the present church, while the lower storeys of the belfry are its south transept, with a fourth-century Ionic capital re-used in the later structure. Arcading and a bull's-eye window of the seventh century can also be seen, and the pavement in front of the doorway of the present church is a rare example from the same period.

In the eighth century the abbey was destroyed, but three centuries later a small priory remained, which survived until the sixteenth century. In the early sixteenth century the present church was built, in the flamboyant Gothic style, by Geoffroi d'Estissac, Rabelais's patron, who was prior of Ligugé; and Rabelais spent some time here.

The present abbey is a Benedictine foundation of 1853, part of the revival of monastic life during the last century which began at the abbey of Solesmes. Even so, for political reasons, the monks were twice forced into exile: from 1880 to 1885, and from 1901 to 1923.

1. Façade of Notre Dame la Grande, Poitiers, Its exuberance of sculpture is controlled by a sober framework of classical arcading; and its composition follows a detailed programme

2. The great hall of the Palais de Justice, Poitiers. Originally part of the twelfth-century castle, it was altered by Jean, duc de Berry in the late fourteenth century, when Gui de Dammartin designed the graceful Gothic chimney-wall

3. (above) Capital showing the death of St Hilaire, from the church of St Hilaire, Poitiers

4. (centre) Detail of lower part of east window in Poitiers Cathedral This twelfth century glass was presented by Eleanor of Aquitaine, who is shown holding a model of the window with her husband, Henry II, and their sons, Henry, Richard, Geoffrey and John. (A later balcony obscures this lower part from view)

5. (below) Capital from the church of St Pierre, Chauvigny: man seized by a devil. The colouring is a nineteenth-century restoration, which makes the sculpture seem harsher and cruder than it really is

Apart from the church, the abbey buildings are all modern. There is a fine library, and an important scholarly periodical on monastic history, the *Revue Mabillon*, is produced here. Other activities include a studio which produces enamels, often based on stained glass or modern paintings. Several distinguished Catholic writers and artists have made long stays in the monastery, including J. K. Huysmans, whose early 'decadent' works gave way to descriptions of religious life, the playwright Paul Claudel, and the painter Georges Rouault.

From Ligugé the road through Smarves joins the N 741; turning right and then left at Roches-Premarié-Andille we come to another abbey in a river valley, **Nouaillé-Maupertuis**, on the banks of the Miosson. In the middle of a tumbledown group of monastic buildings complete with moat the abbey itself is gradually being restored. Founded in the seventh century, parts of the ninth-century church survive in the walls of the present building, and behind the altar is a sarcophagus, said to be that of St Junien, with three great heraldic eagles carved on the side, probably tenth-century work. Rebuilt in 1011 when the abbey was reformed on Cluniac lines, the church was much altered in the seventeenth century. Capitals in the nave and the belfry porch carry masks and fleurs-de-lis, as well as lively but unidentified scenes. The round window in the belfry has a frieze of dwarfs round it. Below the altar is the crypt where the relics of St Junien were originally kept.

Returning along the D 142, you will find a minor road to the right to Les Bordes and La Cardinerie, which leads to the site of the battle of Poitiers in 1356. Here the Black Prince, trapped by the French army while returning from a prolonged raid into French territory, overwhelmingly defeated them and captured the French king, John the Good. Just after the river crossing, at the Gué de l'Omme, there is a monument on the left, half-way up the hill. Away from the road the land forms an amphitheatre with the Miosson curving round the foot of the hill, and it was here that the main action was fought.

The battle began with the French army encamped between the Limoges road and the hamlet of Beauvoir, to the north of the battle-field. As they tried to engage the English forces, who held the two fords across the Miosson, they were ambushed by the English archers stationed on either side of the Maupertuis, a narrow lane which ran approximately along the line of the modern road, and which was then hedged on each side. The English archers cut down many of the French cavalry as they tried to make their way along this. The Black Prince, who had been fighting a guerrilla war, had chosen his position so that he could continue to use small-scale tactics of this kind, without giving the French cavalry an open space in which to form up and charge. His men were therefore stationed in the Bois de Nouaillé, to the east of the road, and between the two fords, the Gué de l'Omme and the Gué de Russan. Under such conditions it was impossible for the French to maintain order in an army which already lacked discipline, and a series of hand-to-hand encounters followed as small groups of French knights tried to achieve glorious feats of arms against a much more down-to-earth enemy, who not unnaturally were better at such fighting. By the afternoon the French realised that the enemy could not be dislodged from the security of the woods south of the Miosson, protected by marshes and the swollen river, and regrouped on the Champ Alexandre to the west of the main English positions. But they were still unable to draw out the Black Prince's troops, and a running battle followed in which the cavalry, already tired and depleted, were harassed by archers and then overwhelmed by a concerted attack by three separate columns of English and Gascon troops.

Jean Froissart describes the closing scenes of the battle:

It often happens, that fortune in war and love turns out more favourable and wonderful than could have been hoped for or expected. To say the truth, this battle which was fought near Poitiers, in the plains of Beauvoir and Maupertuis, was very bloody and perilous: many gallant deeds of arms were performed that were never known, and the combatants on each side suffered much. King John himself did wonders: he was armed with a battle-axe, with which he fought and defended himself . . .

There was much pressing at this time, through eagerness to take the King; and those who were nearest to him, and knew him, cried out, 'Surrender yourself, surrender yourself, or you are a dead man.' In that part of the field was a young knight from St Omer, who was engaged by a salary in the service of the King of England; his name was Denys de Morbeque; who for five years had attached himself to the English, on account of having been banished in his younger days from France for a murder committed in an affray at St Omer. It fortunately happened for this knight that he was at the time near to the King of France, when he was so much pulled about; he, by dint of force, for he was very strong and robust, pushed through the crowd, and said to the King in good French, 'Sire, sire, surrender yourself.' The King who found himself very disagreeably situated, turning to him, asked, 'To whom shall I surrender myself: to whom? Where is my cousin the prince of Wales? if I could speak to him.' 'Sire,' replied Sir Denys, 'he is not here; but surrender yourself to me, and I will lead you to him.' 'Who are you?' said the King. 'Sire, I am Denys de Morbeque, a knight from Artois; but I serve the King of England, because I cannot belong to France, having forfeited all I possessed there.' The King then gave him his right hand glove, and said, 'I surrender myself to you.'

Froissart also records the famous scene at supper on the evening of the victory:

When evening was come, the Prince of Wales gave a supper in his pavilion to the King of France, and to the greater part of the princes and barons who were prisoners. The Prince seated the King of France and his son the Lord Philip at an elevated and well-covered table: with them were, Sir James de Bourbon, the lord John d'Artois, the earls of Tancarville, of Estampes, of Dammartin, of Graville, and the lord of Partenay. The other knights and squires were placed at different tables. The Prince himself served the King's table, as well as the others, with every mark of humility, and would not sit down at it, in spite of all his entreaties for him so to do, saying, that 'he was not worthy of such an honour, nor did it appertain to him to seat himself at the table of so great a king, or of so valiant a man as he had shown himself by his actions that day.'

Poitiers was indeed a spectacular victory, but its effects were relatively short-lived. The English ascendancy over France was prolonged until the end of the century, but the Black Prince's allies were by and large soldiers of fortune, good at this cut-and-thrust warfare, but deeply resentful of any attempt in peacetime to organise a solid basis of sound government on which the English could build. Lacking such a base, the English in France were doomed to eventual defeat.

From this deserted hillside, occupied only by the dim ghosts of the medieval battle, we can either return by the D 12 to Poitiers, or we can continue to **Chauvigny** by the D 142, turning right down the N 147 and then left along the D 1 to the N 151. But if you want to prolong the theme of fourteenth-century warfare continue down the N 147 to Lussac, where one of the heroes of Poitiers met his end. In 1369 the French began the reconquest of Aquitaine from the English, and in a minor skirmish on 31 December Sir John Chandos engaged a small French force. As he led his troops he slipped and fell on the frozen ground and was given a mortal wound by one of the enemy. He was buried at Morthemer, just up the valley of the Vienne beyond Civaux. Taking the road from Lussac to Civaux, we follow, in reverse, the route described on page 40 before reaching Chauvigny.

# Chapter 2

# South-East Poitou

❧

East of Poitiers the rolling plain is broken by the parallel valleys of the Vienne and the Gartempe, which run barely eight miles apart for forty miles, as they flow toward their confluence. It is a spacious landscape of large farms and small market towns. The N 151 from Poitiers runs straight across this undulating country to **Chauvigny**, where an eleventh-century keep dominates the town. By turning left and then right just after the bridge over the Vienne, you can reach the keep by car; but the steep approach on foot is well worth the effort, in which case park in the Place du Marché to the right instead. The rue des Trois Rois leads first to the earliest of the four castles on this one hill, that of the bishops of Poitiers, lords of Chauvigny in the eleventh century. All that remains of this massive building is a hollow shell and towering walls, though it still casts its shadow over the surrounding landscape as it was originally intended to do, perched on the edge of the limestone cliff. Although the bishops of Poitiers remained lords of Chauvigny until the eighteenth century, the real power passed elsewhere. The **Château d'Harcourt** higher up the hill belonged originally to the local family of the viscounts of Châtellerault, but passed to the Norman family d'Harcourt in the fourteenth century, who rebuilt it. The ramparts and a gateway survive, but little else. On the north slope of the hill is the keep of another, twelfth-century castle (Château de Gouzon) belonging to a local lord. Fragments of a fourth castle, that of Montléon, survive just south of the church of St Pierre. Even with the complicated claims to lordship and overlordship which could arise under a feudal system, it is unusual to find such a cluster of castles surviving on the same spot – and, presumably, co-existing in a fairly peaceful manner. One reason why the castles were not demolished is that Chauvigny is the centre of a quarrying industry, and stone is plentiful.

In the midst of all this warlike activity stands the church of **St Pierre**, whose belfry rises above the castle ruins. It is contemporary with the two earlier castles, and the outside of its apse, with its tiers of roofs one above the other, has more than a hint of battlements in

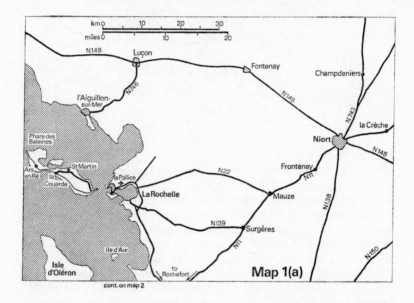

Map 1(a)

cont. on map 2

the upper stages. On the north faces of the chapels which radiate
from the apse pieces of Carolingian sculpture have been re-used:
high on the central chapel there is, badly weathered but still distinct,
a hieratic figure of St Peter which might have come straight out of an
illuminated manuscript. The entrance is to the west, through a
simple arcaded front. The interior is at first disappointing: a simple
Romanesque nave apparently badly disfigured by nineteenth-century
red-ochre painting emphasising the joints in the stonework and
creating irrelevant patterned grounds in the apse. But when it comes
to the real treasure of this church, its capitals, the effect is almost
beneficial. Detailed capitals are all too often difficult to 'read',
tucked away in obscure corners. Here the painting points up the
details and makes them crystal clear, though it perhaps distorts the
emphasis a little in doing so. The capitals in the nave are geometrical
or foliage designs. It is the choir that really repays study. The
subjects do not form a particular sequence: beginning at the southernmost pillar – to the right as you face the altar – they are as follows:

1. Eagles devouring men fill all four faces.
2. 'The great whore of Babylon' is contrasted with 'Babylon
   deserted' on the opposite side. The other faces have the annunciation to the shepherds and the figure of St Michael

38

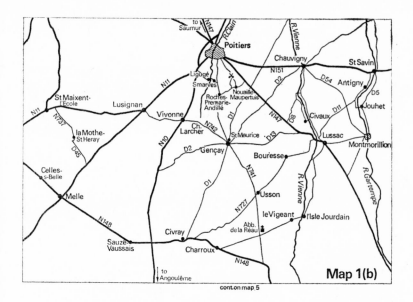

Map 1(b)

cont. on map 5

weighing souls. A man prays urgently to him on the left, while a devil tries to drag down the scales on the right.

3. Dragons devouring men, whose heads are held in their jaws.

4. This is the most striking of all, partly because it bears the name of either the donor or sculptor – *'Gofridus me fecit'*, 'Godfrey made me'. The Epiphany is carved below this inscription, with Mary showing Jesus to the three kings. On one side is the Star of Bethlehem, on the other the hand of God. Two other faces also show scenes of Christ's birth and childhood: the Annunciation, the presentation in the Temple, while the last shows the Temptation, with a massive Devil offering a stone to be turned to bread.

5. Winged lions with two bodies; human heads on the other corners.

6. A riot of monsters, devised with all the inventiveness of the medieval artist: two bearded sphinxes, lions with tails entwined, one of them attacked by the dragon on the next face, and a man with two bodies, dancing, a kind of monstrous entertainer.

7. Two sirens, the mythical creatures who tried to lure Odysseus to his death with their music: here they have become bird-women in Phrygian caps.

8. Satan as Antichrist, holding an altar-stone; demons drag victims to him for sacrifice.

The power of these carvings lies in their directness: the feeling is not of remote and sacred mysteries but of a real and present heaven and hell, expressed in an artistic language which is that of ordinary people, plain French instead of the ritual Latin of the period. It would be hard to match them among Romanesque sculpture for their immediate impact.

Down the hill, **Notre Dame**, on the Place du Marché, has some sculptured capitals in the crossing, and a late-fifteenth-century fresco.

Just south of Chauvigny, on the N 749 to Lussac, a sign to the right to 'Les Eglises' marks a track which runs down to the edge of the Vienne. On the edge of the river, in an idyllic setting, is the church of **St Pierre**. The tenth-century apse contains the fading remains of frescoes which must have once been a remarkable series. The clearest image to survive is that of the Crucifixion, to the left; elsewhere the Visitation, the Adoration of the Magi and a scene from the Apocalypse have dissolved into an impression of urgently moving shadows, against a banded background originally designed to imitate marble inlays.

From Chauvigny the N 749 follows the Vienne valley to Civaux (p. 44).

The N 151 climbs out of the Vienne valley up the rue Bellevue, with one of the best views of the castles. On the other side of Chauvigny it resumes its level course to **St Savin**, on the Gartempe. Just before the fourteenth-century bridge the Hôtel du Midi offers excellent food and simple, old-fashioned rooms; it is a rare example of an unspoilt country inn.

The glory of St Savin is its abbey-church, which contains the greatest surviving series of twelfth-century wall paintings. It is best approached by walking down the bank of the river, and back up into the main square, which gives some idea of the size both of the church and of the former abbey buildings.

The eleventh-century legend of St Savin tells how in the fifth century he and his brother, St Cyprien, were imprisoned and sentenced to death in Greece for refusing to worship idols. They escaped to France, but their executioners pursued them, finally catching up with them on the banks of the river here. The story is almost certainly a monkish invention, to cover up ignorance of the identity of their patron saint.

St Savin's history really begins with the building of a Benedictine abbey here in the ninth century, under the direction of St Benedict himself. Abandoned in face of the Norman raids on Poitou in the late ninth century, it was occupied again early in the tenth century. During the eleventh century a number of benefactors gave the abbey money and lands, including the Countess Aumode, wife of Guillaume the Great, Count of Poitou. This new-found wealth enabled the monks to rebuild on a grand scale at the end of the century.

The exterior of the church, although mainly twelfth-century, takes its character from the lovely fourteenth-century spire, which blends remarkably smoothly with the Romanesque belfry on which it is built, both in its proportions and in its restrained detail. Entering by the door below the belfry, one encounters an interior which is in many ways a surprise. It is one of the few churches to retain its original floor level, well below that of the entrance, and this creates a perspective which emphasises the height of the church and the length of the nave. The architecture of St Savin, almost entirely un- touched since it was first built, is almost on a par with its paintings. The simplicity of the long nave, with its massive pillars, ends in an elaborate choir, with an arcade and five radiating chapels. The transepts are small, almost an afterthought. Before the altar is the crypt of St Savin. As with the exterior, the keynote is simplicity and harmony, as if the idea were to create an elegant and restrained frame which would set off the richness of the paintings. Even the painting on the pillars has the subtlety of watered silk, a far cry from the garish fairground colours of Chauvigny.

The paintings were one of the first treasures to be classified as a *monument historique*; this was done by Prosper Mérimée (better known as the author of the original story of *Carmen*) in 1836. Carried out as the church was built, they had been repaired at different periods, and restoration work went on from 1836 until 1852. However, more restoration has proved necessary, and the visitor will find that, until about 1979, only part of the paintings can be seen. (I myself have not yet been able to see the paintings in the tribune, and the description which follows is taken from repro- ductions, a full-scale set of which is displayed in the Palais Chaillot in Paris. In the church itself, a small pair of field-glasses is a help, as the roof is over fifty feet from the floor.)

The main sequence of paintings is that on the roof of the nave. It portrays the sequence of Old Testament history from the Creation to the giving of the Ten Commandments to Moses. The series begins to the left of the entrance on the upper band of paintings. Parts of the story of the Creation are missing, and the first scene shows the creation of the stars; below it is the creation of Eve. The sequence then continues along the upper part of the vault. Notice the figure of Enoch, being carried up to heaven, half-way along, and the story of Noah at the end of the first row, with two of the best scenes, that of the ark, and of God blessing Noah, one of the most haunting figures. The continuation is on the upper line of the facing vault, reading from left to right and taking the story from the drunkenness of Noah to the building of the Tower of Babel (left of centre) and the story of Abraham. If you read from right to left along the lower line, the story of Abraham continues into that of Joseph, showing his capture, imprisonment, the explanation of Pharaoh's dream and his appointment as governor. The end of the sequence is to the right of the lower row on the north vault; here Moses leads the Israelites across the Red Sea, and in the last painting, receives the tables bearing the Ten Commandments.

In the tribune, above the entrance porch, is a small chapel, originally containing an altar, with a further series of paintings. This arrangement, of a belfry and chapel in a tower over the entrance, is found in ninth-century churches, but is unusual at a later date. The frescoes here were badly decayed due to lack of air during the centuries when the window overlooking the nave remained walled up. They form the New Testament half of the sequence, though the treatment is not so consistently historical. The window wall, toward the nave, carries the story of the Resurrection, beginning with the deposition from the cross above the window, and with the Resurrection scenes inside the arch. In the right-hand wall the first panels show the burial of Christ and a scene from the life of St Denis, with figures of apostles and saints: the left-hand wall shows the flagellation of Christ and the kiss of Judas, another scene from the life of St Denis, and more figures. But only the outlines and an occasional detail of all this survive in anything near their original condition.

Below, in the porch, are scenes from the Apocalypse, including on the tympanum above the west door a Christ in Majesty which underlines the tragedy of the loss of a much larger Christ in Majesty above the apse, destroyed by an incompetent restorer in the 1840s. The remaining paintings are in the crypt: these are the most easily visible and best preserved of all. (For the key, apply to the bookshop in front of the church on the square.) However, they lack the power of the great frescoes of the nave, perhaps for the simple reason that they are designed to be seen at close quarters. A group of saints surrounds Christ on the east wall; the other pictures tell the legendary story of St Savin and St Cyprien, and there is a handsome portrait of

St Savin with his judge.

One last detail is easily overlooked: in the five chapels radiating from the apse the original Romanesque altars survive – square, sparsely decorated slabs with long inscriptions recording their dedications. Interestingly most of the saints mentioned are minor or local ones; valuable documents for the everyday worship of the period.

Leaving St Savin on the D 11, to Montmorillon, the road winds along the Gartempe valley, open farming country with houses grouped in little hamlets. At **Antigny** the church has frescoes which are a dim rustic echo of the glories of St Savin. At **Jouhet** (turn left after Antigny), on the other hand, the frescoes are different in approach, though probably by the same sixteenth-century artists who worked at Antigny. Here they are in a little funerary chapel. (The key can be obtained from the shop on the left of the road, fifty yards before the bridge.) The colours have turned to brown and black due to oxidisation and the blues have faded to white. But there is still drama in the biblical scenes and in the legend of the three men who went hunting, met themselves as dead men, and duly repented of their sinful ways.

Crossing the river, take the D 5 to **Montmorillon**, which lies on either side of the Gartempe, the houses perched above its waters as they run sluggishly between embankments. On the left just before the bridge the Hôtel de France offers excellent local cooking: try their *paupiette de volaille aux pruneaux*. And then, to work off the meal, walk back to the old bridge and up to the church of Notre Dame, pausing to admire the view from the terrace alongside. Here again the jewel of the church is its frescoes. These, in the crypt below the altar (key from the hospital porter across the square), date from the twelfth century, and although the colours echo those of St Savin, the style is much freer and less solemn. The apse of the crypt has a Virgin in glory, receiving St Catherine, to whom the crypt is dedicated. St Catherine carries a strange, round object, probably the 'fruit of life' referred to in the Apocalypse; and, in contrast with her elegance, a powerful portrait of one of the Elders of the Apocalypse – the others have vanished – flanks the central painting. Another scene shows St Catherine confounding the learned men sent to examine her by the Emperor Maxentius.

At the top of the hill behind Notre Dame the rue St Mathelin leads to the Maison Dieu and church of St Laurent to the south-west of the town. The west front of St Laurent has the remains, partly hidden, of a fine carved frieze of scenes from Christ's birth and childhood. In the corner of the great courtyard of the Maison Dieu (or almshouse), to the right of the church, is a curious funerary chapel, which for a long time was called a 'Druid temple'. On the ground floor is a vaulted room with a vent in the centre to the chapel above. This was once painted; now it is derelict and the only feature is the Angevin vault of about 1200. At the entrance four Romanesque statues taken from an earlier building stand guard, perhaps representing the Virtues and Vices.

From Montmorillon the N 727 leads to Lussac-les-Châteaux (see p. 35); and then we turn right up the valley of the Vienne on the N 749 to Civaux. Here we are back at the beginnings of Christianity in France. Excavations have shown that the apse may be as early as the fifth century, built of coarse, small stonework and with narrow keystones above the window. There is an early Christian inscription near the altar, and even the name of the church, St Gervais and Protais, echoes its early foundation. The nave is eleventh-century. To the north just outside the village, on the slope toward the river, lies an early Christian *champ des morts*. Around the edge of a modern cemetery, filled with the usual examples of amazing Victorian undertakers' art, a simple row of inscribed or decorated slabs are a reminder that this has been a burial ground for over twelve hundred years. The Merovingian cemetery was some seven feet below the present ground-level. A small museum near the entrance contains the results of excavations, which have revealed that a Roman temple stood on the site: there are the ruins of a fourth-century Christian baptistery.

Returning to Lussac-les-Châteaux and continuing down the river valley on the D 11, we come to L'Isle-Jourdain. Here turn right across the river on the D 10, to Le Vigeant, whose church has an elaborate small-scale Romanesque doorway. After six miles, a right turn on to the N 741 leads to the ruins of the Abbey of La Réau. (Open Easter–1 October, 10–12, 14.00–18.00; closed on Wednesdays and Fridays; guided tours.) Once one of the richest abbeys of Poitou, it flourished for a century and a half after its foundation at the end of the twelfth century. Burnt in the Hundred Years' War by English raiders, it was rebuilt with fortifications; but in the sixteenth century it was attacked by a local lord (who was eventually executed for this sacrilege), and thereafter fell into decline until 1652, when it was restored. The belfry fell onto the nave in the nineteenth century,

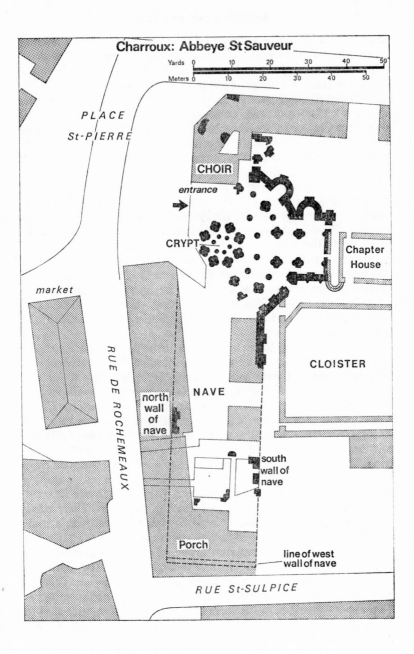

**Charroux: Abbeye St Sauveur**

Yards 0 10 20 30 40 50

Meters 0 10 20 30 40 50

PLACE
St-PIERRE

CHOIR

entrance

CRYPT

Chapter
House

market

RUE DE ROCHEMEAUX

CLOISTER

NAVE

north
wall
of
nave

south
wall of
nave

Porch

line of west
wall of nave

RUE St-SULPICE

and only the apse, the walls and a chapterhouse remain, the latter (with a seventeenth-century staircase) as part of a private house.

From La Réau, turning left on to the N 741 and right on to the D 10, we reach **Charroux**. Here again the abbey stands in ruins, demolished in the nineteenth century. Enough remains to show that this was a disastrous loss, on a par with the disappearance of the church at Cluny or the old cathedral at Limoges at about the same time. Its church was once the largest in Poitou, because it was a great centre of pilgrimage. Founded in the eighth century by Count Roger of Limoges, it was the scene, in 989, of the great assembly which declared 'the truce of God'. This was less an attempt at international peacemaking than a precursor of the Geneva convention on the conduct of war. Specifically, the decrees of the council of Charroux forbade Christians to plunder churches, strike unarmed clergy or to carry off the livestock of peasants. Later refinements of the idea tried to impose a ban on warfare from Wednesday evening to Monday morning, as well as on feast-days. In practice, only Sundays and feast-days were regarded as times of truce, and even that rule was often broken. But that the attempt to regulate war should be made at all shows how tired men had become of anarchy at the end of the tenth century.

The ruins belong to an eleventh-century church, dedicated by Urban II in 1096 to St Maurice as patron saint. It must have been a very imposing and individual building. The impressive tower was situated above the high altar, and its base formed the focal point of the church. The relics, which included a fragment of the True Cross, were housed in a circular crypt below it. The plan was that of a basilica (similar to St Hilaire at Poitiers) in which crowds of pilgrims and imposing processions could be accommodated, but of most unusual form. The tower was the centre of a rotunda, with two rings of pillars and then an outer wall surrounding it (see plan), echoing the circular plan of the Holy Sepulchre. The diameter was 120 feet, and the highest point was the third storey of the tower. There was a small choir to the east, and a broad nave to the west, with a huge entrance porch and twin bell-towers above the façade.

In the cloisters a small museum has been laid out, containing some thirteenth-century sculpture from the façade: note the Christ in Judgment and the figures of the wise and foolish virgins. There is also a collection of Romanesque and Gothic ivories and metalwork. Two abbots' croziers, in the form of a tau cross, were excavated in 1949, and two reliquaries in silver gilt were found in a hiding place in the cloister in 1856.

The N 148 follows the beginning of the Charente valley to **Civray**. Here the church of **St Nicholas,** tucked away in a little square to the right of the main road, has survived after a fashion. It has a striking screen-façade, which was thoroughly restored in the nineteenth century by being entirely dismantled, left on the ground for a year or more, and then rebuilt with a modern tympanum added. Despite this the sculptures still have something of their original glory, though they are no longer painted in brilliant colours, as in the Middle Ages. Themes familiar from other churches in Saintonge include the signs of the zodiac and the labours of the months. On the upper archivolt to the north a delightful group of angels play a whole orchestra of medieval instruments: rebec, bells, harp, olifant, viol, flute, dulcimer, pan-pipes, triangle and castanets. On the corresponding place to the south is St Nicholas flanked by two striking statues of Music and Dancing. Curiously, the façade is late-Romanesque, contemporary with the interior of Poitiers Cathedral, but it seems a world away from the simple, elegant lines of the new style, in its deliberate four-square echoes of classical arches.

Across the N 10 the N 148 brings us to **Melle**, the site of a Roman silver mine which was reopened by archaeologists in 1971. Of its three Romanesque churches **St Savinien** (on the right of the main road after the market square) has had a chequered history, and was used as a prison for many years. Its silhouette above the town promises more than there is. The interior is unrestored, and only the doorway is of interest, with an unusual saddleback lintel, probably from an earlier building, showing Christ between two lions. The finest of the three, **St Hilaire**, a little further along the road to the left, has a riverside setting, its apse and belfry making an attractive composition in the hollow of the valley. Around it are the old paved paths, and the stream flows between gardens to the east. To the west a magnificent staircase descends from the hillside through the west door into the church itself. A much-restored figure of the Emperor Constantine is above the north door. Whether it was originally Constantine is open to doubt. Inside, the high nave and aisles have simple capitals echoing those at Chauvigny; here the donor is named – 'Aimeric asked for me to be made'. The most interesting capital is an unusual scene of a boar at bay in the nave, on the south side – perhaps this was Aimeric's favourite sport?

To the north of the town, above the river valley, stands **St Pierre**. (It is not easy to find: from the N 148 fork right for the station, and then turn right across the river. The first turning left then leads to it.) Constructed on a slightly smaller scale to St Hilaire, it is a simple and well-proportioned building, with echoes of the church at Aulnay (p. 79) in its plan and its details. There is a plain apse, and two chapels in the transepts, a simple barrel-vaulted roof, and only the capitals offer a little decoration, mainly monsters and masks: in the north aisle there is an Entombment of Christ. Otherwise the builders have relied entirely on the balance of architectural details to achieve their effect, as with the west façade and the outside of the apse. Only on the south face is there sculpture, a much-damaged Christ in Majesty.

Four miles north-west of Melle, again on the N 148, the abbey at **Celles-sur-Belle** has a magnificent doorway. Instead of the orthodox arrangement of receding banded arches running down to pillars on each side, forming a vista into the church, the arches are replaced by a series of lobed decorations based on Moorish patterns which draw the attention to the doorway. These vaults occur elsewhere in France along the great pilgrim roads, and remind us that the worlds of Christianity and Islam were far from completely separate. Even more surprisingly, this exotic entrance leads into a simple, very late Gothic church built by Le Duc in the seventeenth century, as at St Maixent (p. 51).

From Celles-sur-Belle we can return to Melle and take the N 150 toward Poitiers, which leads to Lusignan – this is the route we shall follow; or head south for Saintonge, by turning right in Melle for Aulnay and St Jean-d'Angély (see Chapter 4).

6. **(left)** St Savin-sur-Gartempe. Clustered round the great monastic church, the town still has a peaceful contemplative air

7. **(below)** The harbour at La Cotinière, Ile d'Oléron

8. The façade of the church of St Pierre at Aulnay. On the borders of
Saintonge and Poitou, standing at a cross-roads, its subtle harmonies and
outstanding sculpture are enhanced by the clear light of the open country

# Chapter 3

# South-West Poitou and Aunis

✌

To the south of Poitiers, the valley of the Clain forms a small secret country of its own, but beyond, to the south-west, the rolling plain reappears, leading to the flat sea-coast, once marshes, but now well drained and fertile. Here we leave the Middle Ages behind, and the seventeenth century predominates.

The N 741 from Poitiers leads to **Gençay**, where the remains of the castle in which John the Good is said to have been imprisoned after the battle of Poitiers are being restored. A mile to the north, left along the D 1, is **St Maurice**, whose square, fortified bell-tower appears above the trees in the river valley. Here the apse is unusual, divided into three chapels, the central one being very deep. The outside of the apse has blind arcading around the upper part. The frescoes range from the fourteenth to the sixteenth century, and include a Christ in Majesty in the choir.

Along the N 742 toward Lusignan, **Château-Larcher** appears in a dramatic site on the Clouère valley. The church is in fact the chapel of the ruined castle, and forms part of the dominant group of buildings in the middle of the village. A flight of steps leads up to the west façade, built in a rose-tinted stone. The carvings are similar to those at Lusignan, to whose lords Château-Larcher also belonged. In the village cemetery there is a thirteenth-century *lanterne des morts*, where bodies were placed before burial.

Cross the N 10 at Vivonne, where one restaurant, La Treille, offers good food in simple modern surroundings. If you follow the N 742 **Lusignan** appears to the right, crowned by its church. The road running uphill to the left takes you through the centre of the town and on to the end of the ridge, where a skilfully laid-out garden, the work of the Comte de Blossac in the eighteenth century, marks the site of the castle. A miniature in the manuscript known as *Les Très Riches Heures du Duc de Berry* shows it in its fifteenth-century splendour (plate 12); now very little is left of the stronghold of one of the most powerful families in Aquitaine. In the course of the Middle

Ages members of the family of Lusignan became kings of Jerusalem, Cyprus, Armenia and Bohemia, and Dukes of Luxemburg. William de Valence, Earl of Pembroke, was son of a count of Lusignan who changed his name and came to England when the family fortunes were at a low ebb in 1247. This remarkable dynasty claimed an extraordinary ancestress, the fairy Mélusine, whose story first appears in a fourteenth-century romance written for Jean, Duc de Berry. According to this, one of the counts of Poitou, having accidentally killed his uncle while out hunting, met Mélusine as he wandered through the forest in despair at his misfortune. She was a marvellously beautiful fairy, and he at once married her, in a chapel which she built by magic at Lusignan. Her only condition was that he should never see her on a Saturday. After the marriage she built castles at Lusignan, Niort and elsewhere, and bore the count ten sons, ancestors of the various Lusignan lines, who were all deformed in some way but were great soldiers. At length the count was prevailed on by his brother, who suspected Mélusine of being unfaithful, to spy on her one Saturday; he watched her bathing and saw to his horror that she had a serpent's tail. She noticed him, and reproached him bitterly, because she was now condemned to leave him and go back to her unhappy, endless existence as a fairy. Only his constancy to his vow could have released her to lead a human life and die a human death. And she vanished from the castle in the form of a dragon.

This romance, by Jean d'Arras, was invented from vague hints of a fairy who had built the castle; no earlier versions of it are known. There is more than a passing resemblance to the demon ancestress of the Plantagenet family, who would go to Mass but never stayed for the elevation of the Host: when her husband got his retainers to hold her back, she flew shrieking out of the door, leaving her cloak in their hands, never to reappear. Like the Plantagenets, the Lusignans were relatively humble lords who quickly rose to great power: and medieval men, accustomed to thinking in terms of an immutable order of society, looked for some extraordinary explanation for their careers. In the case of the Lusignans, their fall was almost as rapid as their rise. When the French conquered Poitou in the 1240s the Lusignans put up a bitter resistance, opposed to any powerful central rule, whether English or French. But St Louis took ten of their castles; the Countess Isabella of Lusignan, who had once been wife of King John and Queen of England, declared that the nobles were now reduced to slavery. Elsewhere they met with varying fortunes; even in the late nineteenth century there were Lusignan kings in Armenia until they were dethroned in the 1880s. The wife of the heir to the throne thereupon founded a chivalric Order of Mélusine as a fund-raising effort, while the heir himself ended his days as manager of an Italian railway station buffet.

From the site of the castle the town is dominated by the church, an imposing late-twelfth-century building, with a simple and spacious interior. The nave is spacious by Poitevin standards, and the details very restrained. There is a good fifteenth-century half-timbered house opposite the church, and at the east end the river Vonne curls lazily below between meadows and poplars.

The N 11 runs through level country, largely given to mixed arable and dairy farming, to **St Maixent l'École** (*L'École* is the national military school for NCOs). Turn left down the avenue de l'École Militaire at the end of the Place Denfert, and then right at a small church, and you will reach the **Abbey Church**. Destroyed in the Wars of Religion, it was rebuilt in flamboyant Gothic style by François Le Duc from 1670 onward. It is all light and space after the Romanesque churches, an unexpected masterpiece. A few traces of the earlier church remain in the aisle walls and in the west doorway, and the empty seventh-century sarcophagi of St Maixent and St Léger in the crypt are a reminder of the early date of its foundation. The Maurists, a congregation of French Benedictine monks founded in 1621, were responsible for the new building. Their speciality was the study of the history of the Church and in the course of the seventeenth and eighteenth centuries their scholars published editions of the works of St Bernard, St Augustine and many other Fathers of the Church, some of which are still in use today; and they established many of the methods of modern textual criticism. They also produced works on medieval history and literature. When the order was suppressed during the French Revolution they had published 200 huge folio volumes and left over 800 volumes of manuscript material for unfinished projects. Indeed, a great many of the historical details in this book were first established by their researches.

The church reflects much of the Maurist temperament: the choice of a medieval style, the relative simplicity of the detail, and the use of the best possible models for the vaulting and windows. Occasionally a hint of later styles creeps in, as with the nave capitals, and the pattern of the great rose window is a little more rigid than its medieval predecessors. When they wanted to copy exactly they could do so: the sculptors who carved some new capitals for the crypt have made it impossible to tell which are eleventh-century and which are seventeenth-century. The only important change in the interior has been the removal of the rood screen to behind the west door, opening up the vista down the nave. This screen and the choir stalls are very much in the seventeenth-century style, with no concessions to medievalism.

The exterior of the church is less successful, despite its rows of flying buttresses. The rue Anatole France, opposite the west door, has a fifteenth-century apothecary's house, complete with Latin sign saying 'Here is health'. The centre of the town follows the medieval street plan but has nothing very distinguished to offer. Returning to the main road, the old town gate stands at the end of an avenue of trees as we continue toward Niort.

La Mothe-St-Heraye, six miles south of St Maixent, has the ruins of two châteaux, one medieval, one sixteenth-century.

**Niort** was an important medieval market town and port, using the river Sèvre. It was also famous for its glove-making industry. Now the markets and glove-making remain, but the main activity is industrial: plywood, machine-tools, heating equipment, electronics and chemicals. Arriving in the town by the N 11, we come first to the Place de la Brèche, and turn right down to the river. The **Keep** of the twelfth-century castle towers incongruously above the market hall and other modern buildings. It was reputedly built by Henry II and completed by Richard Coeur-de-Lion; but recent historians have questioned this: there is no documentary evidence, and the supposed resemblance to English castles of the period is dubious. The semi-circular buttresses and the double keep are closer to the architecture of Loches or Touffou, in other words to French-built castles. The present building contains the two original keep-towers, linked by fifteenth-century works which filled in the space behind the curtain walls. All the outer works, which were nearly half a mile in circumference, have vanished. The interior now contains a folklore museum: there is one display worth noticing, a reconstruction of a nineteenth-century farmhouse interior, but the rest is uninteresting. A staircase leads to the ramparts, with a view over the river: it requires a considerable feat of imagination to conjure up the original state of the castle among so much twentieth-century activity.

At the top of the hill, behind the town hall, **Notre Dame** has an elegant spire, over 200 feet high, on a Gothic base. The north doorway is a powerful flamboyant Gothic composition, but the interior is gloomy, due to the absence of a clerestory. Next to the town hall, the **Musée des Beaux Arts** (open 10–12, 14.00–18.00; closed on

Tuesdays) contains tapestries, ivories and jewellery on the ground floor and first floor, and paintings on the second floor. The portraits include one of Madame de Maintenon, who, as Francoise d'Aubigné, was born at Niort in 1635, and who became Louis XIV's second wife. There is also a portrait of Madame de Montespan, Louis XIV's mistress, to whom Madame de Maintenon owed her first place at court. Among the nineteenth-century paintings is a Corot landscape.

The **Rue St Jean** leads downhill past a number of old houses of the sixteenth century to the rue Victor Hugo. Crossing this, we come to the old town hall, a delightful little Renaissance building. This was the work of a master mason, Mathurin Berthomme, between 1530 and 1535. There is a distant hint of the keep in its plan, but the details, including ornamental battlements, are entirely sixteenth-century. It houses a collection of sculpture, coins and archaeological remains (key from 1 rue Yver, behind the old town hall; open 10–12, 14–18 (17), closed on Tuesdays).

Opposite the market hall the **Cloche d'Or** restaurant offers a good meal in scruffy surroundings: it is not as cheap as it looks. Try the *soufflé glacé à l'angélique* – angelica being a local speciality. If you have ever wondered what it is, it is the candied rib of the leaf of a herb, called the 'angelic herb' in Latin because it was good against plague and pestilence – a seventeenth-century poet called it 'that happy counterbane, sent down from heav'n'.


From Niort the N 11 goes through Frontenay to Mauzé. The direct road to La Rochelle is the N 22, but it is well worth taking the longer route via **Surgères**. The castle has vanished, except for its outer wall, which contains a Romanesque church and the one memorial to its sixteenth-century owner, Hélène de Surgères, in the shape of an elegant Renaissance gateway, which now leads to a shady garden laid out on the site of the keep. Hélène de Surgères was one of the maids of honour of Catherine de Medici, and was the inspiration of Pierre de Ronsard's famous *Sonnets pour Hélène*, in which he wooed her in vain. W. B. Yeats paraphrased one of these in a poem which is now as well known in English as the original is in French:

> When you are old and grey and full of sleep,
> And nodding by the fire, take down this book,
> And slowly read, and dream of the soft look
> Your eyes had once, and of their shadows deep;

How many loved your moments of glad grace,
And loved your beauty with love false or true,
But one man loved the pilgrim soul in you,
And loved the sorrows of your changing face;
And bending down beside the glowing bars,
Murmur, a little sadly, how Love fled
And paced upon the mountain overhead
And hid his face amid a crowd of stars.

Though Yeats has changed Ronsard's central theme, that Hélène's beauty will live in his poetry long after it has vanished, the course of Ronsard's love for her was as Yeats described it: for she left the court, and Ronsard consoled himself with the poetic joys of Parnassus and of the Pleiades, as he and his fellow-poets were called. She retired to Surgères, where she spent the rest of her life doing good works and running her brother's household.

The church has changed little since her day, apart from the restoration of the façade in the nineteenth century. It is a spacious Romanesque building, whose formal arcading must have been admired by Renaissance eyes. It is an unusually wide façade, extended beyond the real width of the church. The geometrical ornament of the arcades contrasts with the swarm of creatures who inhabit the two friezes running across the whole width: on the lower one you can make out the signs of the zodiac, interspersed by show-men, acrobats, monkeys playing instruments and mythical creatures, while the labours of the months are the theme of the upper band. Two figures of horsemen flank the central window, of uncertain identity: one may be the Emperor Constantine, the other Christ triumphant over evil. Above the façade rises a sixteen-windowed belfry, with multiple columns which seem to reach upward to a missing higher storey. The interior is airy: the original barrel vault of the nave was replaced by a Gothic roof, but the choir retains its intimate original proportions. There is a small funeral crypt below the apse, lit by a double window, where Hélène de Surgères was probably buried.

The gardens behind the present *mairie*, part of the seventeenth-century rebuilding of the château by the Rochefoucauld family, run from the ramparts down to the edge of the river Gères.

On the main square opposite the entrance to the castle, the Trois Piliers restaurant provides a good meal at reasonable prices.

South of Surgères on the D 114 **Vandré** has a church with a restrained but engaging façade – a hint of the polylobed doorway at Celles and of Surgères's own more formal composition. **Genouille**, a mile or two to the south on the D 212, has a slightly more elaborate version of Vandré's façade, showing how local masons tended to copy from available models – or indeed that the same team would move on to another church when one had been completed.

From Surgères the N 139 leads to **La Rochelle**, whose huge bypass and approach roads warn us that we are back in the twentieth century. Fortunately, most of La Rochelle's industry – ship-building, engineering and fishing – is sited away from the old centre, at La Pallice and south of the town. But La Rochelle is a relatively new town by the standards of the region. Its first certain appearance in history is about 1126, when Châtelaillon, six miles to the south, was destroyed. The inhabitants fled to La Rochelle, and by the end of the twelfth century it had become a commune under the protection of Eleanor of Aquitaine, who is said to have rebuilt the port. In 1224 the town was captured by Louis VII, and remained in French hands until the Treaty of Brétigny in 1359. In 1372 an English fleet was defeated outside La Rochelle by a combined Castilian and French force, and the inhabitants managed to overpower the English garrison.

Despite constant English raids, La Rochelle remained loyal to the Crown until the Reformation. The Protestants became numerous in the town after 1560, and in 1568 the threat of military occupation by royal troops led to a *coup d'état*, as a result of which La Rochelle declared itself an independent Protestant republic on the model of Geneva. Charles IX entrusted its recapture to Blaise de Monluc (see p. 226), but before he could lay siege to it peace was signed at Longjumeau.

La Rochelle now became the chief Protestant stronghold in France, and not only from a military point of view. A college was founded by Jeanne d'Albret (see p. 222) in 1571, with professors of Greek, Latin and Hebrew; and in 1571 a synod of all the French Protestant churches was held there. As such, it was the obvious target for a royalist counter-attack, and at the end of 1572 a besieging army under the Duke of Anjou encamped around the town. But the besiegers were unable to penetrate the very strong defences, and when ambassadors arrived to announce that the Duke had been elected King of Poland a peace was arranged. (The Duke refused to take part in the celebrations to mark the peace, and when the citizens of La Rochelle presented him with rare creatures, parrots and monkeys, one of the monkeys bit him on the finger!) A period of

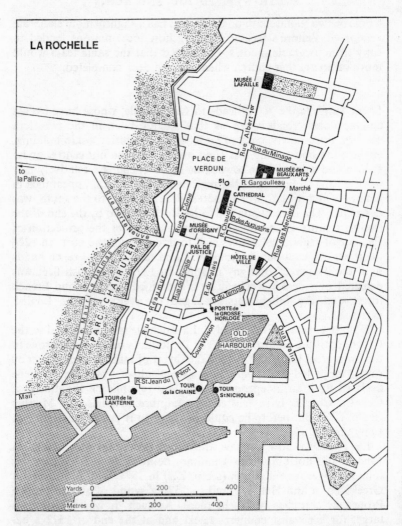

LA ROCHELLE

MUSÉE LAFAILLE

Rue Albert 1er

Rue du Minage

PLACE DE VERDUN

MUSÉE des BEAUX ARTS

St O  R. Gargoulleau

Marché

CATHEDRAL

R. St Côme

R. Chaudrier

R des Augustins

MUSÉE d'ORBIGNY

PAL DE JUSTICE

HÔTEL DE VILLE

Rue Réaumur

Rue de l'Escale

R. du Palais

R. du Temple

PORTE de la GROSSE HORLOGE

Cours Wilson

OLD HARBOUR

Quai Valin

Ave Mauro Delmas

PARC CHARRUYER

Rue Porte Neuve

to la Pallice

Mail

R St Jean du

Perot

TOUR de la CHAINE

TOUR St NICHOLAS

TOUR de la LANTERNE

Yards 0     200     400
Metres 0     200     400

peace followed, during which the Grand Temple was built in its original form, a huge octagon with a wooden roof covered in lead, the largest Protestant church in France.

From 1612 onward there was a series of disputes over religious liberty, which led to the famous siege of 1628. Louis XIII decided to reduce the town to obedience by force and laid siege to it in October; and the inhabitants responded by enlisting the help of George

Villiers, Duke of Buckingham, the favourite of Charles I. However, the English intervention lasted only a few weeks: Buckingham withdrew from his encampment on the Ile de Ré, and was assassinated by his valet Felton soon afterwards. For the moment La Rochelle had to rely on its own resources. Under the leadership of Jean Guiton, a stubborn resistance was offered to the huge army of 30,000 men which Louis XIII commanded in person. By July 1629 the town was very short of food, and only the arrival of a new English fleet, under the Earl of Lindsay, prolonged the siege. But the English ships were in poor condition, and made no serious attempt to break down a dyke which had been built to bar access to the port. At the end of October Guiton admitted defeat: La Rochelle became an ordinary French town once more.

The old harbour is at the centre of the town. It is now used almost entirely by pleasure craft, particularly yachts, this being one of the most active sailing centres on the Atlantic coast. The powerful fortifications contrast with this peaceful scene. Looking seaward, the entrance is guarded by the **Tour St Nicholas** on the left and the **Tour de la Chaine** on the right. Both have fourteenth-century origins, but the Tour de la Chaine has been much altered. From the latter, as its name indicates, a huge chain was hung across the harbour mouth and attached to the Tour St Nicholas to close the entrance against surprise attack. For until the nineteenth century privateers, official or unofficial, plagued this coast. Both towers can be visited (in summer 9–12, 14.00–18.00, in winter 9–12, 14.00–17.00; closed on Tuesdays and in October). The Tour St Nicholas is the more elaborate, with a large vaulted central room and an outside gallery half way up. At the foot of the Tour de la Chaine there is a model of La Rochelle with a *son et lumière* commentary explaining its history.

From the Tour de la Chaine a road along the top of the wall leads to the Tour de la Lanterne (hours as above), the highest and most elegant of the three towers, built in the fifteenth century and used as a lighthouse and later as a prison. The guardroom now contains an exhibition of pictures of La Rochelle from the sixteenth to the nineteenth century. The upper floors were used as the actual place of confinement, and innumerable graffiti record the names, and often the stories, of prisoners. The most famous of these graffiti bear the names of two of the 'four sergeants of La Rochelle', executed in 1822 for their part in organising a radical secret society similar to that of the Carbonari in Italy. Louis XVIII, no lover of such movements, is said to have asked, when a plea for clemency was presented to him, 'When are they to be executed?' 'At four in the morning, sire.' 'Then I will pardon them at five.' Many other inscriptions record English and Dutch captives from privateers or from warships, from 1660 onward. One tragedy in miniature reads: 'To the memory of William Freethy Gunner of the Lively Privateer who in attempting to escape from this prison was unfortunately shot dead the night of XV Oct 1778.'

Further up the staircase there is a fine view over the town and the shore from a precarious balcony round the lantern. About half a mile from the harbour entrance, at low tide, are the remains of the immense dyke built for Richelieu by the architect Métezeau and the master mason Thiriot. This effectively blocked off the port during the siege, with a space left to allow the tide to flow through and thus ease the pressure on the structure. The inhabitants refused to believe that it would stand up to a storm, and did not take it seriously: but it proved to be the key factor in defeating them.

On the old harbour, a number of seventeenth-century houses survive, with arcades below which once led to warehouses. There are several good restaurants specialising in seafood, none of them cheap: the best and most expensive is Serge (46 cours Wilson), while the Bar André in rue St Jean is more modest but also good. From the harbour the Porte de La Grosse Horloge leads into the town. Turning right along the rue du Temple you come to the Hôtel de Ville. Much restored in 1879, the Gothic front, complete with battlements and a belfry, conceals a heavy Renaissance front, built under Henri IV at the end of the sixteenth century. His initials and those of his wife, Marie de Medici, appear as monograms between the classical ornaments. Its interior (open in summer 9–12, 14.00–17.30, in winter 10–12, 14.00–16.00; apply to concièrge) contains one or two rooms with original details, including the office of Jean Guiton, mayor during the great siege of 1628. An apocryphal but famous story tells how when he was appointed, soon after the siege had begun, he agreed to accept the post and then, drawing his dagger, said that he would plunge it into the heart of the first man to talk of peace, and thrust it into the table in front of him. His house is just round the corner from the Hôtel de Ville, at 3 and 5 rue des Merciers, a street which still retains the spacious arcades that are one of La Rochelle's most pleasing features, even though shop displays now tend to invade them and block off the long vistas. Crossing the market square, the rue du Minage (whose name commemorates an old feudal tax on corn grown on the lord's estate) has a sixteenth-century fountain at one end and another fine set of arcades, which continue into the Place de Verdun. Here the Café de la Paix survives with its late-nineteenth-century interior in fine condition. The square itself marks the site of the medieval castle. The cathedral is a heavy and dull eighteenth-century building, a severe reminder of orthodoxy to any would-be Protestants who remained. Just off the Place de Verdun, in the rue Gargoulleau, is the Musée des Beaux Arts, whose own collections are frankly uninteresting, except for one or two paintings of Algeria by Eugène Fromentin, better known as a novelist and author of *Dominique*, a pastoral romance set in the country around La Rochelle. However, there are also temporary exhibitions, and these are often worth seeking out.

If you return toward the rue du Minage, the rue Albert Ier runs north to the **Musée Lafaille** (open 10–12, 14.00–18.00 (17.00 in winter); closed on Sundays a.m., Monday, holidays). This elegant Louis XVI house stands in its own botanic gardens. Inside there is an extraordinary collection, mainly eighteenth-century, of natural history; but the chief glory is the study of the founder of the museum, Clement Lafaille, who left the house to the *Académie* of La Rochelle in 1770. His study has been preserved intact, with marvellous panelling and specially-made cabinets to hold his collection of shells. The carving is decorated with scientific objects, and the whole room is a perfect reflection of the eighteenth-century scientist, a man of taste and learning who regarded science much as his neighbour might have regarded art or literature.

The **Rue du Palais**, with more arcades, runs beside the cathedral; just off it, down the rue des Augustins, is a house in the mid-sixteenth-century style of the reign of Henry II; built for a local lord in 1555, it has two asymmetrical wings, a gallery and a loggia, echoing in miniature the great Renaissance châteaux on the Loire. An unusual feature, copied from classical models, are the oxen's heads or *bucrania*. Back in the rue du Palais, the Palais de Justice itself is in the late-eighteenth-century classical manner which dominates Bordeaux, and which lingered on through the nineteenth century. The Hôtel de la Bourse, a few yards further on, is a much more interesting building, with its open portico where merchants could discuss business as they walked up and down. There are suitably naval details in its carved decorations.

At the end of the rue du Palais we are back at the Porte de la Grosse Horloge; just before, we turn right and then take the cobbled rue de l'Escale, part of which used to be the aristocratic quarter. Here the arcades give way to houses with private courtyards, reserved and aloof. Turning left into the rue Reaumur, the Musée d'Orbigny (hours as Musée Lafaille, above) has in its garden the chain which used to be hung across the harbour mouth. Inside the ground floor illustrates the history of La Rochelle, including mementoes of the great siege. The eighteenth-century china factory, which functioned spasmodically from 1722 to 1728 and from 1752 to 1788, is represented by a good collection of pieces in eighteenth-century showcases on the first floor. The **Rue Porte-Neuve** leads to the **Parc Charruyer**, whose paths wind between trees planted along the old city moat, where a stream runs down to the sea. At the southern end it leads to the Mall and casino, and a further series of parks and avenues along the sea front.

Beyond the old town sprawls a vast complex of industrial building and modern housing, of which the drive to **La Pallice**, the embarkation point for the **Ile de Ré**, gives a more than adequate idea. The N 22 crosses the southern end of the Parc Charruyer, and the way to the car-ferry (*bac*) is well signed. Boats leave at frequent intervals, and even in winter a wait of more than twenty minutes is unlikely. The crossing takes about ten minutes.

As with La Rochelle, there is little trace of any settlement on the Ile de Ré before the eleventh century. In the Middle Ages it was famous for its wine and its salt, but it is now mainly a farming community, though tourists are rapidly becoming an important industry in July and August. It is a low-lying island, edged by dunes; the brilliance of the sunlight in the sea air and the little white-washed houses have earned it the name of 'the white island'. The road along the south shore (D 201) runs along the sandy coast, though there are few good bathing beaches. It rejoins the N 735 at Couarde; crossing a narrow neck of land joining what are really two separate islands, we come to Ars-en-Ré, which has a fifteenth-century church steeple, once used as a landmark and look-out, with a fine view; the garrulous sexton is usually somewhere nearby and will unlock the door. In the tightly grouped houses is a Renaissance seneschal's house.

At the very end of the island the **Phare des Baleines** rises to a height of 170 feet, dwarfing its seventeenth-century predecessor which stands beside it. Some 250 steps bring you to the lighthouse-keeper's bedroom, a mahogany-panelled Victorian cabin, perched like an eyrie just below the lantern. A gallery gives a spacious view over the island, down to La Rochelle and the Ile d'Oléron. Northward, the flat marshland or Marais Poitevin stretches toward Les Sables d'Olonne.

On the way back, turn left in Couarde for St Martin de Ré, the largest village on the island. In 1625 the island was recaptured from the Protestants at La Rochelle by the royalist governor Toiras. He built fortifications round the town, and repulsed attacks by the English invading force who had encamped at the western end of the island, near Ars-en-Ré. Although the English forces were almost successful in starving out his garrison, relief arrived just in time; and when Louis XIII sent reinforcements across from the mainland the besiegers withdrew. The present fortifications date from the mid-seventeenth century and are the work of the great military engineer Vauban. Entering from the west, cross the outer line of fortifications near the Campani gate and you will come first to the old quarter and the port, now a yacht harbour. There are restaurants along the quay, including the St Hubert – more excellent sea-food.

The citadel, which lies to the east of the town, is not open to visitors, but it is worth walking along the Avenue Bonthillier past the naval museum in the Hôtel Clerjotte, the old town house of the lords of Ré. From the rue de la Citadelle can be seen the triumphal gateway, embellished with appropriate martial trophies, and the much smaller defensive entrance to the citadel proper. As you come back and turn along the Champ de Mars there is a good view of the citadel, and the Cours Vauban then leads to the Porte Toiras, which like the Porte Campani preserves all its original features, including the wooden portcullis lowered into the gateway by a winch. From the Porte Toiras the Cours Toiras leads back into the old quarter of the town: in the centre is the church of St Martin with remains of fifteenth-century fortifications. The formality of the eighteenth-century Place de la Republique and the narrow streets by the port reflect St Martin's dual existence as a naval garrison town and as a simple fishing village, both now largely matters of history.

Taking the ferry back to the mainland, bear left in La Pallice toward the aerodrome, and this will lead on to the bypass around La Rochelle; at the far end of the bypass the N 137 will take us south into Saintonge.

Chapter 4

# Saintonge and the Ile d'Oléron

✤

The Atlantic coast, with its wide sweep of marshes and dunes, is a very different landscape from that of Saintonge inland, a country of pastures and small villages, whose richness is echoed in the sculpture that decorates its churches.

From La Rochelle the busy N 137 runs parallel to the coast toward Rochefort. A turning to the right leads to the little port of **Fouras**, used mainly by yachtsmen. From the end of the Pointe de la Fumée a passenger ferry runs to the Ile d'Aix, departing every half-hour. The crossing lasts about 20 minutes. There is a small restaurant on the island, but little other shelter, so a fine day should be chosen.

The **Ile d'Aix** is another of the line of forts built by Vauban to protect the coast from English attacks in the seventeenth century. It commanded the approaches to Rochefort, and was reinforced by Fort Enet, a massive building that apparently rises sheer out of the water, and which can be seen looking toward the Ile d'Oléron as you cross to the Ile d'Aix. Further west is a similar structure, Fort Boyard.

From the landing stage there is a short walk along the quay to the main gate. The massive seventeenth-century ramparts did not prevent an English raiding party from capturing the island in 1757; a battle off the island in 1809 led to heavy French losses, and Napoleon ordered the building of the Fort de la Rade, to the left of the entrance, in 1810. He had visited the island in 1808, and had built himself a house there; and it was to Aix that he came at the end of his rule in France, in July 1815, after his defeat at Waterloo and abdication in the previous month. His situation was becoming desperate when he reached Rochefort on 3 July, with the Prussians in pursuit, the country around declaring in favour of the Bourbons. But he found his hope of escape by sea to America cut off by an English fleet. He debated for some days whether to try to slip away under cover of night and evade the English, as he had done when leaving Elba in 1814, to be taken aboard a Danish ship, *La Magdeleine*, bound for America. A scheme was even mooted whereby he was to be hidden in a specially padded brandy cask, in the event of the ship being searched by the English; but his valet Marchand recorded in his memoirs that 'the Emperor felt it undignified to be found hiding in the hold of a ship if he was captured', and the plan was abandoned. In the end, he was persuaded by his advisers to surrender to Captain Maitland of the *Bellerophon* on 15 July.

The house in which he spent the preceding three days is now a museum (open 10-12, 14.00–18.00), on the left at the end of the street which opens off the yew-lined Place d'Austerlitz. It houses a mass of relics of the Emperor, assiduously collected by the great-grandson of one of Napoleon's counsellors and companions in exile, Baron Gourgand. These present a different view to the English judgment of Napoleon as 'old Boney', a tyrant unloved by anyone; for Napoleon still has his followers in France. The Bourbons, the old royal family, arouse nothing like so much enthusiasm. The Emperor's bedroom is preserved almost exactly as it was when he left it for the last time.

At the end of the street the ring of fortifications is closed by ramparts and a water-filled moat; beyond, the island curves away to the Fort Liedot, two miles away to the north.

Continuing down the N 137 we reach **Rochefort**, the seventeenth-century rival to La Rochelle, which replaced it as a naval base. It was built for the latter purpose by Colbert in the 1660s, and its grid lay-out betrays its origin as a planned town. It was originally entirely made up of wooden buildings, but was rebuilt in stone under the supervision of Michel Bégon, better known for his introduction of the begonia plant to Europe. Of the vast dockyard built by Colbert only the main gateway remains, used as the entrance to the new docks created in 1830, at the end of the rue de l'Arsenal. Next to it the Hôtel de Cheusses, with another imposing gateway, houses a naval museum. Along the rue Toufaire an eighteenth-century garden has a terrace overlooking the Charente. A few other mementoes of the days when Rochefort was the centre of a great ship-building industry, producing 300 sailing ships a year, survive in the Musée Municipal (open 10–12, 13.30–17.30 (16.00 in winter); closed on Mondays), which also has a small picture collection. Pierre Loti was born at 141 rue Pierre Loti. He was a naval officer who used his experiences of distant and exotic places to write a series of very successful travel books, set in such places as Tahiti, Senegal and Japan; but his best books are probably the three he wrote about Breton deep-sea fishermen, one of which is the famous *Pêcheur d'Islande*. The museum contains his collection of exotic souvenirs from his travels.

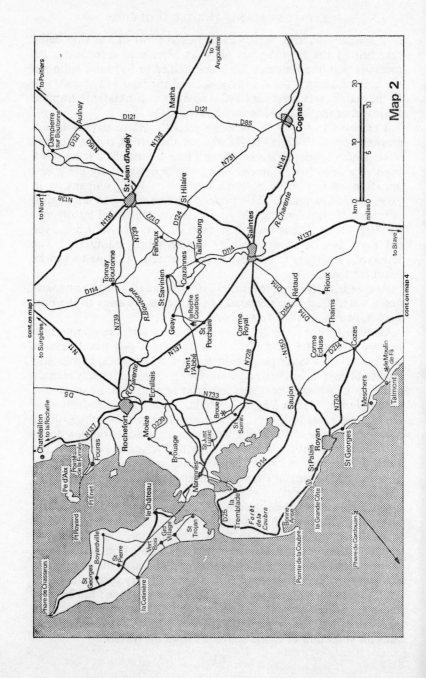

Map 2

cont. on map 1

cont. on map 4

**(right)** The Roman arch
[a]t Saintes; it stood originally
[o]n the bridge over the Charente,
[b]ut was rebuilt in 1842 on its
[p]resent site

[1]0. **(below)** The church at
[T]almont, on the Gironde
[e]stuary. Although part of the
[c]hurch has crumbled into the
[s]ea, it is still an impressive
[m]onument to past pilgrimages,
[o]n the route to Santiago in
[S]pain

[1]1. **(overleaf)** In the depths
[o]f the Saintonge countryside,
[th]e **lanterne des morts** at
[F]enioux is the most elaborate
[o]f these curious yet evocative
[st]ructures, found only in this
[r]egion

Taking the N 137 to Saintes and turning left after 15 miles, you will reach the château of **La Roche Courbon,** a much worthier monument to Loti. As a schoolboy in the 1870s he had come to know and love the château and its park, neglected since 1817. Its present owner had inherited it in 1856, and had never even visited it, while the only inhabitant was a caretaker whose instructions were to prevent anyone from entering the grounds. In 1907, when Loti had made his name as a writer, and was a member of the Académie Française, he heard that the castle was for sale, the owner having died; and the following year he wrote a famous appeal in a newspaper for someone to come forward and save La Roche Courbon, which he called 'the castle of the Sleeping Beauty'. He recorded how 'as I travelled all over the world, the barricaded castle and the depths of its forest of oaks still haunted my mind'. A buyer came forward, but he proved to be a confidence trickster, and twelve years later the château was for sale again. At last it was bought by a friend of Loti's, M. Chenereau, who restored and refurnished the castle, and tended the grounds and the forest beyond.

The original château was a square keep, built in the fourteenth century; a series of divided inheritances in the sixteenth century led to its neglect, and the present building is largely the work of Jeanne Gombaud in the early seventeenth century. She not only rebuilt the château but also reassembled the lands which had once belonged to it. It was further modified in the mid-seventeenth century by her grandson Jacques de Courbon, and half of the fourteenth-century keep was demolished soon after. A fire in about 1780 led to further alterations which were still in progress at the Revolution.

The entrance to the castle is a seventeenth-century gateway at the end of an avenue of trees (car park at entrance, open 9–12, 14.30–18.30 (17.30 in winter); closed on Thursdays; *son et lumière* July and August, weekends). Cross the moat and go into the inner courtyard through the gatehouse, part of the sixteenth-century castle remodelled in the eighteenth century: it contains a small museum of prehistoric finds from nearby sites. The tour of the interior begins at the doorway to the west wing, which has a simple early-seventeenth-century façade. In the first room, a library, are a number of local engravings. In the base of the tower a lavishly decorated bathroom presents a remarkable sight, covered in paintings on walls and ceiling. The ceiling paintings show stories from the Greek myths, with Jupiter in the centre, and the same themes provide the subjects for most of the paintings around the walls, with the exception of a series of little landscapes in the Dutch style. The arms and mottoes on the ceiling show that this cabinet was the work of Jacques de Courbon in the 1660s. The bath seems to be original, though the parquet floor and the portrait over the mantelpiece are both later.

The drawing room has a fine seventeenth-century painted ceiling and a picture of the château as it was at the end of that century. Beyond the fine Louis XVI staircase the dining room has not only a painted ceiling but also the original chimneypiece. The centrepiece of the kitchen is a clockwork spit of the eighteenth century which is still in working order. From the kitchen you go up to three rooms in the roof, two of which are devoted to a collection of religious art including a twelfth-century figure of the Virgin. The third is a remarkable chapel, framed by the massive roof-timbers whose inverted keel structure serves as a vault.

On the lowest level there is a series of rooms behind an Italianate loggia: one contains a collection of armour. From here you go out into the gardens. From the front of the château an ornamental staircase descends to a formal garden and to the lake, which was created to replace the unhealthy marsh in the valley in the 1920s. Another staircase leads to the beginning of a huge avenue into the forest on the other side of the valley; looking back, the château and its gardens might be an illustration from a Victorian book of fairytales.


North of La Roche Courbon on the D 122 **Geay** has a very simple Romanesque church, with beautifully balanced arcading on the exterior, set in an avenue of lime trees. The restraint of the decoration, the harmony of the detail and the warm yellow stone make a perfect small-scale composition, an enlargement perhaps of a little ivory casket of the period.

The D 128 leads to Crazannes, which has a castle built by the bishops of Saintes; only the outside can be visited, the best feature being a flamboyant Gothic doorway in ecclesiastical style on the main building.

A little further on turn left across the Charente into **Taillebourg**. All that remains of the feudal keep besieged on several occasions by Richard Coeur-de-Lion is a broad and peaceful terrace overlooking the river with a few crumbling piles of stone. An enchanting overgrown eighteenth-century garden accounts for the fine stone balustrades at the edge of the terrace. The lord of Taillebourg was not particularly important, nor was his castle militarily very important; but he was typical of the southern French lords, always eager to find an excuse to defy the central authority. It is difficult to imagine warfare in this drowsy pastoral scene: but Taillebourg was also the scene of Louis IX's victory over Henry III of England in 1242, the first skirmish being on the bridge, followed by a full-scale encounter two days later between Taillebourg and Saintes. This was indecisive, but Henry III beat a retreat to Saintes and then embarked at Blaye for fear that the French would attack again.

From Taillebourg the D 114 leads to **Saintes**, the chief town of the old province of Saintonge, named after the Gaulish tribe of Santones. When Caesar invaded Gaul in 58 BC the Santones lent him ships to attack the Breton coast; and they only joined Vercingetorix's rebellion in 52 BC at the last moment. Their pro-Roman attitude meant that their capital was one of the earliest towns in Gaul to be remodelled by the conquerors, and it became the capital of western Aquitaine as *Mediolanum*, 'the city in the centre'. It was later known as '*Mediolanum Santonum*' to distinguish it from other towns of the same name, and this became Saintes. Of its Roman remains the most conspicuous is the famous **Arch of Germanicus,** built before AD 19 by C. Julius Rufus. Old engravings show it standing on the bridge in the centre of the town. When this was demolished in 1842 Prosper Mérimée (see p. 41) succeeded in arranging for it to be rebuilt on the west bank of the river. It was a votive offering to the Emperor Tiberius, his son Drusus and his adopted son Germanicus, rather than a triumphal arch; the donor was a leading Gaulish citizen, possibly the descendant of a chieftain, and perhaps also the builder of the amphitheatre at Lyon. Its new setting is not so dramatic, and it is best seen from the other bank of the river. Just by it is a small archaeological museum (apply to caretaker), principally a collection of Roman carvings found in and around the town. Many of the pieces have a depth and freshness of detail which surviving monuments (including the Arch of Germanicus) have lost through weathering, because they were used as rubble in building a defensive wall round the town in the fifth century, and were only recovered in the last century.

On the opposite bank to the Arch of Germanicus lies the old quarter of the town. The spacious quays are bordered by eighteenth-century houses, many with elaborate ironwork: on the quai de Verdun there are gardens between the houses and the river, and there is relatively little traffic. The river, too, is peaceful, used mainly by pleasure boats – there are day-trips to La Rochelle in the summer – and by rowers. At the end of the quays turn across the Place Blair and back into the rue St Maur, where there are some private town houses in the eighteenth-century classical style: note a fine gateway at No 17, and a pilastered front at No 8. Off the rue St Maur an alley leads to the Musée Dupuy-Mestreau, another house of the same period complete with furnishings. Its façade, a miniature version of a grandiose classical composition, is charming. The rue Clemenceau leads to the cathedral, a late Gothic building. The huge belfry over the porch was never completed because of its vast scale. Much damaged in 1568, during the wars of religion, the interior was rebuilt in the seventeenth century; but the portal at the entrance, nestling between the massive buttresses, with its tiers of saints, angels and prophets, was largely spared by the Huguenots. The flying buttresses have delicate tracery and details.

From the cathedral the Place du Synode and the narrow rue de l'Evêché bring us to the foot of a flight of steps up to the Place du Capitole, a little irregular tree-lined square straight out of a nineteenth-century Romantic drawing. At the top of the steps there is a good view over the town. The rue des Jacobins runs down past the huge Gothic west window (dated 1446) of the **Chapelle des Jacobins** to the **Rue Alsace-Lorraine** where we turn left. In the **Place de l'Echevinage**, the old town hall (*échevinage*) has a classical façade visible through an eighteenth-century wrought-iron gate, flanked by a sixteenth-century belfry. Turn right into the Grande Rue, where the **Musée des Beaux Arts** occupies a well-restored seventeenth-century house. Its collection of ceramics, on the ground floor, ranges from the medieval to the nineteenth century; upstairs the pictures include a Breughel ('Allegory of the Earth'), a Salvator Rosa landscape and a portrait by Rigaud.

Returning via the quays across the bridge to the Arch of Germanicus, the rue Arc de Triomphe brings us to the Place de la Caserne and the entrance to the **Abbaye aux Dames**. Dedicated in 1047, the apse was rebuilt in the early twelfth century, the vaults toward the end of the twelfth century. The original church was built with the help of Countess Agnes of Burgundy, who was a benefactor of St Hilaire at Poitiers at about the same time, and both churches have the same spaciousness. But the Abbaye aux Dames is very different in its present appearance. Instead of the Byzantine intricacies of the pilgrimage church at St Hilaire it is airy and simple, as befits a nunnery. The façade must once have been more richly ornamented. Only the carvings on the vault of the doorway are original, where friezes of animals and flowers alternate with figures. The outer arch portrays the elders of the Apocalypse; then comes a theme often found in Saintonge, men fighting with axes and swords and grappling with each other, perhaps a memory of Viking raids, which were recent events when this doorway was built. The Lamb and the four symbols of the Evangelists follow, and finally the hand of God blesses the churchgoer from the keystone of the inner vault. Inside, there is an immediate change of style, for the severe straight lines of the façade do not even hint at the huge rounded cupolas which cover the nave. Sadly, the domes themselves are missing, destroyed by a fire in 1648, but their shape and that of the massive broken arches which supported them still dominate the church, dwarfing the little Romanesque apse. There is very little decoration. Perhaps this was because of the death of the master mason, Berengar, whose epitaph ends, in a complicated play on words beloved of medieval writers, '*quem petrum defunctum celat celare volebat petras cui petrus petra deo ante favebat*'. ('He who is covered by a stone now that he is dead wished to carve stones. It was through his rock that Peter once gave glory to God.') There is a powerful twelfth-century head of Christ in the south transept.

The loveliest part of the Abbaye aux Dames is its central tower, best seen from the outside of the east end. Its lowest storey rises four-square and solid from the mass of the building, above the gently crumbling curve of the apse, as if to support some massive plain structure above. Instead, a graceful rotunda with slender pillars rises out of it and vanishes into a simple conical spire of stone. On the corners of the lower storey four little pyramids echo the shape above.

The remains of the abbey buildings, used as a garrison from the early nineteenth century until 1924 (during which time the church became a store), lie to the right of the façade; it is a far cry from the days when the abbess was one of the great ladies of France and known as 'Madame de Saintes'. Madame de Montespan, Louis XIV's mistress, was educated here.

At the opposite end of the town, off the N 137 to Bordeaux, down the rue St Macoult and the rue Bourignon, lies the **Roman amphitheatre**, lying in a natural hollow in the hillside running down to the Charente valley. Built in the first century AD, it could hold 20,000 spectators on the tiers of stone seats, a huge number even by modern standards. Although it has suffered much at the hands of later builders, who used it as a gigantic quarry, its plan remains clear. The arena itself at the foot of the seats was six feet below the present ground level: at either end the gladiators or animals entered it through tunnels. At the east end the natural circle was made up by a massive stone structure whose ruins are now the most impressive feature of the amphitheatre. Although they appear to be built of rubble this is only a surface coating and conceals huge stone blocks within.

Following the rue Lacurie, and turning left into the rue St Eutrope, we arrive at the **Church of St Eutrope,** named after the supposed first bishop of Saintes who is said to be buried here. This was a favourite stopping-place for pilgrims on their way to Compostela; St Eutrope also had a great reputation as a shrine where miraculous cures took place, and Louis XI attributed his recovery from dropsy to a visit to this church. In gratitude he built the flamboyant Gothic belfry and the east end, a not entirely happy addition to the relatively simple Romanesque church. The façade is modern, for half the church was pulled down in 1802–3, and where we enter is in fact the far end of the nave. The original façade was at the far side of the square in front of the church, and the wall to the south of the open space is in fact that of the south side of the church. Like St Hilaire at Poitiers, the transept and choir were separated by a great flight of steps, so the nave would have been about six feet lower than the present ground level. It was another church designed for crowds of pilgrims to watch almost theatrical rituals: and all that remains today is the 'stage'. Built by a master mason named Benoit for Cluniac monks, the church was consecrated by Pope Urban II on his journey through France in 1096. The choir is sober and dark, with narrow side aisles lit by slit windows and small oculi above. The capitals are stylised versions of the Roman capitals, which must have been in evidence everywhere in Saintes at that period. In the crossing these formal carvings give way to exuberant fantasies. The height of the crossing makes them difficult to read, even with the lighting provided, as does the entangled riot of real and unreal figures and foliage. Three scenes can be made out, two from the story of Daniel and one showing St Michael weighing souls; but these are less carefully done than the decorative elements. The preference for shapes and patterns is typical of the sculpture of Saintonge, and we shall meet similar carvings even in quite humble churches.

The south side of the outside of the choir, though overshadowed by the mass of the belfry, has a section of the original Romanesque wall; the traditional arcading on the projecting chapel gives way to the less usual pattern made by the windows of the choir, with the oculi above included in a single arch springing from a pillar. The decoration is all severely geometrical. The south doorway leads to the crypt, which has survived unchanged, a massive vault with grouped, truncated pillars crouched to carry the weight of the church above. The little ambulatory at the east end has complex vaulting, designed to ensure the strength of the whole, and possibly arrived at by experiment rather than previous design. The massive capitals are forerunners of those in the church above, each consisting of leaf patterns, treated with varying degrees of complexity but with a sure feeling for line and form. Here for once is an untouched Romanesque ensemble, with nothing to distract the eye.

Saintonge is so rich in Romanesque churches that it is difficult to know when to stop describing them and to leave them as possible discoveries, tucked away down a byroad. Even toward the coast they are still thick on the ground. Leaving Saintes by the N 150 to Marennes, **Corme-Royal** is off the road to the right. Its façade has strange decorated pillars, whose textured surfaces have a faintly Moorish air, and vaults which seem to be made up of fully three-dimensional figures, so deep is the relief. These vaults show, to left and right, the combat of the virtues and vices, and round the central window, the seven wise virgins. Above the doorway, in an archaic, late classical style, roundels show adoring angels below Christ presenting the Gospel to the evangelists.

The splendour of the sculpture both here and at the neighbouring church of **Pont l'Abbé d'Arnoult** may be due to their being attached to the Abbaye aux Dames in Saintes. At Pont l'Abbé the façade is hemmed in by buildings and by a busy main road, so that its three wide arches lose their effect; most of the upper part has been rebuilt, and a tympanum added over the doorway. But the figures on the vaults have survived, and the central arch retains its play of light and shade on the receding curves of the vaults. The scheme is similar to that at Corme-Royal: the inner line is of adoring angels followed by the combat of virtues and vices and a vault decorated with saints. The outer vault shows the seven wise and seven foolish virgins. To the south, the supple carving of these figures is replaced by formal foliage around a tympanum of St Peter's crucifixion.

From Pont l'Abbé the D 18 and a right turn on to the N 733 lead to **Echillais**, just beyond the bridge across the Seudre, on the right. On a fine day the clear sea air and bright light emphasise the square outline and deep carving of the façade, which clearly echoes the triumphal arch at Saintes. Much of the rich detail has crumbled, but the bold patterns of the upper arcade still stand out: it is the flat face of each arch which is carved, rather than the vault, repeating the love of textured surfaces at Corme-Royal. To the left of the doorway a strange monster-mask seems to swallow the rising pillar. The outside of the choir has powerful pillar-buttresses instead of the usual slender vertical lines.

Return southward and take a turning just before the river, to the right, which leads across the marshes to **Moëze**, on the edge of a low-lying coastal plain which stretches to the far bank of the Seudre. In the little cemetery on the edge of the village is a curious 'hosanna cross' of the sixteenth century. Each Palm Sunday palm branches were carried in procession from the church and placed on this monument, which has no parallel anywhere else. A Latin inscription round the frieze commemorates the purpose of the shrine, which looks more like a delicate classical folly than anything religious.

The road winds south across the marshes to **Brouage**, once a flourishing harbour, now a deserted seventeenth-century fort in the most peaceful surroundings imaginable. Used as the royal arsenal during the siege of La Rochelle, its fortifications were built on Richelieu's orders from 1628 onwards. In its final form Brouage could hold a garrison of 6,000 men, but the silting-up of its harbour led to its gradual abandonment during the eighteenth century in favour of Rochefort and La Rochelle. Its only appearance in history was not warlike, but as the setting for the end of a royal love affair. Louis XIV, when he was only twenty, fell in love with the niece of Cardinal Mazarin, Marie Mancini, and wanted to marry her; but the Cardinal wished to cement his proposed alliance with Spain by the marriage of Louis XIV and the Infanta. Marie was sent into exile for a time at Brouage; when she failed to reply to a letter from Louis she was allowed to return to court, and soon after the Spanish marriage took place at St Jean de Luz. But Louis had not forgotten her, because on the return journey he played truant and spent a few days at Brouage in the same room that she had once occupied.

The massive archway of the Porte Royal pierces the ramparts and brings us to the Grande Rue. The town is laid out on a grid pattern within a square of defences. Steps beside the Porte Royale lead up to the ramparts, where the old sentry path survives on the north and west sides (*son et lumière* in summer, four nights a week). From the north side the site of the old harbour can be seen, while just below the ramparts is the old armoury. In the south-west corner is one of two old powder-magazines, the other being at the centre of the east rampart. The elms which now grow along the top of the walls have changed the once spartan appearance of the fort into something nearer to that of a landscaped terrace, with long views across to the sea and to Moëze. If only the débris of war was always as well-camouflaged and peaceful as this forgotten corner!

Traces of much earlier warfare survive at **Broue**, a dozen miles away across the marsh, to the north of St Sornin, off the N 728 from Saintes to Marennes. An unsigned left turn just after crossing the canal de Broue runs along a spur of land overlooking the plain, on the end of which the ruins of the square keep are perched, commanding the whole countryside.

**Marennes** is a great centre for oysters: the beds extend over thousands of acres in the estuary of the Seudre, which is not really an estuary but a shallow valley long since flooded by the sea. Its church, which is faintly English in appearance, has a 250-foot spire which served as a landmark for ships in the narrow channel between Marennes and the Ile d'Oléron. This passage is now crossed by a huge bridge (toll).

The **Ile d'Oléron** has two very distinct coasts. The north is a continuation of the plains and marshes of the mainland, with harbours such as **Le Château d'Oléron** which look like canals. This is the practical – farming and fishing – side of the island. Here you may still see old ladies wearing the traditional *quichenotte*, a large black bonnet said to get its name from a corruption of 'kiss not', because it protected the wearer very effectively from the attentions of raiding English troops. Toward the tip of the island, at Boyardville, dunes appear – the beach is good but very popular – and the south coast is entirely dunes and pine forests, a continuation of the **Côte Sauvage** on the mainland (p. 74). **St Georges d'Oléron** has a Romanesque church with a façade based on that of Pont L'Abbé, with purely geometrical decoration. Just outside the village the Trois Chapons restaurant offers a reasonably priced meal. At the tip of Oléron the lighthouse of **Chassiron** matches the **Phare des Baleines** on the Ile de Ré, which can be seen from it on a clear day. The whole island was once a great trading centre, but the dangers of the coast also made its ships an easy prey for wreckers. The Rolls of Oléron are the earliest surviving attempt at laying down a law of the sea. They were set down, so the story goes, on the command of Eleanor of Aquitaine in 1199, and throughout the Middle Ages and sixteenth century these customs were respected as the laws governing shipping in the English Channel and Bay of Biscay.

Before the lighthouse was built the spire of the church at **St Pierre d'Oléron** served as the chief landmark; from it there is another fine view over the island. On the south coast the little harbour at La Cotinière is a busy fishing centre; along this coast bass and bar can be caught with rod and line in the surf (a map can be bought locally showing suitable places). The coast road from La Cotinière south is now largely built up, for Oléron is popular as a holiday resort. There are two good beaches at Vert Bois and at the Grande Plage, though bathers should beware of undercurrents. At St Trojan a miniature railway runs in summer to the otherwise inaccessible Pointe de Maumusson, deep among the dunes and pine forests.

From Marennes the new Pont de la Seudre (toll) leads across to the peninsula of the Forêt de la Coubre, a huge pine forest planted to stabilise the sand dunes of the **Côte Sauvage**. Vast stretches of sandy beach are pounded by the full force of Atlantic waves and winds, and even on a calm day there are treacherous currents close inshore; but there is more than enough space for everyone. On the Pointe de la Coubre a lighthouse marks the opening of the Gironde estuary, with one of the most powerful lanterns on the French coast. Ring the bell for the keeper, who will let you in; there are 300 steps, but the view is the most rewarding of the four lighthouses along this coast, and it is worth taking a map to get bearings.

From the Forêt de la Coubre we come back gradually to civilisation past the little fishing harbour of Bonne Anse, sheltered by a spit from the south-westerly gales, and more beaches (bathing again dangerous). At La Grande Côte there is a viewpoint from which the **Phare de Cordouan** can be seen, on a rocky bank far out in the estuary. A light was first placed here by order of the Black Prince in the fourteenth century, when there was a small village on an island there. In the early seventeenth century this island was swept away, and a new tower had to be built on a stone platform. It was a remarkable octagonal classical building, complete with porticos, pediments and blank windows, a monumental folly with a purpose. Inside there are state rooms, including a royal apartment and a chapel. Sadly the upper part was rebuilt in less exotic and more practical style in the eighteenth century. All this can only be seen properly by taking a boat from Royan: these leave about once or twice a day in calm weather in July and August.

Beyond La Grande Côte **St Palais** has an attractive harbour; this old-fashioned resort gives something of the atmosphere of **Royan** before the last war. Originally a small harbour and pilot station for ships going up to Bordeaux, Royan became a resort after 1825, when the new fashion for seaside holidays began to develop. In 1875, a railway link was completed, and it became popular with Parisians. It was quickly developed in the latest style, and boasted two casinos, one with a Renaissance campanile, the other in a baroque Italian manner, besides hotels in every grandiose style imaginable. Today Royan is now almost entirely a new town, because this (like La Rochelle) was one of the places to which the German army in France retreated in 1944. Unlike La Rochelle, the French liberating armies met stiff resistance here; and in January and April 1945 they were forced to bombard the town heavily. The second bombardment almost completely destroyed the place, and the Germans surrendered. Rebuilding began almost at once, and apart from the suburb of Pontaillac on the way in, we are in a completely different world from the rest of this coast. On the whole the result is very successful, the sweeping line of the front emphasised by the curving modern buildings behind it. By the harbour is the casino, while down the central axis of the new buildings behind it an avenue ends in the dramatic concrete dome of the market. The best-known of Royan's new features, and justly so, is the cathedral of Notre Dame, designed by Guillaume Gillet and Hébrard and begun in 1955. Buildings using the architectural possibilities of concrete are commoner now than when the cathedral was first built. This has diminished the dramatic impact of the exterior, though it is unorthodox enough, with the highest point of the church at the east end. The interior is astonishing, a vast space filled with colour and light from the mass of stained glass, the lines of perspective converging on the altar as focal point.

South of Royan a corniche road winds between the pine forest and the rocky coastline, past the little harbours of St George de Didonne and of Meschers sur Gironde. At Meschers the curious caves where the inhabitants used to live – often because they were outlaws or refugees from persecution – are now restaurants. Beyond Meschers the road crosses the coastal plain to the little village of **Talmont** perched on a rock on the edge of the Gironde. Its narrow streets of stone houses lead to the church of Ste Radegonde, on the very edge of the estuary. Built as a stopping-place for pilgrims on the way to Compostela, it is in fact half of a church, because the nave has disappeared long since into the water, and what we now see is a fifteenth-century façade built to close off the remainder. The castle, too, disappeared into the sea, and even now work has to be done regularly on the foundations. There are rich carvings on the capitals, though the north façade is badly weathered. The church suffered from being fortified in the Hundred Years' War as well as from the ravages of the sea, but if anything, this wear and tear has merely added to the impression of defiant isolation. Yet it is not a grandiose site, and the church and village as a whole are friendly and familiar in scale, and a world away from the resorts further up the coast.

Inland, at the abandoned windmill of Moulin du Fâ, are the remains of a massive circular temple dedicated to Mars, dating from the second century AD. Only a few details remain, apart from the foundations: note the basin near the entrance where pilgrims washed their feet before entering the sanctuary barefoot.

From Talmont the D 114 leads to Cozes and then to a group of fine Romanesque churches in the countryside toward Saintes. **Corme-Ecluse** (D 241, on the left) has a graceful façade, with bands of ornamental foliage in which little figures appear and disappear and smiling animals face one another. The capitals include one of a pilgrim and one of a centaur drawing his bow. The golden-yellow of the stone makes this façade particularly worth seeing in the evening light.

At **Thaims** the church is bordered by an avenue of lime trees leading to an eighteenth-century manor house, and the building has something of the pastoral charm of its setting. It is built on the site of a Roman temple, and in the north wall a bas-relief of Bacchus has been inserted, in the fond belief that it showed the crucifixion of St Peter. A plaque showing Epona, goddess of horses, was also found on the site, and excavations to the south of the church have revealed part of the Gallo-Roman foundations. The apse has a fine double arcade, with unusual inverted 'V' arches copied from a Roman source and square pilasters on the south wall. The ornament on the outside is again mostly in the form of arcading on the little central tower and the exterior of the apse. The tower has the typical Saintonge pattern of a square base with an octagonal upper storey.

Rétaud (on the D 114) and Rioux (to the west off the D 142) offer two very similar churches, famous for the rich ornaments of their apses. **Rioux** is the more resplendent of the pair, with a powerful façade as well. The façade is a curious mixture of restraint and artistic abandon: a single round window or oculus, a line of arcading, one sculpture, a single doorway. The absence of any other figures emphasises the mandorla of the Virgin and Child, but the arcading is covered in luxuriant tracery, and the pillars are twisted or textured. The vault of the doorway carries a series of geometrical patterns above relatively simple pillars. However, it is the apse that brings out the full flower of the sculptor's art. Here the stone itself seems to form into patterns: only the vertical lines of the pillar-buttresses and the wall behind the blind arcades are plain. Otherwise every kind of geometry and foliage is pressed into service: plain crosses, elaborate echoes of polylobed doorways, bold leaf-curls. Under the cornice a row of glum heads with their eyes shut look as though they were suffering from visual indigestion from the riches below.

Rétaud, overpowered by a plain fifteenth-century tower, is not quite so lavishly ornamented; though the sculptor evidently knew the work at Rioux, the patterns are different, and are concentrated round the cornice. Only a small part of the façade remains.


We take the D 114 into Saintes and cross the town, to find the N 138 to St Jean d'Angély, which passes through wooded country to St Hilaire. A left turn on to the D 124 and, after six miles, a byroad to the right, lead to the hamlet of Fenioux, on the side of a wooded valley deep in the country. The little church is a simple rectangle in plan, and dates back to Carolingian times: parts of the ninth-century walls remain. In the twelfth century a façade was added, with multiple pillars flanking a single, richly carved doorway, making the building very imposing, despite its small size. On the vaulting the outer band, carefully labelled, shows the labours of the months, separated by the signs of the zodiac: then the theme of the wise and foolish virgins, followed by angels adoring the Lamb. The elegant warriors of the inside vault are virtues fighting vices, the little demons being trampled underfoot. To the north, a smaller doorway has rich foliage decorations.

The real treasure of Fenioux is across the road from the church, in a green meadow which was once a cemetery. This is a Romanesque *lanterne des morts*, one of those strange structures which are found only in France. They are most frequent in the old diocese of Limoges, and grow less common as they radiate out from that centre. Their exact purpose is uncertain; there seems to be some relationship between the Benedictine monks and the building of these towers. Documents indicate different ideas as to what they were used for: a text of 1187 says that they were to contain lights burning all night, 'to remind all who saw it that the soul was immortal', while another writer says that they were used for vigils and services at night in the cemeteries. First built in the twelfth century, they were replaced from the thirteenth century onward by funerary chapels. That at Fenioux is beautifully preserved, and shows the typical lay-out: a chamber, probably for the coffin or for holding the service, with a slender lantern tower above, to the top of which a ladder, or, as here, a slender staircase gives access so that a light can be lit there. The Fenioux *lanterne* is in the form of eleven columns forming a single pillar, capped by the lantern chamber and a steep-pitched stone roof. At dusk it is easy to imagine the effect of the light shining down the long wooded valley stretching away to the south, in a world where the darkness at nightfall was usually absolute.

**St Jean d'Angély**, a few miles to the north, offers a very different kind of church – urban, grandiose and ruined. Turn left after crossing the river and park on the Square de la Liberation, for the centre of the town is a maze of narrow one-way streets. The rue Pascal Bourcy leads through a fifteenth-century gate and clock tower, flanked by the old town hall. In the centre of the town stands the Fontaine du Pilori, dated 1546; it in fact belonged to the nearby château of Brizambourg and was re-erected here in 1819. Following the road round to the left the twin towers of the abbey, which crown the sky-line of the town from a distance, but disappear in the narrow streets, re-emerge like some great cliff-face. The abbey, once a great place of pilgrimage, as well as a halt on the road to Compostela, was destroyed by the Huguenots in 1562, and the attempts to rebuild it in the eighteenth century were so ambitious that they were never completed; so the façade of 1741 is strictly speaking not a ruin, for its rook-haunted heights are much as they were when building came to a halt at the Revolution of 1789. Nearby, the old abbey buildings, behind a fine wrought-iron gate, are used as a school.

The D 127 north of St Jean d'Angély winds up the pleasant Boutonne valley to **Dampierre-sur-Boutonne**, where, in a wooded island in the river, is a lovingly-cared-for little Renaissance château. This is a much more delicate version of the town hall at La Rochelle; the open-air architecture of this style is better suited to a pastoral setting. The low arcades on the ground floor and the open air gallery on the first floor are divided into a mass of little compartments. As so often with decoration of this period, the details include initials and badges. The initials here are unusual: they refer to Henri II and Diane de Poitiers, and Diane's emblem of three crescent moons also appears, but only because the builder of this part of the château was her protégé. Other little carvings refer to proverbs, and Latin quotations also abound, while 'devices', a kind of visual motto, recur throughout the château. The interior is well furnished, mostly with appropriate Renaissance pieces and tapestries.

The Renaissance building replaced the old keep of the castle, and the two west towers are part of the fifteenth-century château, their powerful defensive aspect in sharp contrast with the light-hearted air of the front. They overlook the river Boutonne, which formed one side of the square moat.

The D 121 brings us to the main road from Poitiers to Saintes. At the crossroads is sited one of the finest Romanesque churches in the area, that of **Aulnay**. It stands on the borders of Poitou and Saintonge, and draws on the different styles of the two provinces to achieve an almost perfect harmony of its own. It was a pilgrims' church, on the road to Compostela, and in a sense still is; but now they come by coachloads, and are addressed by recorded commentaries over loudspeakers.

St Pierre d'Aulnay was probably built by the canons of Poitiers Cathedral *circa* 1150–1200. It remains almost untouched, except for some fifteenth-century repairs to the façade and spire. What is unusual is that the whole church seems to have been built at once; it is more common to find that the transepts or apse have been added to an earlier building consisting of the nave only.

The façade is best seen in the afternoon light. The upper part is part of the fifteenth-century remodelling: a statue of Constantine occupied the central arcade until the Revolution. The lower vaults have survived untouched, filled with marvellous sculpture. To the left, the centre of the vault shows the crucifixion of St Peter (to whom the church is dedicated), with the executioners setting up the inverted cross. This and the right-hand vault, where Peter and Paul sit in glory to the right and left of our Lord, are framed by a deeply-cut flowing foliage pattern, as powerful and rich as any to be found in Saintonge. Among the leaves on the outer vault crouch wild beasts.

The central doorway is the original of the group of similar compositions on the churches west of Saintes. On the inner vault the angels adore the Lamb; then the virtues trample on the vices, and the seven wise and seven foolish virgins stand in attitudes of joy and despair. The outer vault, sadly mutilated, portrays the signs of the zodiac and the labours of the months. But here we have the work of an original master, while elsewhere, though this or that detail may have been finer or better preserved, the figures are imitations. Look at the lively rendering of the angels on the inner vault, joyous, moving beings with bold gestures; above, the virtues are portrayed as solemn knightly statues, triumphant over the vices rather than actively locked in combat with them. Note that 'largesse' (*largitia*) or generosity is given the key place on the arch: this was the knightly virtue above all others.

79

The entrance was originally up a flight of five steps, so that you entered the nave down a flight of steps, giving an illusion of greater height. This was removed by the architect Abadie (see p. 134) in 1855. The interior is dark; it was probably painted in the Middle Ages, but only very faint traces remain. The columns of the nave are each made up of four pillars, giving a monumental effect in a relatively small space; sharply defined foliage patterns, some of the loveliest examples of Romanesque patterns in stone, adorn the capitals, and a pair of pillars reach up from them into the vault. A very simple apse rounds off the perspective.

In the crossing and transepts are a number of lively scenes on the capitals, not easy to see except on a bright day: it helps to open the south door. In the south transept elephants and eagles appear on one pillar, carefully inscribed 'here be elephants'; other capitals show sphinxes and monsters. At the crossing, Delilah cuts Samson's hair on one side, while devils swallow sinners on the other. In the north transept Cain slays Abel; opposite, the giant figure of Eve occupies two sides of a capital. In the little apse chapels there is the miser with his moneybag, and a St George.

The outside of the south transept is the glory of Aulnay. Here is a complete Romanesque façade with the carvings largely intact; the upper part reminds one of what the main façade must have looked like before the fifteenth-century restoration. Above the upper window four virtues echo the theme of the main west doorway, though these are sterner figures, not triumphant but ready to do battle. The oculus, with its bold cross tracery, strikes an unexpected note, placed between the vertical lines of pillars. On the vaults of the doorway below, ranks of human figures are framed by a decorative band of animals and foliage on the inner vault, and a varied selection from the book of beasts on the outer half-circle. Here are centaurs, an ass playing the harp, man-headed monsters and monster-headed men, a motley crowd compared with the ordered lines of figures within. The most solemn of these inner ranks is that of the Elders of the Apocalypse, holding flasks; they are supported by kneeling men with wide-open eyes, perhaps representing witnesses; and below these are pairs of apostles and prophets, supported in turn by giants holding up the ground on which they walk.

The outside of the apse is less impressive in its lines than the rest of the church, and from this aspect the fifteenth-century slate spire is at its most intrusive. But there is delicate carving around the outside of the east window, figures climbing through twining leaves, carved in low relief like the patterns on ivory caskets of the period.

12. The castle at Lusignan has long since disappeared, but its medieval aspect is preserved in this miniature by Pol de Limbourg in the **Très Riches Heures du Duc de Berry** in the Musée Condé at Chantilly (near Paris)

13. **(overleaf)** The castle of La Roche-Courbon, in the wooded country between Saintes and the coast; one of the few seventeenth-century examples in the south-west

And indeed the whole church is like such a casket; the decoration, both inside and out, is more important than the overall lines, but it is a treasurehouse none the less.

Aulnay is the culmination of our tour of the churches of Saintonge, for those who like to end on a crescendo. This makes an appropriate point to take the road north to Poitiers, and we are indeed already on the borders of Poitou, as the open landscape shows. But the rest of Saintonge, if it has nothing to equal Aulnay, has very different pleasures in store.

Chapter 5

# Cognac

❧

South-east of Aulnay the countryside changes gradually as we
approach the chalk slopes which run down to the Charente. Beyond
Matha these become a broad expanse of vines, their regular pattern
stretching into the distance like a huge net thrown over the landscape.
This open country has long been known as the **Champagne**, meaning
an area where fields predominate, 'champaign country' in Elizabethan
English. Until the eighteenth century it was a mixture of arable land
and vineyards, the vines growing on the poor soil at the crest of the
ridges, where the underlying chalk came close to the surface. The
wine from these was of no particular merit, a basic *vin ordinaire*
which was largely sold locally or to merchant ships trading with La
Rochelle which wanted a cargo to take back on their homeward
voyage. Imports of wine from La Rochelle appear in English records
from the fourteenth century on, though they were on a very small
scale compared with the trade with Bordeaux. Locally the wines were
also distilled as *eau-de-vie*, a practice which first appears on a commercial scale in the fourteenth century. At some time in the seventeenth century both Dutch and English traders began to take an
interest in these *eaux-de-vie*, because there was no risk of their spoiling during the voyage. As a result of the demand for Cognac *eau-de-
vie*, the vineyards expanded rapidly in the eighteenth century, and
now cereal crops have all but vanished from the area.

From Aulnay the road to Cognac leads first to Matha, which
possesses two good twelfth-century churches. The remains of the
abbey church at **Marestay**, just north of the town, consist of the apse
and crossing only; the nave seems to have disappeared as long ago
as the twelfth century. The outside of the apse is remarkable for the
rich decoration of the window arches, contrasting with the sober
rounded pillars which form the vertical divisions. All the decoration
is rich and arabesque, but the most striking pattern is reserved for
the east window, where a frieze of remarkable heads, some crowned,
some horned, are interspersed with writhing creatures. These strange
apparitions seem to belong to the head-cult of ancient Gaul rather
than sober twelfth-century Christianity. The capitals inside the

church present an array of monsters in the same vein, interspersed with scenes from the Old Testament: Samson killing the lion, and Daniel in the lions' den. A capital of St Michael conquering the forces of evil, which would originally have appeared at the beginning of the nave, is now on the outside, to the west.

The parish church, St Hérie, to the south of the town, has a Romanesque façade with arabesques like those at Marestay. Here the grotesques are more extreme, their contortions emphasised by the presence of a radiant statue of a richly dressed lady to the right of the façade. The first window on the north side nearest to the façade has a vignette worthy of Hieronymus Bosch as its arch: a demon's head with grotesque teeth from which two of the damned are trying to escape. It is all the more disturbing for being carved upside down.

The road to Angoulême from Matha brings us to Neuvicq-le-Château. There, above a wooded valley, the château occupies a lovely position on the edge of the village. Its present use is surprising: it is now the local post office! The main part is fifteenth-century, with elaborate gable windows: on one a hunter armed with a spear sets out on a boar-hunt, while on another a man embraces a lady who holds a rosary.

From Neuvicq the D 23 and D 15 bring us to Cognac; a more direct route from Matha is the D 121 and D 85, which run through the open vineyards of the Borderies, part of the Cognac region. Just outside Cognac the road descends into the deep wooded valley of the little river Antenne. At Cherves de Cognac a road to the right leads to the Château de Chesnel (not open) on the edge of this valley. The château was built in 1610 in an old-fashioned Renaissance style, with an elaborate gateway. Its square plan is echoed in the four square towers, and parapets hide the roofs of the buildings within, giving it a solid and unified silhouette which was copied many times in this area. After the junction with the N 731 a narrow road drops steeply down to the right and skirts the enormous façade of the castle at Richemont, a plain curtain wall towering above the valley. At the southern end are the remains of an earlier feudal castle, including the church, which has an eleventh-century crypt with archaic capitals. It has all the right ingredients for a romantic site – ruins, deep woods, and a river lost in the bottom of the valley. While I was there two local horn-players were doing their best to bring to life Alfred de Vigny's famous line:

*Dieu! que le son du cor est triste au fond des bois!*
(Lord! how sadly sounds the horn beyond the woods!)

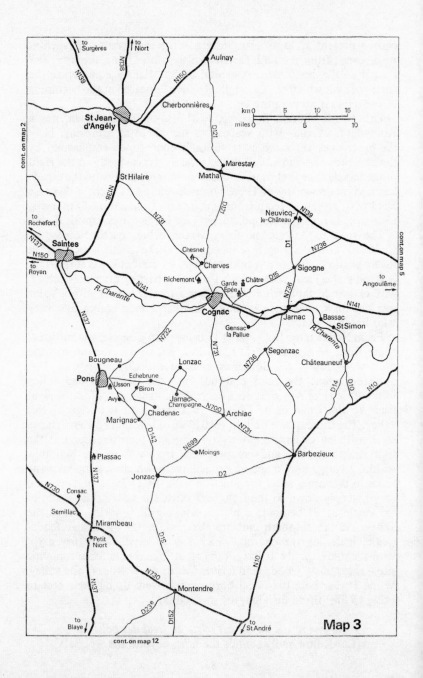

cont. on map 2

cont. on map 5

cont. on map 12

to Surgères
to Niort

N139
N138
N150

Aulnay

Cherbonnières

St Jean-
d'Angély

km 0    5    10    15
miles 0    5    10

Marestay

D121

St Hilaire

Matha

N138

Neuvicq-
le-Château
N139

to
Rochefort

N731

D1

N736

N137

Chesnei

Saintes

N150

Cherves

D15

Sigogne

to
Royan

Richemont

Châtre

to
Angoulême

R. Charente

N141

Garde
Epée

N736

Cognac

N141

Jarnac

Bassac
St Simon

Gensac
la Pallue

R. Charente

N732

N731

Segonzac

Châteauneuf

Bougneau

Lonzac

N736

D1

D14

D10

N10

Pons

Echebrune

Usson

Biron

Jarnac
Champagne

N700

Archiac

Avy

Chadenac

N731

Marignac

D142

N699

Moings

Barbezieux

Plassac

Jonzac

D2

N137

N730

Consac

Semillac

Mirambeau

Petit
Niort

D15

N10

N730

Montendre

N137

D23e

D152

to
Blaye

to
St André

**Map 3**

Their efforts were only *triste* in the playing; they were obviously enjoying the ringing echoes they produced.

We come into **Cognac** by the bridge over the Charente. Along the south bank of the river are reminders of Cognac's golden age, long before brandy became the focal point of the town's life, when Francis I patronised the town which was his birthplace and held his court at the **castle**, to the right of the road. The traffic cuts off the castle from the huge park to the right. This was planted in Francis I's time and has altered little since then, but the castle is much changed. It was originally a small tenth- or eleventh-century castle, rebuilt by the Lusignan family in the days of Isabella of Angoulême, and much used in the 1360s by the Black Prince. This made way for a late medieval castle, more of a residence than a stronghold, built for Jean de Valois in the 1450s. The so-called 'Salle du Casque' has a twelfth-century wall and thirteenth-century arcades; but the rest of the buildings are largely those of Jean de Valois. They were allowed to decay quietly until 1795, when an enterprising Scotsman named Otard realised that the massive walls of the building would provide the steady temperature and conditions needed for the maturing of brandy. Although a good deal of destruction was done in the process of conversion, the most regrettable being the loss of the chapel with its della Robbia enamels, in recent years the building has been carefully restored, and a *son et lumière* system has been installed inside the castle (1 June–30 September, 9.30–11.30, 14.00–18.00). The visit serves a double purpose: both the castle and an old-established brandy house can be seen at the same time, as the former dungeons are filled with casks, and the visit ends with a tour of the larger storage-rooms, with their subtle aroma of alcohol. This is due to the slight but steady evaporation through the casks, which also encourages the black lichen that grows on the walls of many of Cognac's buildings.

Otard is only one of a dozen or so brandy houses open to visitors. (It is interesting that, for no very obvious reason except perhaps native fondness for brandy, several others have English names – Hine from Dorset, Hennessy from Scotland.) The full list is available from the Syndicat d'Initiative in the Place de la Corderie. However, one house is much like another; apart from Otard, Martell, which preserves the original building of 1715, is the most interesting. There is little to be seen besides the immense vats and barrels made of oak from the forests around Limoges. The 'making' of brandy is a relatively simple process: its ageing and blending are much more subtle. The basic material is the local white wine, an acid product of low alcoholic strength. The best brandy is said to come from the worst wine, meaning that the less palatable the wine the more likely it is to distil into a good *eau-de-vie*. The wine is made in the ordinary way, and allowed to ferment, but it is not then 'racked' or removed from its lees before being distilled. The resulting spirit is stored in oak casks until bottling, the only addition being a small amount of caramel for colouring: brandy would normally be as pale as gin. The word 'brandy' derives from the Dutch *brandijwein*, or 'burnt wine', a good matter-of-fact description of it.

The only recognised grading of cognac is by the area from which it comes, the best coming from the Cognac region itself. Like the delimitations of other wine-growing areas, they mark off physical differences in the soil, so that they represent only one factor in the process. Whether a brandy labelled *Grande Champagne* is actually better than a *Fines Bois* depends on the grower and distiller; but it starts with the advantage of the best soil and growing conditions, so that when the furthest parts of the region, the *Bois Ordinaires*, are reached, it is unlikely that anyone will try to make a first-class brandy from their products. Vintage cognac is no longer obtainable in France, as official records are not kept after the brandy is five years old: but English merchants can still supply it by shipping in cask and keeping their own records. The only real guide to quality is the reputation of the house whose name it bears; stars, 'Napoléon' and other symbols are by and large decorative. (I have found that a sound principle is the old adage that 'a good wine needs no bush'. The plainer and more tasteful the label the better the contents – a rule which often applies to wine as well!)

Looking at brandy casks is not a very exciting pastime, but Cognac has other attractions to offer. Just beyond the castle is the old quarter, with the squat towers of the Porte St Jacques on the riverbank. Winding, cobbled streets climb between half-timbered houses: here the black lichen sometimes appears in abundance. The Grande Rue and the Rue Saulnier have the finest houses, ranging from the fifteenth to the seventeenth century. The Grande Rue leads into the modern centre of the town; beyond this, to the north, is the museum, set in one of the most pleasing and well-kept public gardens I have seen – a mixture of formal beds, curving paths and surprisingly green lawns. In the centre is a little Victorian Hôtel de Ville, looking more like a folly in the garden of some great house than a place of business. The Museum is in the southern corner of the park; it houses both a local history collection and a small art gallery. On the ground floor there is a good reconstruction of an eighteenth-century interior from the region, while in the basement a display devoted to the traditional methods of making brandy is being mounted. The rest of the ground floor contains prehistoric finds and a range of local pottery from the Roman period to the nineteenth century. The pictures, on the first floor, include an extensive group of minor mannerist canvases of the sixteenth and seventeenth century, and some dramatic Art Nouveau pieces of glass by Gallé.

From Cognac the main road to Angoulême runs south of the Charente. The D 49, to the right, leads to **Gensac-la-Pallue,** '*pallue*' being the marshland by the river; here the church has a simple but elegant façade, on which two sculptures in high relief stand out like jewels: to the left the Virgin, her hands held out in prayer, and to the right St Martin. Both are surrounded by a mandorla and adoring angels: those accompanying the Virgin stoop to do homage, while their companions treat St Martin as an equal. Despite weathering, the quality of the sculpture is at once evident.

The D 158 takes us back to the main road: crossing it, we reach Bourg-Charente, with a seventeenth-century castle much restored about 1900, and a church on the hillside to the east of the village. Both the apse (set in open lawns) and the façade of the church have arcades as their chief decorative feature, without elaborate ornament. The same style is to be seen nearby, at **La Châtre,** on the other side of the river. This church was once that of an Augustinian abbey, destroyed in the sixteenth-century wars of religion. It is hidden in the fields to the north of the château of Garde-Épée, about half a mile down a rough track: its elegant, restrained façade rises out of water-meadows whose long grass is starred with buttercups, and brambles grow over the apse and the scant remains of the monastic buildings. It seems like some great abandoned ship left to decay in a quiet creek. To north and south discreet buttresses and cornices provide the only variety of surface, as if to emphasise the façade. Here there is an interesting blend of styles: the pediment and upper arcade have a strongly classical flavour, while the decoration – rich bands of irregular interlaced foliage – and the main doorway, with its poly-lobed inner arch, are Arabic in inspiration, a reminder of the inter-national style of the pilgrim roads.

The château of Garde-Épée, at the top of the lane leading to La Châtre, has been entirely rebuilt, but the gateway remains, with its

Renaissance decoration, as does the curtain wall. A turning to the right leads to the dolmen of Garde-Épée, a huge slab supported on five smaller stones to form a burial chamber whose sandy earth-covering has long since been blown away.

Rejoining the main road, we turn toward Jarnac; on the far side of the town, the D 22 leads to the abbey of Bassac. On the left of the road, a small stone pyramid marks the spot where the Prince de Condé was stabbed to death after being wounded at the battle of Jarnac in 1569, leading the Huguenot troops against the Catholic army under the command of the Duke of Anjou.

**Bassac** was once a wealthy Benedictine abbey, one of the group which enjoyed a revival under the reforming leadership of the congregation of St Maur in the seventeenth century. The Revolution left its mark both spiritually and physically: on the façade are engraved Robespierre's words: 'The French people acknowledge the Supreme Being and the immortality of the soul.' It was only in 1947 that it was re-established as a religious community, and it now houses a group of missionary nuns. Behind the Romanesque façade of the church the nave is thirteenth-century, with 'Angevin' vaulting. The appearance of the choir is largely eighteenth-century, the date of the magnificent woodwork which accords surprisingly well with the simplicity of the church itself. For once the often feeble and over-loaded classicism of church furnishings of that period is absent. The eagle lectern is particularly striking, and there are elegant rails dividing off the sanctuary. To the right of the church a classical gateway frames the tunnel-like entrance to the monastic buildings, the most important of which is the seventeenth-century cloister square. Although the cloister walk vanished in 1820 there are still good details on the gable-windows: the interior can be visited on request.

The D 22 continues along the river, through St Simon, whose plain Romanesque church stands on the riverbank, to **Châteauneuf-sur-Charente.** This was an important crossing-place in the Middle Ages: under the terms of the treaty of Brétigny of 1360 the English were careful to keep it, but it was taken by the French in 1380. In 1568 it was the scene of a struggle between Huguenots and Catholics and on both occasions the church suffered during the fighting. It stands on what is now the western edge of the town (on the D 84). The interior is spacious and aseptic with its pure white stone; there are elaborate capitals high in the nave. The nave ends in a Gothic choir. But it is the façade, modelled on that of the Abbaye aux Dames at Saintes, which impresses. The central doorway has three richly carved vaults, with the Lamb as centrepiece, and the decoration is in the style found on the churches of Saintonge: human figures alternate with strange animals. The whole composition is dominated by the central statue of a horseman, now generally agreed to represent Constantine triumphing over paganism: the latter appears, a much-mutilated figure, below his horse's hooves, while the statue to the right represents the church. The sweep of the horseman's cloak shows the sculptor's skill, and makes the mutilation of his work all the more regrettable.

From Châteauneuf we turn south to Barbezieux, on the N 10. Only the gateway of the castle, built by Marguerite de la Rochefoucauld in 1453, survives, in one corner of an empty square at the top of the town. The medieval plan of the town is unchanged, but its peaceful streets have few old houses. Its chief claim to fame is the Hôtel Boule d'Or, which retains its traditional appearance and a kitchen to rejoice the heart of any hungry traveller.

Turning west the D 2 runs through rolling farmland to Jonzac, on the river Seugne. The curious, much-rebuilt castle in the centre of the town houses the *mairie*. Between here and Pons lies a wealth of little country churches, remarkable in their variety. As a foretaste, there is the church at Moings (on the N 699 to the north) with an elaborate, arcaded but foreshortened bell-tower. Turning left at Archiac on to the N 700 we come first to **Jarnac-Champagne**, with an apse whose height is emphasised by triple pillar-buttresses on the outside which rise unbroken to just below the roof, where all the decoration is concentrated around the head of the arches. Inside, the east end has unique interlinked pillars woven into zigzag links. Below, bands of half-rounded stones continue this strange manner, more reminiscent of Art Deco than the twelfth century.

Across the N 700 the tower of the church at **Lonzac** is quickly apparent above a line of poplars. For this part of the country it is a rarity, a late Gothic village church, but once we arrive beneath its lofty mass and look at the details it is clear that it was built for a special reason. The bell-tower is over 120 feet high, and the building is indeed higher than any measurement of its ground plan, though it has a nave and transepts. The clue to the mystery lies in the band of Renaissance motifs which encircle the church just above the buttresses. Here two initials are repeated, K and I, with the device '*j'aime fort une*' (meaning either 'I love one greatly' or 'I love fortune'). These are the initials of Jacques de Genouillac and his wife Katherine, and it was in order to provide a suitable burial place for Katherine, who was daughter of the Lord of Lonzac, that this remarkable building was designed. Jacques de Genouillac was master of the royal artillery under Francis I, and his feats of war are alluded to in the bas-reliefs of Hercules over the main door, where Francis's salamander emblem also appears. He was a patron of the arts, as is evident from these carefully planned details. The interior is disappointing, largely due to later furniture and decoration, which destroys the spacious effect originally intended.

The plain church at **Echebrune,** along the main road toward Pons, has a façade which is relatively simple but very satisfying in its harmony of proportions. It is divided into two stages instead of the usual three, and the wide arch of the door is balanced by elongated arcading above with quadruple pillars; the polylobed pattern usually found on the doorway is transferred to the central window above. The cornice separating the two parts is supported by bold figures of men and oxen. Nearby, at Biron, the church stands in water-meadows: the façade is a humbler version of that at Echebrune, enlivened by amusing and largely secular carvings. A frieze of animals, real and fabulous, runs round the door arch, while the capitals to each side house more examples from this zoo, and at the extreme left a farmer is being scolded by his wife.

South-east of Biron there is yet another interesting façade at **Chadénac.** This was once the finest in the area, with a wealth of statues and rich detail; but weathering, restoration, and even official vandalism have wrought a good deal of damage. Only the lowest of the three tiers is original, the upper part being a poor nineteenth-century rebuilding. To the right the standing figure in the arcade was cut in half to make way for a letterbox. Above the door on the inner-most vault, Christ – a surprisingly small figure in the composition – is worshipped by angels, while around him the virtues (angels) triumph over the vices (demons), and saints and apostles look on from the outer vaults. The theme of the struggle between good and evil is continued on the archways to left and right: the tympanum of each is occupied by wrestlers, while above two leaping wolves or monsters try to seize a lamb. The figures flanking them are too mutilated to be clearly identified, but might represent the already familiar theme of a knight or soldier triumphing over evil to deliver a lady, the symbol of the Holy Church. The lady wears a dress which is in the height of thirteenth-century fashion, with long 'bell-bottomed' sleeves. On the capitals below, to the left, the same theme reappears, while to the right the three Marys are shown at the empty sepulchre. On the south wall is an inscription which, if the reconstruction of it is correct, underlines the esteem in which the façade was held from the very first: 'Here lies William the Poitevin, clerk to William. He was the architect, but not the sculptor.'

South of Chadénac, off the road from Jonzac to Pons, **Marignac** stands on a hilltop, clustered round the church. Originally a priory of the abbey of Charroux, the church shows its monastic origins in the unusual trefoil plan of the east end. (The nave was rebuilt in the fourteenth century.) The three equal bays are linked by a central cupola; the importance of the eastern bay is emphasised by an arch made of rounded stones, and by a rich frieze of foliage in which simple figurines, beasts and birds pursue each other. There is more than a hint of Eastern inspiration, perhaps the tracery of Moorish buildings, in the lions with cat-like faces and sinuous tails or in the little archers; but it is all interpreted in a homely style, because it has reached this humble corner of France by way of the great churches at Saintes, who in turn borrowed it from other sources further south. The outside of the church, a pleasing harmony of rounded pilastered apse and chapels and square bell-tower, has a similar frieze interrupted by supports for the heavy, almost battlement-like, cornice. The roofs have been lowered, but without spoiling the overall effect.

Nearer to Pons, **Avy** has a weathered and altered façade, whose composition and carving are rustic and echo only remotely the richness and balance of those of Saintonge. The theme is one found elsewhere in Saintonge, the Elders of the Apocalypse singing in honour of the Lamb: here they are a slightly comic concert-party, reduced from the usual 36 to 24, but their simple enthusiasm still captures the spirit of praise. On the edge of Pons itself turn back to Cognac on the N 732 to reach Bougneau, whose church appears as a long silhouette in an overgrown graveyard to the left of the road. This takes one back to the mid-eleventh century: the apse and choir have simple, early arcading which echoes the architecture of Charlemagne's day. Two of the arches are replaced by inverted 'V's of carved cornice, a device which goes straight back to the Roman architecture from which 'Romanesque' takes its name, as do the square, fluted pillars of the blind arcades to north and south.

After this feast of country churches we come to **Pons**, whose narrow streets contain little to hold one's attention (except for the Auberge Pontoise in the main street, plain and modern, but offering excellent value for a meal). At the south end of the town the streets open out into a square, above which the huge square keep of the old castle rises majestically. It was once the centre of a complex of buildings occupying the whole of the square and running out to the edge of the spur of the hill, now a little public garden. All that remains of the other buildings is part of the seventeenth-century living quarters, now the *mairie*. There are fragments of walls, as well as the little chapel of St Gilles at the end of the promontory. The keep itself, built between 1179 and 1186, was restored at the beginning of this century. Its battlements are perhaps not quite as they should be, and old engravings show a much simpler arrangement. However, it is a fitting monument to what was once one of the most powerful lordships in eastern France. The barons of Pons held their lands directly of the king, as tenants-in-chief, on a par with such families as the Lusignans. Indeed, after the treaty of Pons of 1242, between the French king and the Lusignan rebels who had sided with Henry III of England, the Lusignan power was eclipsed, and the lords of Pons were without rivals. Their eventual downfall, like that of so many other families of the region, was brought about by the religious wars of the sixteenth century.

At the extreme southern end of the town is a building of even greater interest: the gateway to the New Hospice founded in the mid-twelfth century by Geoffrey, Lord of Pons, to provide shelter for the pilgrims on their way to Santiago de Compostela. This is one of the very few surviving buildings (other than churches) connected with the pilgrimages: the endless procession of piety or penance that wended its way across Europe has left surprisingly little trace. Even here the buildings have vanished, and only the vaulted gate remains, with its perspective south across the shimmering landscape, a foretaste of many weary miles on rough roads. On either side of the road are the stone benches on which pilgrims sat while they waited for admission to the shelter of the Hospice, where simple food and a floor to sleep on were available to all who bore the pilgrim's staff and scallop-shell badge. As the pilgrims waited they scratched graffiti on the walls, the most prominent being horseshoes, reflecting their anxiety about finding means of transport; for most pilgrims would travel on mules or horseback, as did Chaucer's pilgrims to Canterbury.

On the opposite bank of the river from Pons is the **Château d'Usson**, which was dismantled from its original site near Lonzac and removed here at the end of the nineteenth century. The courtyard has all the trappings of the Renaissance: a gallery with medallions of the twelve Caesars, mottoes and emblems, a tower richly ornamented with the arms of the original owners and a frieze just below the roofline. The interior, which can only be visited by writing in advance to the owner, contains white and gilt Louis XV woodwork brought from another château.

Six miles to the south the château at Plassac offers a different interpretation of classical art. It was built from 1772 on by the archbishop of Lyon, while its architect was Victor Louis, whose masterpiece was the Grand Théâtre at Bordeaux. Only the outer court can be seen, but this gives a good idea of the severe and formal manner of Louis's work, a far cry from the gaiety of Renaissance classicism.

Near Mirambeau there are three churches with eleventh-century features, of interest to the enthusiast. The church at Petit Niort has a most unusual pierced stone slab as a window. Semillac has good arcading in the apse, while Consac has a series of geometric capitals on the crossing, forerunners of the twelfth-century richness of patterned carving in the Saintonge, though they are concealed under many layers of whitewash.

South of Mirambeau the estuary of the Gironde begins to come into view as the pilgrim road takes us to **Blaye**. The modern town is uninteresting, but to the north of it stands the **citadel** built by the great engineer Vauban in 1689. It stands on a key point commanding the river, and has a long military history, beginning with the *praefectus militum garonnensium* in the fourth century, who commanded a kind of local militia raised to counter possible pirate attacks on the rich trade of Bordeaux. In 1126, the Duke of Aquitaine, William IX, was killed while besieging one of his rebellious vassals at the castle of Blaye. William was the grandfather of Eleanor of Aquitaine, and was renowned as a troubadour: and in the next century an even more famous troubadour poet was to appear at Blaye: Jaufré Rudel. In the heart of Vauban's citadel there still stands the ruined castle of the Rudel family, where Jaufré probably wrote his songs. Later stories told how he fell in love with the Norman Countess of Tripoli in the Middle East merely by hearing tales of her overwhelming beauty, and how he sent her love-songs without ever seeing her face. At last he succeeded in making his way to Tripoli, where he died in her arms only a moment after he had seen the lovely form which had inspired his dreams. Alas, the story is romance rather than history; Jaufré himself was more down-to-earth, if we are to believe one of his poems about how he was caught in bed with his beloved and out of shame vowed to pursue a higher kind of love. For troubadour poetry disdained the idea of physical solace, but preferred to scale the heights of spiritual love. Jaufré's idea of *amor londhana*, love from afar, in the poems to the Countess of Tripoli, was a brilliant way of exploring this theme: in such a situation physical love was impossible, and the lovers could only unite in spirit. But this abstract ideal did not prevent him from writing poems which still speak across the centuries. Here is the opening of one of the most famous of them:

> When the days grow long in May
> I love to hear the distant bird;
> When I have left off listening
> It reminds me of my distant love
> And I go dull and bent with longing
> So that song, flower and hawthorn
> Might as well be winter frosts for me.

The citadel owes its present appearance to Vauban. The entrance is through a massive gate defended by a ravelin, and by the immense earthworks which are the hallmark of Vauban's work. The gate bears the fleur-de-lis on a shield, but is otherwise severe and practical. The fortifications are more or less complete: turning north, past the ruins of the medieval castle, we come to the Tour de l'Aiguillette, which looks out across the Gironde to the other two links in this scheme of defence: Fort Paté on an island in midstream and Fort Médoc (see p. 118) on the south bank. The western side of the citadel is a cliff, rising sheer from the river, which explains the choice of the site. In the heart of the defences are the garrison buildings, the commandant's house and the parade ground, all much as they were in Vauban's day.

If you want to follow the pilgrim road south cross the river at Blaye (either by ferry or hydrofoil). Otherwise turn inland, along the river, past the Bec d'Ambes with its vast petrol refinery at the point where the Garonne joins the Dordogne to form the Gironde. This road leads to Bourg, through the outer edge of the wine-growing districts of Bordeaux, known as the **Côtes**. The Côtes de Bourg is probably the best known of these areas, ranking with the Côtes de Fronsac further inland. From the terrace in the upper part of the town there is a good view over the estuary. To the east of the town is an isolated prehistoric site, the Grottes de Pair-non-Pair, with engravings of the New Stone Age period on the limestone walls of a cave.

Just before St André de Cubzac the Château du Bouilh stands in its vineyards, another of the works of Victor Louis, the Bordeaux architect. Planned on a vast scale, it was never completed. Even so, its pillared front with an arcade below is very imposing. The cellars are cut into the limestone, with pillars left to support the roof, and are open to the daylight.

At St André de Cubzac, with its three huge bridges, two for the road and one for the railway, we cross the Dordogne toward Bordeaux.

Chapter 6

# Bordeaux

✿

Bordeaux has always been a commercial town, and, in common with
so many centres of trade, has been too active a place to preserve
much of its past, which is now the province of the archaeologist and
historian. It has an immensely rich past, as the imposing series of
purple and gold volumes of the *Histoire de Bordeaux* reveal; but it
is not much in evidence in the busy city of today. Hence a good deal
of this chapter will be pure history: for Bordeaux is distinctly more
interesting if you can appreciate its past and, for instance, conjure
up the ghost of the medieval Château de l'Ombrière where there are
now only car parks.

Bordeaux has the unusual distinction of appearing as a trading
centre from the very start of its recorded history. The Greek geogra-
pher Strabo, writing at the very beginning of the Christian era, notes
that the Bituriges, a tribe from the north of Gaul, were the only
strangers living in Aquitaine, and that they inhabited the *emporium*
or market town of Bordeaux. They paid no tribute to their neigh-
bours, so Bordeaux was evidently a kind of free port; and it was on
the important tin-trading route from Britain and Brittany to the
south of France.

Under the Romans Bordeaux became a centre for the wine trade.
At first, this was in a very different way from today; the wine came
down the Garonne from Toulouse and the Midi, and Bordeaux was
merely an entrepôt. In the first century AD, however, the possibilities
of cultivating the lands round Bordeaux as vineyards were realised,
and with the creation of a new type of vine-stock, adapted to the
harsher weather of the Gironde while giving greater yields, the
Bordeaux vineyard owners flourished to such an extent that Bordeaux
became not only the economic but also the political capital of
Aquitaine, and was promoted to the rank of an imperial city. Far
from the frontiers of the Empire, it was probably without walls and
only lightly garrisoned until the invasion of AD 276, when the
German tribes overran Gaul and plundered it unchecked until the
Emperor Aurelian arrived in the following year and drove them out.

14. The tomb of St Junien, the work of a twelfth-century master, in the collegiate church at St Junien near Limoges

15. St Michael and the dragon was a popular theme with medieval sculptors; this tympanum, from the pilgrim church at St Michel d'Entraygues, near Angoulême, is one of the most striking versions of the subject

16. **(right)** The cathedral of St Pierre at Angoulême: apparently an untouched romanesque façade, closer examination shows how heavily it was restored by the architect Abbadie in the mid-nineteenth century

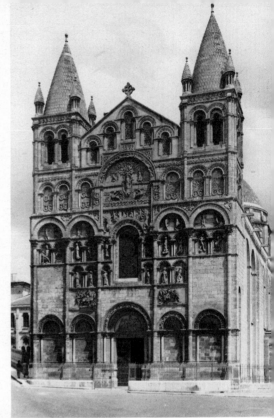

17. **(below)** Part of the grandiose eighteenth-century rebuilding of Bordeaux, the Bourse stands on the quayside, next to the wharves where the ships that made the city's trading fortune used to tie up

Under Diocletian, at the end of the third century AD, Bordeaux was given permission to build a wall around the city. Parts of the wall have been excavated, and although, as at Saintes, pieces of temples and monuments were used in its construction, it was not hastily erected. The massive foundations show that it was carefully planned and built.

Despite these signs of insecurity, Bordeaux and its inhabitants continued to flourish. The wealth of the city depended on the products of the surrounding land, and links between city and country were very close, because the landowners were in many cases also the chief citizens. Their images stare out at us from surviving memorials, touching in their mixture of luxury and simplicity. Occasionally we catch a more vivid glimpse of life in late Roman Bordeaux. The poet Ausonius, born here about AD 310, son of a doctor from Bazas, wrote:

> Bordeaux's my native soil where heaven's mercy
> Is mild, and large the watered earth's good bounty,
> Where spring is long and a young sun warms the winters
> And under hills of vines swirl tidal rivers
> Foamswept: the way of seas that rise and fall.
> Here four-square breadth of walls with towers is tall
> And cleaves the clouds light-lost above it all.
> Look admiring on the regular streets, the homes
> Well-plotted, spacious squares that suit their name,
> And gates directly opposite the crossroads,
> The springborn stream whose channel cuts the town,
> When Ocean brims it with returning tide:
> You watch a whole sea with its fleets come gliding . . .

Ausonius's memoirs, written in the 380s, give some idea of what life was like in fourth-century Aquitaine. He had a brilliant career, setting up as a teacher of rhetoric at the flourishing university at Bordeaux when he was only twenty-five and making such a reputation that in the 360s he was called to Rome by the Emperor Valentinian as tutor to the heir-apparent, Gratian. He and his pupil became firm friends, despite the difference in age, and when Gratian came to power he made his old tutor consul, in 379, even though Ausonius was more scholar than politician. Four years later Gratian was assassinated, and Ausonius retired to Bordeaux. If we are to judge from his poetry he left Rome with few regrets, and settled down to a peaceful retirement. Learned authorities have called him 'a man of letters rather than a poet'. Gibbon roundly declares that

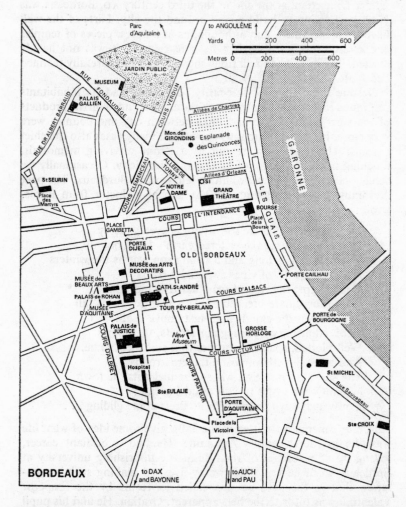

BORDEAUX

'the poetical fame of Ausonius condemns the taste of his age', but Helen Waddell's delightful versions of his lyrics belie the accusation. Besides, even where Ausonius's verse is bad, the subject of it still intrigues us; and without it we would have lost many vignettes of a corner of Roman civilisation in peaceful and uneventful times. Here is the opening of his version, the earliest on a seemingly perpetual theme, of 'Gather ye rosebuds while ye may':

Spring, and the sharpness of the gilded **dawn.**
Before the sun was up a cooler breeze
Had blown, in promise of a day of heat,
And I was walking in my formal garden,
To freshen me, before the day grew old.
I saw the hoar frost stiff on the bent grasses,
Sitting in fat globes on the cabbage leaves,
And all my Paestum roses laughing at me,
Dew-drenched, and in the East the morning star,
And here and there a dewdrop glistening white,
That soon must perish in the early sun.

Some of his letters and poems to his friends also survive and reinforce the image of a leisured and privileged age. A present of oysters or wine changed hands accompanied by a few lines of verse. The frontiers between his world and our own seem distant again. Even Ausonius's brother-in-law in far-off Britain is having to deal only with brigands on the roads to London. And this is still a pagan world; when Ausonius hears that his friend Paulinus of Nola has become a Christian, he is dismayed and bewildered.

After Ausonius's death in 395 this ordered Roman and pagan world quickly gave way to a Frankish and Christian chaos of warring tribes and wandering saints. Commerce needs peace, and if not peace, order. From the early fifth century on there were neither. In 412–13 the Visigoth chieftain Atheulf took Bordeaux, but was driven south into Spain by the Roman armies. The Visigoths returned six years later, and this time were accepted as Roman confederates. From their alliance with the Romans stems the medieval duchy of Aquitaine. At first the Roman system of government continued with little alteration, save that the real power was in Visigoth hands. By 480, however, the Visigoth princes were independent of Rome, and the Roman traditions were weakening; the capital of the Visigoth kingdom was at Toulouse. Even after Clovis defeated and killed the Visigoth prince Alaric II near Poitiers in 507 Toulouse remained the centre of southern political life, while Bordeaux was distinguished only as the see of the archbishop. Roman traditions were preserved by the archbishops and the poet Venantius Fortunatus, who came here in 565–7 before settling at Poitiers. Under the descendants of Clovis Bordeaux changed hands frequently in internecine wars, though in 629 we find it in the hands of a Saxon duke, and in 731 it fell to invading Saracens. Charles Martel defeated Abd-er-Rahman at Poitiers in 732, and soon after tried to expel the Duke of Aquitaine from Bordeaux, but it was only in 768 that his successor, Pépin the Short, succeeded in capturing the town.

Something of the Roman organisation of Bordeaux survived all these vicissitudes, only to be wiped out in the ninth and tenth centuries. The new threat came from the Norsemen, and Bordeaux was the first town in Aquitaine to experience this new horror. In 844, 845 and 847 raids aimed at the town failed; but in 848 the chronicles record that 'the Danes burnt Bordeaux after they had captured it and massacred the population', blaming the treachery on those universal scapegoats of the Middle Ages, the Jews, for this disaster. It was a major triumph for the Norsemen, for Bordeaux had the unenviable distinction of being the first walled city of any size to fall before their attacks. In 870 we find the archbishop in exile at Poitiers and most of Aquitaine abandoned by the kings of France to whoever could make himself its master.

It was only in the orderly days of the twelfth century that Bordeaux began to revive. In the middle of the century the population had once again grown to a point where the space within the old city walls was filled, and early in the thirteenth century an additional wall was built to protect the new suburbs. Politically, the old duchy of Aquitaine was now centred on Poitiers, while the rulers of Bordeaux acted as dukes of Gascony. The series of dukes of Aquitaine called William – William VIII, IX and X – were both dukes of Aquitaine and of Gascony, but the distinction between their territories was maintained. When Eleanor of Aquitaine inherited this vast domain in 1137 it was to Bordeaux that Louis VII came to marry her, in the newly-built cathedral of St André. But the reunion of the southern lands to the crown of France was brief: in March 1152 Louis divorced Eleanor, and two months later she married Henry II of England.

From this marriage derived the English claims to Aquitaine and Gascony. If the French kings accepted the English presence here as well as in northern France they were reduced to mere puppets in the face of their immensely powerful vassals; if they pressed their claims to effective overlordship they had to be prepared to take on an enemy with far greater potential resources. This struggle for power dominated English and French history for three hundred years, and because Gascony remained in English hands for so much longer than the north Bordeaux was the main English base throughout much of this period. In 1206 King John tacitly recognised the existence of a commune at Bordeaux, a self-governing body of citizens, and he encouraged them to remain loyal to the English by exempting Bordeaux wines from all customs duties. By 1260 a complex administrative system was based in the city, doing its best to rule the rebellious lords of the south and to collect the king's revenues. Much of this organisation was the work of Edward I, who, as the Lord Edward, had been made ruler of Gascony in 1254. The chief officer was the king's seneschal, assisted by a small council, while the constable of Bordeaux was responsible for finances (the castle of Bordeaux was the home of the Gascon exchequer). But though the English were better versed in administrative skills than any other nation in Europe the politics of Gascony prevented them from securing an effective hold on the hinterland, and Bordeaux remained the centre of a relatively small political unit in real terms.

Bordeaux was none the less extremely important to the English Crown, both as the base for its Continental operations and as a source of revenue. The wine trade with England yielded immense revenues for the royal coffers, and formed the basis of one of the great trade-routes of the Middle Ages. The endless rolls of the constable of Bordeaux containing the customs registers reflect the activity of the town's growers and merchants. Between 1305 and 1309, an average of 90–100,000 tuns of wine were exported each year, though in the years of warfare at the end of the fourteenth century, the volume had dropped to a tenth of this level. But compared with the trade in wines from the Rhine and elsewhere, 'the Gascon merchant vintner enjoyed a virtual monopoly of the market' under the protection of the Crown, and he was a familiar figure at English fairs, even as far afield as Berwick or Cornwall.

This trade, conducted on favourable terms, explains the generally pro-English attitude of the inhabitants of Bordeaux. When the city was seized by the French king in 1294, its return to the English nine years later was due not to an English army but to a citizens' revolt led by Arnaud Canillau. In 1324, when most of Gascony fell into French hands, Bordeaux remained loyal; and under English rule it was as prosperous as it had been under the Romans. The population grew to over 30,000, the walls of the city were again enlarged and the castle of l'Ombrière, at once the government centre and key to the defence of the town, was remodelled and enlarged. The new walls enclosed an area four times that of the town of the twelfth century.

But at the end of the fourteenth century renewed warfare, famine and the Black Death reversed the rise in Bordeaux's fortunes. The population dropped to 10,000, and rose to only 20,000 early in the fifteenth century. Worse was to come. With the expulsion of the English in 1453, the English market for wine seemed to be lost, and Charles VII put a heavy tax on wine exports. But the advantages of peace outweighed such handicaps, and trade was soon back to normal levels. At Bordeaux itself, where the inhabitants were acknowledged to be 'all in favour of England', two huge forts, the Château Trompette and the Fort du Hâ, were built, ostensibly to protect the city against attempts to recapture it, but in fact to over-awe the possibly rebellious citizens. Louis XI relaxed the levies on the wine trade, and in 1462 created a *parlement* at Bordeaux, con-tinuing its role as an administrative centre. The French *parlements* were more concerned with the carrying out of the laws than the making of them, and ratified, rather than shaped, the royal edicts. By the eighteenth century, posts in the *parlement* had become hereditary, but the presence of such a body and its attendant lawyers was none the less an important element in the life of Bordeaux. Montaigne was mayor of Bordeaux from 1581 to 1585, and Montes-quieu an officer of the *parlement* in the mid-eighteenth century (see pp. 270 and 263).

During the wars of religion, Bordeaux escaped with little damage, remaining a Catholic stronghold throughout the period. The seven-teenth century, however, saw a series of revolts against increased taxes on trade and against the notorious salt tax, or *gabelle*. The worst outbreaks were in 1635 and 1675; the latter revolt began in March and was not finally suppressed until the late summer, the causes being new taxes on tobacco, pewter and *papier timbré*, the paper used for all legal documents and bills. Between these two episodes Bordeaux also played a prominent part in the revolt known as the Fronde, directed against the heavy hand of the royal govern-ment during Louis XIV's minority, when Cardinal Mazarin was effective ruler of France. Bordeaux was one of the bases of the Prince de Condé, who made use of the provincial capital's disquiet at the domination of Paris. But there were more complex factors at work as well, including the curious republican society called the Ormistes, who used to meet in an avenue of elms (*ormes*) near one of the churches. Their programme was aimed largely against the city's ruling class, a closed, hereditary caste; but they were encouraged by a former leader of the English Levellers, Edward Sexby, sent by Cromwell to make contact with them. Sexby helped them to draft a republican constitution, and spent a good deal of money – he was paid £1,000 for expenses on his return to England – but the Ormistes disappeared after the royalist victory over the main body of the rebels in 1653.

*

Now is the point at which to begin our visit, for of all Bordeaux's history only two aspects are immediately visible if one walks round the city: the eighteenth and the twentieth centuries. Once you have penetrated the seemingly endless and often poorly signposted roads through the suburbs the best way to approach the centre is to drive along the **quais** – the delight of eighteenth-century engravers – the huge sweep of waterfront with its classical façades built to screen the medieval slums behind. Tourny was unable to pull down the buildings behind these gracious fronts for lack of funds, so the vista was made by adding a new row in front. It was this sight that made Victor Hugo exclaim, 'Take Versailles, add Antwerp to it, and you have Bordeaux.' Since then wharfs have appeared along the front, and only in the centre is the vista free of these intrusions: and the forest of masts which Hugo would have seen has given way to a few rusty cargo-ships. But it is none the less a view that few ports can offer.

The **Esplanade des Quinconces**, in the centre of the eighteenth-century quarter, is a starting point from which to explore the city. The Allées d'Orléans and de Chartres, on either side of it, are now car parks, convenient perhaps, but ruining the green space created by careful planting. The Esplanade is all too often a sprawling mess of amusement fairs or ordinary markets. Toward the river the view is blocked by a modern warehouse, and the balustrades and flights of steps lose their intended effect. The western end of the Esplanade has suffered less; the crescent of houses retain their classical façades, and the monument to the liberal deputies of the Revolution, the 'Girondins', is a splendid late-nineteenth-century finishing touch to an equally monumental piece of landscaping. The four famous bronze horses, the 'Chevaux des Girondins', were removed during the German occupation, and lawns and gardens mark their place.

From the centre of the crescent we reach the end of the Allées de Tourny, newly resurfaced and replanted after the creation of an underground car park. It feels open and windswept as yet, but will doubtless improve as the trees grow to their full size. The rue Montaigne leads to the circular Place des Grands Hommes, with, just off it, the church of Notre Dame, a replica of the 'Gesù' at Rome built in the late seventeenth century. It contains some good eighteenth-century ironwork and furnishings.

Look across to the great range of eighteenth-century houses, and here is evidence enough that the eighteenth century was a period of great prosperity for Bordeaux, as both the wine trade and the trade with France's overseas colonies began to flourish. The quantity of wine was not much greater than in the past, but new methods of vinification, and the sale of wine to be matured, gave claret a high reputation which was reflected in the prices paid for it. The colonial traffic was a new development, and the effect of this new-found wealth is best seen in the appearance of Bordeaux today. Scarcely anything of the medieval town remains, save the streets around the Grosse Cloche (p. 109), while the whole of the centre, with its sweeping avenues and crescents, flanked by buildings in the classical style of the period, is a monument to the wealth and confidence of the city, whose population doubled between 1715 and 1790. This was chiefly the work of the *intendants* Boucher and Tourny between 1720 and 1757. Though the city revenues made such schemes possible, there were often protests from the city fathers, and much of the town remained medieval until the nineteenth century. By the end of the century, however, Bordeaux had made the classical style its own, and it no longer required an *intendant* to impose it. Private houses and above all the Grand Théâtre, were built in similarly impressive classical designs. Arthur Young visited Bordeaux in 1787 and found its glories even greater than its reputation. He was particularly impressed by the theatre and the high style of life at Bordeaux:

> The establishment of actors, actresses, singers, dancers, orchestra, etc., speak the wealth and luxury of the place. I have been assured that from 30 to 50 louis a night have been paid to a favourite actress from Paris. Larrive, the first tragic actor of that capital, is now here at 500 livres (£21. 12s. 6d.) a night, with two benefits. Dauberval, the dancer and his wife (the Mademoiselle Théodore of London), are retained as principal ballet-master and first female dancer at a salary of 28,000 livres (£1225). Pieces are performed every night, Sundays not excepted, as everywhere in France. The mode of living that takes place here among merchants is highly luxurious. Their houses and establishments are on expensive scales. Great entertainments, and many served on plate: high pay is a much worse thing; and the scandalous chronicle speaks of merchants keeping the dancing and singing girls of the theatre at salaries which ought to import no good to their credit. This theatre, which does so much honour to the pleasures of Bordeaux, was raised at the expense of the town and cost £270,000.

He also noticed how much Bordeaux's prosperity depended on peace:

The new houses that are being built in all quarters of the town mark, too clearly to be misunderstood, the prosperity of the place. The skirts are everywhere composed of new streets, with still newer ones marked out and partly built. These houses are in general small, or on a middling scale, for inferior tradesmen. They are all of white stone, and add, as they are finished, much to the beauty of the city. I inquired into the date of these new streets and found that four or five years were in general the period, that is to say, since the peace; and from the colour of the stone of those streets next in age, it is plain that the spirit of building was at a stop during the war. Since the peace they have gone on with great activity.

At the end of the Allées de Tourny we reach the façade of the **Grand Théâtre**, the masterpiece of the classical style in Bordeaux. It replaced a genuine classical building, on the site of the Roman forum, the temple of la Tutelle, or 'the Guardian Spirit'. Seventeenth-century engravings of this graceful monument present a charming scene; but it was demolished in 1680. The Grand Théâtre was begun in 1773 and completed in 1780, to plans by the Bordeaux architect Victor Louis. It has survived unchanged, and each year is the centre of the Bordeaux festival, the 'Mai Musical'. The façade has the strongest echoes of antiquity, with its colonnade surmounted by statues of the nine Muses and of Juno, Venus and Minerva. Each side has a long arcade echoing the design of the façade proper. Between the peristyle and the façade is an elegant coffered ceiling. A spacious colonnaded foyer leads to the staircase of honour, lit by a glass dome. The huge semicircular auditorium can be seen on request (concierge in vestibule). The ceiling was repainted to the original designs at the end of the last century.

Before we continue on our way let us complete Bordeaux's recent history. The first year of the Revolution, as elsewhere in France, saw little real change in the structure of power, though Bordeaux quickly set up its own city council to replace the old order. Apart from a brief attempt by the so-called 'girondin' liberal deputies to set up a kind of federal system in the south-west after they were banished from Paris in 1793, the political scene at Bordeaux was controlled by events in the capital; and any extremists to be found in Bordeaux were usually foreigners to the city. For the economic policy of the Republic and the abolition of slavery in the colonies had brought ruin to Bordeaux's trade, already impoverished by the disastrous harvests of the period. Bordeaux, besides its export trade,

105

was also a great wholesale and distribution centre, and much of the discontent in times of shortage focused on grain merchants. The almost total lack of trade by sea during Napoleon's war with England continued to depress the city's economic life. It was not surprising that Bordeaux was quick to declare allegiance to Louis XVIII in 1814, hoping for peace and a renewal of trade. But these hopes were deceived, and Bordeaux in the nineteenth century shared what a recent history of the region called '*les somnolences aquitaines*', which lasted until the Second World War. In 1870, 1914 and 1940 the French government moved briefly to Bordeaux in face of the German threat to Paris but the hold of the capital on France's political, economic and cultural life continued unchallenged and undisturbed by these temporary interruptions. In the last decade Bordeaux has begun a conscious policy of industrialisation to counteract the relatively static traffic of the port and the uncertainties of the wine trade, now depressed after years of extravagant prices. A huge new exhibition centre, provided with hotels, has been built north of the town, near the Pont d'Aquitaine, and the city has a new air of dynamism.

This new commercial activity shows in the Cours de l'Intendance, which runs west to the Place Gambetta from the Grand Théâtre, its eighteenth-century façades largely replaced by expensive shops. The Place Gambetta is too overwhelmed with traffic to be attractive, though its houses, some the work of Tourny's architects (1750), and its central garden merit a quieter existence. To the south-east is the classical arch of the Porte Dijeaux (1748) whose name is a corruption of the 'Porte de Jews', a piece of medieval Franglais. From the opposite corner the Place des Martyrs brings us to **Saint-Seurin**, one of the few medieval buildings to survive in Bordeaux, though much altered in the course of the centuries. Its appalling mock-Romanesque façade might be enough to deter any visitor; but immediately behind it is the base of the original belfry-porch with a remarkable set of capitals. The earliest are those flanking the doorway into the church itself, where monsters of strangely Scandinavian appearance contort themselves to bite a mysterious mask or grow into foliage. They probably date from before 1075, while the other capitals are early twelfth-century. Again, the décor consists of animals and foliage, save for one pillar, to the left, showing Abraham sacrificing Isaac. The alteration in floor level means that these capitals are close to hand and easy to examine in detail. Inside, the rather gloomy nave was rebuilt in the eighteenth century after the earlier Gothic vaults collapsed. A flamboyant Gothic chapel to the north shows what may have been lost in terms of richly worked masonry. There are good furnishings of the sixteenth and seventeenth century, but it is the crypt that is of prime interest. This ninth-century structure contains four fine seventh-century sarcophagi. When the roof collapsed the crypt was damaged, and the vaults are eighteenth-century. The seventeenth century cenotaph is that of the legendary St Fort, whose only claim to fame is the tradition of bringing young children to his tomb between 15 and 19 May so that they will grow *forts* (strong).

To the south of the church, behind a Renaissance porch facing the square, is a handsome Gothic doorway, with thirteenth-century sculptures of the Last Judgment. Excavations have shown that the square and surrounding streets are on the site of a huge Christian burial ground of the fourth century; the church of St Seurin may go back to a building connected with this cemetery. The only tangible architectural evidence of Bordeaux's Roman past is half a mile to the north, in the rue Dr Albert Barraud. The so-called **Palais Gallien** is not a palace at all, but the remains of a Roman amphitheatre, much of which was destroyed during the Revolution. Dating from the third century, the surviving arches are perhaps an eighth of the whole; but they still dwarf the houses which hem them in. Excavations are in progress, and only the outside can be seen.

Turn right into the rue Fondaudège, and the Jardin Public is down a street to the left. It was laid out after 1746 by Tourny, though its present appearance is due to its nineteenth-century restoration; in the 1840s it had become a rubbish dump. Instead of Tourny's original formal lay-out, with the classical portico of the orangery as its central point, it is now a 'parc à l'anglaise', with winding paths and a winding stream. The splendid wrought-iron gates are also nineteenth-century, though the original gates survive at the Place Champs-de-Mars. The eighteenth-century town house by the western gate contains a natural history museum.

To the south of the Grand Théâtre the Cours de l'Intendance runs down to the river. On the quayside is the **Place de la Bourse**, the most appealing of Bordeaux's squares. Open on one side to the river, it was built in 1776 beside Tourny's 1749 Hôtel de la Bourse (Exchange), which is now the Chamber of Commerce. It has richly decorated pediments by Claire Claude Prome, representing the greatness of Princes, Neptune inaugurating trade, the confluence of the Garonne and Dordogne rivers, and Time discovering Truth. The square itself was designed by Jacques-Ange Gabriel and his son, and though less elaborately decorated is carefully planned to avoid the monotony of formal architecture laid out on a rigid plan: the corners are angled, and the Hôtel de Tourny (housing the Musée de la Marine) is set back between two streets which lead into the medieval quarter of the city. Originally called the Place Royale it was renamed Place de la Liberté, then Place Impériale, Place Royale again at the Restoration in 1815, and finally Place de la Bourse in 1848. In the centre stood a statue of Louis XV on horseback, which was melted down in 1792. Napoleon III's statue, which succeeded it almost a century later, met an even more undignified end: it was thrown in the river.

On the quays beyond the Place de la Bourse are two fine gateways: the Porte Cailhau, much restored in 1882, was built in 1493, its sturdy Gothic mass a contrast to its classical surroundings. Behind it once stood the palace of the dukes of Aquitaine and of the English kings. The Porte de Bourgogne is more in keeping with the atmosphere of the quayside, a classical triumphal arch. From it the Cours Victor Hugo cuts through the old medieval quarter of narrow streets, now a relatively poor and ill-kept area of the city. To the south rises the spire of the belfry of **St Michel,** the highest in south-west France (370 feet). The belfry was built in 1472–92, and the spire added by Abadie in 1862. From the platform half-way up there is a wide view over the city; at present the whole tower is being restored. St Michel itself is also Gothic, built from 1350 on with flamboyant buttresses and a central doorway with angels, sibyls and apostles below a great rose window. The original glass was destroyed by bombing in 1940.

To the south of St Michel the rue Sauvageau winds its way to **Sainte Croix,** whose façade stretches along one side of an irregular cobbled square. A monastery was founded here outside the city in the seventh century. Sacked by the Saracens and later by the Vikings, it was rebuilt in the late tenth century. The walls of the nave probably date from this period, while the triple bays of apse and transept chapels are early twelfth-century, and the façade is twelfth-century. But little of this is in anything resembling its original state. The gloomy interior is mainly the work of nineteenth-century restorers, while Abadie rebuilt the façade from 1860. The result 'amply justifies the laments of four generations of archaeologists'. Only the central doorway and the south tower survived without drastic alteration: the upper part and the north tower are entirely Abadie's own invention. The tower has rising tiers of arcading, and little decoration; Abadie's wide-eaved roof cuts off this progression all too abruptly. Round the central door are much-restored sculptures in the style of Saintonge, including men linked by a rope – the faithful united by faith – and the elders of the Apocalypse. Figures on the blind arcades on each side represent Lust and Avarice.

Retracing our steps to St Michel and the Cours Victor Hugo, we will find on the right the **Grosse Cloche,** once part of the old city hall. Its foundations are thirteenth-century, but most of it is fifteenth-century. The inner clock dates from 1592, the outer being eighteenth-century. The Latin verses on it read, in translation,

> My strokes mark the time, my voice is a call to arms,
> My sounds chase away the dark-lined clouds
> I have songs for every joy,
> A tear for every death.

The verses reflect the important part played by bells in the life of a medieval city. Any great event was marked by their tolling, and this one had a special function, for it was used to signal the day on which the vintage was allowed to begin. Beyond its arch stretches the rue St-James, whose name echoes Bordeaux's English past. The road comes out on the Cours d'Alsace, where we turn left to the cathedral.

At the east end of the **Cathedral** is the **Tour Péy-Berland,** a separate belfry built between 1440 and 1446. Its original upper part was destroyed by lightning, and a poor statue has replaced it. Otherwise it is richly decorated, almost to excess: the detail suppresses the lines of main design. The cathedral of St André itself is also partly in the decorated Gothic style. The choir and transept, built on a massive scale by Bertrand de Goth in 1300, echo the design of contemporary English cathedrals as much as those of northern France. The project of rebuilding the whole church in the new manner proved too much for the archbishopric's resources after the decline in Bordeaux's fortunes in the 1450s, and the Romanesque nave remains, reinforced by a Gothic exterior of buttresses. Much-needed restoration is being carried out, both inside and outside, and it will be interesting to see the result. The interior appears dull, but cleaning may lighten the gloom and reveal the soaring lines of the choir. The simple Angevin vaulting of the roof is an attempt to bridge the styles of nave and choir, but the vista between the two fails to impress because of the relatively low nave. The Romanesque walls of the nave have been drastically restored.

Outside, the western façade, once very close to the city wall, is little more than a blank wall. The north and south doors are in desperate need of cleaning; their elegant thirteenth-century statues stand disconsolately under a heavy layer of grime which makes them almost impossible to decipher. To the north, the subjects can just be made out: St Martial on the central pillar supports a tympanum depicting the Last Supper, the Ascension and the Triumph of Christ. The south doorway, the 'porte royale', is flanked by ten large-scale figures of apostles; the tympanum shows the Last Judgment. That this work is close in style to that of the cathedrals around Paris is not surprising when we remember how little Gothic work there is in the south-west. There was no local Gothic style of note, and sculptors had to be brought from elsewhere.

To the west of the cathedral is the palais de Rohan, once the residence of the Archbishop of Bordeaux and now the city hall. A single storey surrounds three sides of the courtyard, forming a prelude to the main block, with its monumental staircase in pure white stone. The ironwork, as everywhere in Bordeaux, is elegant and distinguished. The western façade overlooks gardens flanked by two museums, the Musée des Beaux Arts and the Musée d'Aquitaine.

The **Musée des Beaux Arts** is strongest on Renaissance paintings, displayed at the far end of the long single gallery. In Section I a group of Italian primitives includes a *Madonna with St Jerome and St Augustine* by Perugino. Veronese is represented by a number of minor works, and there is a *Toilet of Venus* from Titian's studio. An imposing portrait of a seventeenth-century *jurat* (member of the city council) of Bordeaux is in sharp contrast with these polished Italian works: every detail underlines his pride in his rank. There is a striking chiaroscuro work by the 'Maître de la Chandelle', *St Sebastian tended by St Irene*, a manner more familiar in the works of Georges de la Tour. Section II contains two Rubens, *The Martyrdom of St George* and *The Martyrdom of St Just*. Two curious little scenes by Magnasco show the embarkation of galley slaves and torture scenes in a Turkish bagnio. Nattier's portrait of Henrietta, daughter of Louis XV, seems a world away from such horrors: it leads in to the predominantly French collections which follow in Section III, with works by Greuze, Vernet and Tischbein. Isabey's huge *Burning of the steamer Austria*, in the manner of Géricault's *Raft of the Medusa*, looms over Section IV; there is a fragment of *A Lion Hunt* by Delacroix, while in the cases are *animalier* bronzes, including six by Rosa Bonheur, born at Bordeaux in 1822. The last section includes some evanescent symbolist sketches by Odilon Redon and plaster maquettes by Rodin, as well as more recent French canvases.

The **Musée d'Aquitaine**, opposite, should be the collection which brings together many of the themes of this book, a starting point for exploring the art and architecture of the region. Alas, at the moment, most of the collection is in store; but a start has been made on a new museum in what used to be the Faculty of Letters at 20 cours Pasteur, south of the cathedral. The first stage of this is due to open in 1978. At the moment a well-thought-out display indicates the kinds of theme which the new museum will try to explore using its 600,000 catalogued items. The entrance hall underlines the problems a museum faces. Acquisitions are all too often either through chance discoveries during roadworks or from demolished buildings, gifts, or purchases; these need to be supplemented by research programmes aimed at building up holdings in definite areas and by archaeology. Conservation problems are illustrated by case-histories, as are problems of documentation and dating. The famous Venus à la Corne, from Laussel in the Dordogne, acquired as a gift, is on display to the right of the entrance hall.

The display continues with the museum's relations with historians and with its public, showing that the ideal programme must involve the visitor in history through the objects in front of him. This is followed up in two displays: the first explores the Romanisation of Aquitaine, in which two items in particular stand out, the stela of the sculptor Amabis and a statue of Diana as huntress. The second shows educational exhibitions on the subjects of town planning and architecture in the fifteenth to seventeenth centuries and on the Church and religious life in the Middle Ages in and around Bordeaux. If the new museum is planned with as much care and imagination one can only look forward eagerly to its opening.

Round the corner, toward the Place Gambetta, at 39 rue Bouffard (amid a host of antique shops) is a museum of the old-fashioned type, the **Musée des Arts Décoratifs.** Its rich collections are mainly eighteenth-century, though one room is given to medieval religious art and includes a fine twelfth-century Limoges enamel crucifix from the abbey of La Sauve Majeure. On the ground floor the rooms have eighteenth-century panelling: among the exhibits in room III is a remarkable terracotta bust of 'Young America' from the first American consulate at Bordeaux. The rooms upstairs contain metalwork, including the locks (room XII) and wrought-iron work for which Bordeaux was famous. The china includes plates with revolutionary mottos; their changing themes are a history in miniature of those troubled times. Room VII has a collection of *pots jacqueline*, the French version of Toby jugs.

To the south of the Musée d'Aquitaine the Cours d'Albret leads to the one remaining tower of the Fort du Hâ, the twin of the now vanished Château Trompette, built just outside the old city walls in the fifteenth century. To the south again is the church of Ste Eulalie, outside which the Ormistes (see p. 102) used to meet; and we end our exploration at the busy crossroads of the Porte d'Aquitaine, the gateway which marks the southernmost point of the eighteenth-century city.

From the city itself, we turn to the countryside around, which provides Bordeaux with what is still its most important product: wine. We will begin to the west, with the area along the Gironde estuary which is the heart of claret country, the Médoc.

18. Landscape in the Médoc; tractors are now as common as horses, even in the vineyards

19. Wine labels of Chateau Mouton-Rothschild; these headpieces are for 1947, 1955, 1958, 1964 and 1970, and are designed by Cocteau, Braque, Dali, Henry Moore and Chagall

1947

1955

1964

1958

1970

20. The castle of Hautefort was rebuilt in the seventeenth century; it still stands defiantly on a hilltop, but otherwise there is no visible link with its most famous owner, the troubadour Bertran de Born

21. The courtyard of the castle at Rochechouart

# Chapter 7

# The Médoc

✤

The landscape of the Médoc is shaped by vineyards; there seem to
be vines in every conceivable corner, from the crests of the chalky
ridges facing north to the Gironde down to the sheltered corners of
the village walls. So it is appropriate to begin with a short dis-
course on the making of wine and on the famous vineyards of the
Médoc.

Vines have been grown here since Roman days, and possibly even
earlier. Vines flourish in relatively poor but well-drained soil, and
these hillsides, with the chalk lying very close to the surface, are
ideal territory. The climate, too, is favourable: a reasonable but not
excessive heat in summer, and not too many late or severe frosts in
winter. Too great a heat tends to produce a stronger, coarser wine,
while the vines themselves will not survive bad or unseasonable frost.
The other important element in the character of the wine produced
is the type of vine; since Roman times the Médoc had developed its
own vine type, specially adapted to the prevailing conditions. Most
of this long heritage was wiped out in the great phylloxera epidemic
of the 1870s, when American vines were brought to Europe, and
with them four serious diseases, to which European vines were not
immune. Oidium, mildew and blackrot were fungus diseases which
were relatively easy to control with chemicals. Phylloxera was caused
by a minute insect, and before an answer was found it had laid
waste most of Europe's vineyards. And the solution itself was
drastic; almost all modern European vines have American root-
stocks, which are immune to the dreaded disease, with the old
varieties used as a graft above. The results were twofold: an increase
in quantity – the abundant harvest from American vines was the
original reason for their introduction – and a decline in the length of
life of the wine. Whether pre-phylloxera wines are actually better
than later vintages is now almost impossible to say. There was
certainly an immediate drop in quality, but a century of careful
breeding has done a great deal to repair the damage. The great age
of the pre-phylloxera wines, and their rarity, means that comparisons

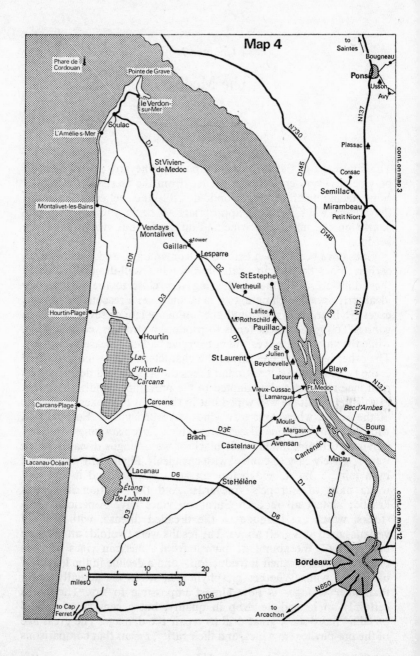

Map 4

Phare de Cordouan

Pointe de Grave

le Verdon-sur-Mer

Soulac

L'Amélie-s-Mer

St Vivien-de-Medoc

Montalivet-les-Bains

Vendays Montalivet

*tower

Gaillan

Lesparre

St Estephe

Vertheuil

Lafite

M Rothschild

Pauillac

Hourtin-Plage

Hourtin

Lac d'Hourtin-Carcans

St Julien

St Laurent

Beychevelle

Latour

Blaye

Carcans-Plage

Carcans

Vieux-Cussac

Lamarque

Ft. Medoc

Becd'Ambes

Brach

D3E

Moulis

Margaux

Bourg

Lacanau-Océan

Lacanau

D6

Castelnau

Avensan

Cantenac

Macau

Étang de Lacanau

Ste Hélène

D1

D2

D3

to Cap Ferret

D106

Bordeaux

N650

to Arcachon

km 0       10       20
miles 0    5    10

to Saintes

Bougneau

Pons

Usson

Avy

N730

Plassac

Consac

Semillac

Mirambeau

Petit Niort

D145

D146

D9

N137

N137

cont. on map 3

cont. on map 12

are difficult; but there was certainly a change in the nature of the finished product when phylloxera was conquered.

The quality of a vineyard's wine depends on so many factors that it seems a miracle that the result is ever a success. The vines have to be selected according to the type of soil, pruned and nurtured; each year constant watch has to be kept for disease; and above all the year's vintage depends on the weather. A cold, wet summer will delay the ripening of the grapes, so that they may never reach the proper degree of ripeness. Too hot a summer will mean that the wine has to be made while the weather is too hot. In 1921 the vintage at one of the great châteaux, Lafite, was spoiled by excessive heat while it was fermenting, and had to be sold off as *vin ordinaire*. The vintage records which have been kept since 1795 reflect the trials of the wine-grower: good vintages are all too often small in quantity, while abundance will go hand in hand with poor quality. Then there are disasters: a late vintage in 1816 (27 October) produced a quarter of the normal yield, of 'detestable' quality; a great frost on 6 May in 1861 reduced the yield to a minimum; the disease oidium gave three bad years from 1854–6. In this century devastating frosts in February 1956 brought two very small harvests in 1956–7. Against this, remarkable years bring much higher prices to the grower: 1921, 1929, 1961, 1970 and 1971 are examples, the harvest in 1970 being 'very abundant' as well. Recently, however, prices have been upset by speculative buying; the very high prices commanded by the great names lured buyers into regarding wine as an investment. Price-levels rose steeply until 1973. A natural reaction has set in, but it may be some years before the market returns to its normal course, particularly as recent abundant good vintages have produced something of a glut.

The wine-making itself is a very slow and patient process, and all that most visitors will see is the equipment of what looks like a modern factory, apparently idle for much of the year. The wine-grower is naturally least interested in visitors at his busiest period, the vintage, though some châteaux allow you to see this first stage of the process. For visits to châteaux, the best approach is through the Maison du Vin, 1 cours du 30 Juillet, Bordeaux (near the Grand Théâtre), where you can find out which châteaux are open and when. What you will see at vintage time is not the traditional image of barefooted men rhythmically trampling the grapes but tractors bringing in baskets from the vineyards, which are emptied into a virtual production line. For a red wine the grapes are first separated from their stalks (unless these are left in to increase the tannin in

115

the wine which tends to make it slower to mature). They are then passed through a mechanical crusher which is designed to extract the juice without breaking the pips; these would give a bitter flavour. This juice, or must, is then left to ferment, throwing up a crust which has to be broken up at intervals. As the fermentation proceeds the crust sinks to the bottom, and when the process is complete the wine is drawn off. The remains of the crust are then put through a wine press, and this pressed wine is added to the wine drawn off in the proportion 1–10; again, its merit is that it contains chemicals like tannin which preserve the wine. The object of these elaborate processes is to extract the colour and 'body' of the grapes. For a white wine the grapes are pressed immediately, as no colour is required.

Once the wine has been fermented it is put into cask, and the slow and complex process of ageing begins. Originally this took place in oak vats, whose porous sides allowed a natural reaction with the atmosphere. Now it is more often done in glass-lined reservoirs, where the atmospheric changes are exactly controlled. The fermentation continues very slowly, and the by-products of this form the lees. These are impurities, and the wine would suffer if left in the same cask. So it is drained off the lees two or three times in the first year, and again in the following year, in case the wrong type of fermentation begins: this would make the wine acid. Two further processes are also needed: ullage, or refilling of the casks, so that there is no air space where the microbes which produce acid can breed, and fining, which is done to ensure that the lees do not remain suspended in the wine but sink to the bottom. Only when these processes are complete and the ferments in the wine have come to a halt is it ready for bottling. Then there is nothing more to be done except to store it carefully and watch its development, so that it is drunk at the right moment.

A fine wine depends on all these processes being carefully carried out; lesser wines can be made by simpler methods. In the Médoc our interest must centre on the great vineyards, but first we must look briefly at the vineyards of Bordeaux as a whole (see map). Médoc and St Emilion are the main producers of red wine, with Pomerol and the area called the Côtes (Côtes de Fronsac, Côtes de Blaye, Côtes de Bourg and others) making up the balance; Graves produces excellent red wine, but a far larger quantity of white; Entre-Deux-Mers yields equal quantities of red and white, while Sauternes specialises in sweet white dessert wine. Each area has its own 'honours list', but Médoc is generally acknowledged to be the home of the finest clarets. Partly for this reason the tentative list of its wines drawn up in 1855, dividing the different vineyards according to their excellence, has never been revised. At the head of it were three names, the *premiers grands crus*: Château Lafite, Château Latour and Château Margaux. Château Mouton-Rothschild, listed in 1855 as a *deuxième grand cru*, was promoted by special decree of the Minister of Agriculture in 1973, and the name of Château Haut-Brion in the Graves (see p. 263) was 'associated' with these Médoc wines. As the original listing was never intended to be an official one such a decree was a remarkable tribute both to the continuing tradition of quality of the three first growths of 1855 and to the mystique attached to the classification. This mystique all too often confuses and baffles someone trying to learn to appreciate the finer points of claret. To make matters worse, the lower ranks of the classification are in many cases very out of date, and many a 'fifth growth' can rival a 'second growth'. The efforts of those with experience to justify their opinions by describing in extravagant prose what they taste in a particular wine do not help. It is hardly surprising that the result is either an inverted snobbery about wine or mere bewilderment. The sole object of both classification and description should be to guide a would-be purchaser as to the relative merits of a wine, to praise the good vineyards and ignore the poor ones. A new classification and less flowery prose would be a step in the right direction; fortunately, there are signs that both are on the way.[1]

None of this, except the rows of vines, each centred on a particular château, is much in evidence as we drive out of Bordeaux toward Lacanau. Notice, by the way, that 'château' is a purely technical title here, and that the buildings are rarely of any architectural interest; it means no more than 'farm' might mean elsewhere. Just outside the suburbs the D 2 branches to the right, between the northern edge of the great forest of the Landes to the left and the marshes of the Garonne to the right. We come first to Macau, whose wines have long been popular in England, and then to Cantenac, with two or three vineyards of importance, in particular Brane-Cantenac, Kirwan, Cantenac-Brown and Palmer. Château Palmer, under the name of Château de Gasq, was a favourite of both Richelieu in the seventeenth century and Louis XV in the eighteenth century. Beyond these, on the heights of the ridge overlooking the

---

[1] A revised classification was proposed by the national body for *appellations controlées* in 1960, but never endorsed. However, with the revision of the first growths there is hope for the rest.

river, is the area of **Margaux**. The labelling of its wines has often led to misunderstanding, because while ordinary Margaux is a blended wine from the surrounding district which enjoys no more than *appellation controlée* status (a guarantee of origin and quality), **Château Margaux** is one of the first growths. The cellars and a museum of early bottles are open to visitors, and the outside of the delightful porticoed house and its gardens built by the Marquis de la Colomella in 1802 can be seen. It stands on the site of much earlier buildings, going back to the fifteenth century, when it was a castle called Lamothe. Margaux's great reputation goes back to the 1750s; its older neighbour, Rauzan-Segla, was well known in the 1660s, but now ranks second with Rauzan Gassies among the wines of this area.

Just short of Lamarque we turn inland to **Moulis**; this is still an important wine-growing area but not the equal of the Margaux sites where the vines have 'their feet in gravel in sight of the river', as the local saying sums up the ideal aspect for a vineyard. Our theme here and at Avensan is very different, for the Médoc also contains a fine group of Romanesque churches, as individual as its wines. At Moulis the church is fortified, with arrow-slits and a defensive chamber below the belfry. The outside of the apse is amazingly rich in its ornaments, with a tiered double blind arcade on which are carved interlaced birds, and a frieze on which a hare is hunted by hounds. Scallop-shells in other friezes remind us that we are on a pilgrim road which began at Soulac (see p. 121). Avensan, where the body of the church was rebuilt in the nineteenth century, has a much simpler version of this decoration, relying on elegance of line rather than on rich sculpture. Nearby the church at Castelnau has a rare fifteenth-century English alabaster of the Crucifixion.

Back on the road along the Gironde, we find a track to the right at Vieux Cussac. This takes us to **Fort Médoc** on the bank of the river, the counterpart to the fort at Blaye (p. 94). Built by Vauban in 1689, it is being restored, and its star-shaped outline is emerging from the trees and undergrowth which masked it. The entrance is magnificent, a doorway with all the hieratic grandeur of the gateways of Karnak, bearing the sun in splendour, worthy of a temple. Even at this provincial fort the Sun King's magnificence had to be blazoned forth. Behind this triumphal entrance the peaceful central square, with the Gironde at the foot of the far wall, is an anti-climax.

The next wine-growing area we reach is **St Julien**, which, although small in area, has many distinguished châteaux; the seven most important are the two Léovilles, Gruaud-Larose, Ducru-Beaucaillou, Langoa-Barton, Talbot and Beychevelle, all of which can produce wines of the first order in a good year. Gruaud-Larose was founded in 1757 by a M. Gruaud, eccentrically devoted to his vineyard. He lived among his labourers, supervising the least detail of their work, and when he was not in the vineyards, he surveyed them from a specially built tower at the château. If he was satisfied with the quality of the vintage he would hoist a flag on this tower. Talbot owes its name to Sir John Talbot, the English commander at the end of the Hundred Years' War, who was killed at Castillon (see p. 269). The impressive château of Beychevelle has an even longer history, going back to the fourteenth century, when a fortified château belonging to the counts of Foix stood here. It passed to the family of the ducs d'Épernon, one of whom was High Admiral of France. Ships passing down the Gironde dipped their sails as a mark of respect when they sailed by; hence the château's name, a corruption of 'baisse-voile'. The cellars are open to visitors.

From St Julien we continue to **Pauillac**, where Ausonius (see p. 97) had a country villa. This is the greatest of all the wine-growing communes of the Médoc, with three out of the four first growths: Lafite, Latour and Mouton-Rothschild. **Lafite** appears in exalted company from the first, at the royal table and at those of Madame de Pompadour and of Richelieu. Bought by an English banker in the mid-nineteenth century, it was resold to its present owners, the Rothschilds, in 1867. Many writers have ranked it the first of the first growths, and it has always commanded the very highest prices. The Château Lafite of 1811 has become a legend, the finest wine of a peerless vintage; but any vintage of this château must remain legendary for most wine-drinkers because of its price. The cellars can be visited, and contain a vast collection, not only of Lafite vintages from 1797 onwards, but also of the produce of other Bordeaux châteaux. **Latour,** on the border between Pauillac and St Julien, has its partisans who would rank it as high as Lafite; its history goes back to 1670. And if no one would dispute the motto of **Mouton-Rothschild** before its recent promotion: 'First I cannot be; second, I disdain to be; Mouton is what I am' (an imitation of the motto of the ducs de Rohan), it too has its supporters who would now claim for it the rank of 'first of the firsts'. Mouton's distinction dates from the mid-nineteenth century, and has been upheld, save for a brief period before 1914, by its owners since 1853, another branch of the Rothschild family. Besides the cellars, there is a small museum (open only by prior arrangement through the Maison du Vin at

Bordeaux or by writing), containing works of art connected with wine, not least of which are the château's own labels, designed in different years by such distinguished artists as Chagall, Braque, Dali, Cocteau and Henry Moore – payment being in bottles of the relevant vintage.

The other Pauillac wines, which would be outstanding anywhere else, are too numerous to mention; there is only space here to mention the two Pichon-Longuevilles, and a personal favourite of mine, Château Lynch-Bages, on one of the highest sites in the district.

To the north of Pauillac, on the Gironde, is the last important wine-growing district, St Estèphe. Just opposite Lafite rise the strange Oriental pagodas of Château Cos d'Estournel. Calon Ségur, nearer to St Estèphe, has one of the longest histories of any of the vineyards: it was originally a Gallo-Roman village, and in the Middle Ages it was an important fief of the lords of Lesparre, fifteen miles to the north-west. There have certainly been vines here since the fourteenth century, and possibly since the fourth century.

The main road to Lesparre leads us away from the river, and the vineyards soon fade out. The church at Vertheuil has a fine Romanesque south doorway; the sculptures show the elders of the Apocalypse and, on a more familiar plane, peasants pruning vines. Beyond the town, marshes appear to the right, and the northern edge of the forest of the Landes to the left. **Lesparre** still has the fourteenth-century keep of its castle to the west of the town, the only remaining part of a powerful fortified ensemble dating back to the eleventh century. Its lords had rights over most of the Médoc under Edward III, and eighteenth-century drawings show that their castle was on a scale to match their domains.

A mile or so outside Lesparre a road to the right leads to the church of Gaillan, where an octagonal Romanesque tower survives beside a nineteenth-century church. Rebuilt with the original materials in 1847, it is a most unusual form for Romanesque art, as it continues in octagonal storeys to the top. Eight-sided bases to towers are not rare, but these usually become square as the storeys progress. Each stage has a different variation of arcading and columns. Begadan, further toward the Gironde, has a Romanesque apse in the style of those in Saintonge; the main difference is that the geometric patterning favoured by the Saintonge masons is absent, giving a severer appearance. Among the little capitals of the upper arcades is the lively figure of a minstrel, who reappears on the cornice.

Returning to the main road, we reach **St Vivien de Médoc**, whose church was probably the prototype for that at Begadan. Here the solitary minstrel of Begadan becomes two tableaux on the tympan of the blind arcades: in one two musicians play the lute and psaltery, and a girl performs a fantastic, acrobatic dance, while next to them a lady approaches a seated lord. The scenes are so secular in style that it is at first difficult to give them any Biblical context, but they must surely be Salome dancing before Herod, the long-sleeved lady of the second scene being Herodias. The decoration is closer to that of Saintonge, and the capitals inside the church are also in the style of those to be found north of the Gironde.

The road reaches the coast at **Soulac**; five miles to the north the Pointe de Grave marks the mouth of the Gironde. Soulac stands on the site of the Roman city of Noviomagus, swallowed up by the sea in the sixth century AD; it was once an important point on the pilgrims' route from England to Compostela: here they disembarked and made their way down the Landes, which were then mosquito-infested marshes. The alternative was to face the storms of the Bay of Biscay, which in medieval ships must have been a frightening prospect indeed. Eleanor of Aquitaine came here in 1199, aged nearly eighty, on her way to Castile to arrange the marriage of her granddaughter Blanche of Castile to Louis VIII. It was after this voyage that she retired to the abbey of Fontévrault 'worn out with the toils of her journey and with old age'. In the sixteenth century the port, which was to the east of the present town, was silted up, and Soulac became an unimportant village until the nineteenth century, when it was developed as a holiday resort. Now it welcomes a different kind of pilgrim: its population is little more than 1,000 in winter, and can be as many as 70,000 in summer.

All that remains of old Soulac is the church, once that of the priory of Notre Dame de Fin des Terres (Our Lady of Land's End). Overwhelmed by sand dunes in 1744, it was dug out and restored at vast cost after 1860. It is a huge building, obviously designed for large parties of pilgrims. The nave was originally nearly ten feet higher, but changes in the water-table have made it impossible to dig out the floor to the original depth. It is probably that recorded as being built in 1079, while the choir is twelfth-century. Four striking capitals in the sanctuary are remarkable not only for their execution but also because they repeat the same theme, Daniel in the lions' den.

South of Soulac the vast solitudes of the Landes coast begin. After L'Amélie-sur-Mer (with a good restaurant at the Hôtel des Pins), badly surfaced roads run through pinewoods and dunes to Hourtin-Plage; the main road goes inland to Hourtin, on the other side of the Lac d'Hourtin-Carcans, which, like the Étang de Lacanau to the south, is well-equipped for water-sports. The coast itself is not suitable for swimming and sailing, because of the very strong currents which sweep along it close inshore. From Lacanau straight roads through the forest bring us back to the outskirts of Bordeaux.

# Chapter 8

# Angoulême and the Angoumois

.♣.

Before we continue from Bordeaux southward to the Landes and east to the Dordogne, we must return to the borders of Poitou. Instead of taking the road south-west to Saintonge, we turn south-east, to the Vienne valley, which we last crossed in Chapter 2. The Angoumois, centred on Angoulême, is wooded country, but its hills are relatively tame compared with the forests further south. There are attractive corners, little lakes and quiet river valleys, but nothing spectacular: it is a domestic, comfortable landscape.

Our starting point is the little town of **Confolens**, spanning the Vienne, at the north-east corner of the old province of Angoumois. It is a quiet backwater, the river spanned by a fourteenth-century bridge, now shorn of its towers and drawbridge. The centre of the town is a maze of narrow alleys between old houses. At 12 rue du Soleil is a great timber-framed house variously called the Hôtel of the Prince de Condé (a leading figure in the troubles of the mid-seventeenth century) or of the Duc d'Épernon. It was here in 1619 that Marie de Medici's escape from custody was planned, Louis XIII having temporarily managed to gain the upper hand over his formidable mother and her entourage. Beyond this the steps of the rue des Francs Maçons climb between steep-roofed houses to the old castle.

To the north of the town, the Church of St Barthélémy (on the N 148) has an interesting, if crude, Romanesque doorway.

The Auberge de la Belle Étoile, on the road toward Angoulême, offers a good meal in plain modern surroundings. The road then runs through wooded, empty country to St Claud, where if you turn right along the N 739 you reach the hamlet of **Cellefrouin,** tucked away in the bottom of the valley of the river Son. Here in the eleventh century the Augustinian canons built a church, or *cella*, on land given by the local lord, Frouin. The building survives more or less unchanged, though it suffered during the sixteenth-century wars of religion, and was clumsily repaired during the next two centuries. The tower was shortened, and the nave re-roofed, but the severe

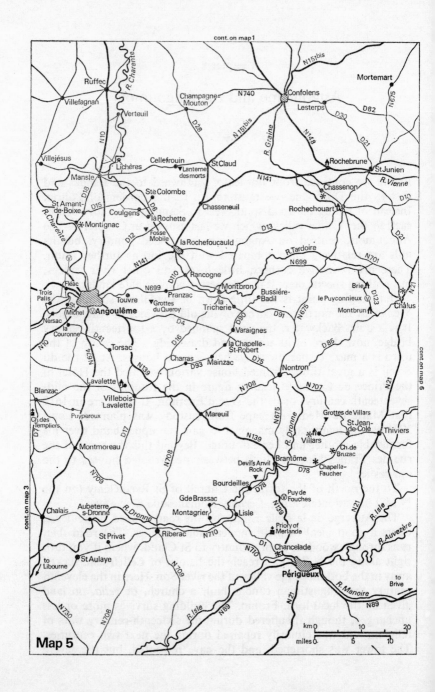

cont. on map 3

cont. on map 6

**Map 5**

Mortemart

N151 bis

Ruffec

Villefagnan

R. Charente

Champagne-Mouton

N740

Confolens

Lesterps

D82

N675

Verteuil

D28

N151 bis

R. Graine

N148

D30

D21

Villejésus

N10

Cellefrouin

StClaud

Rochebrune

St Junien

Lichères

Lanterne des morts

N141

Chassenon

R. Vienne

Mansle

D15

Ste Colombe

Chasseneuil

Rochechouart

D10

St Amant-de-Boixe

D6

Coulgens

la Rochette

D13

D21

Montignac

D12

Fosse Mobile

la Rochefoucauld

R. Tardoire

Brie

N701

D123

Châlus

N21

Trois Palis

Fléac

N141

D10

Rancogne

N699

Pranzac

Montbron

Bussière-Badil

le Puyconnieux

N699

D21

St Michel

Angoulême

Touvre

Grottes du Queroy

la Tricherie

Montbrun

Nersac

la Couronne

D4

D30

D91

N675

N21

Torsac

D16

Varaignes

D85

Blanzac

D41

N614

Charras

D93

Mainzac

la Chapelle-St-Robert

D75

Nontron

N708

N707

N10

Lavalette

N139

Villebois-Lavalette

Grottes de Villars

St Jean-de-Côle

Thiviers

Ch. des Templiers

Puyperoux

D17

Mareuil

N139

N675

R. Dronne

Villars

Ch. de Bruzac

Montmoreau

Brantôme

D78

Chapelle-Faucher

N709

Devil's Anvil Rock

Chalais

Aubeterre-s-Dronne

R. Dronne

Bourdeilles

D78

Puy de Fouches

N21

R. Isle

Gde Brassac

Montagrier

Lisle

N139

St Privat

Riberac

N710

Priory of Merlande

Chancelade

R. Auvezère

St Aulaye

to Libourne

N709

N710

N89

R. Isle

Périgueux

R. Manoire

to Brive

N89

N730

N708

N21

km 0 — 10 — 20

miles 0 — 5 — 10

D1

façade survived, one of the very earliest in the region. Compared with the façades of Saintonge, it is puritanical. Only a hint of decoration appears on one capital; otherwise the effect is achieved entirely by a simple harmony of proportions and lines. Inside, the pillars of the nave seem foreshortened, because the floor was raised by four feet in 1789, and since the original proportions of the nave were all-important in such a simple building some of the impact is lost. The quietness and remoteness of the church is emphasised when you climb up the hill to the left to Cellefrouin's other monument, a fine *lanterne des morts* in the cemetery above the valley. It is less elaborate than that at Fenioux (p. 77), as the slender column has no stairway within and the lantern must have been lit from a ladder; but its light would have been visible for a long distance around.

From Cellefrouin the N 739 runs east to the N 10; turning right, a small road to the right after a mile or so leads to **Lichères**, whose church stands on a hilltop to the north of the few buildings of the hamlet. It is a simple building of mellow grey stone, with sparse but carefully composed decorations. The bell-tower collapsed in 1750, and the north transept and north wall, damaged by the falling masonry, were properly restored only in 1905. The west doorway has a lovely tympanum formed by two arches of different radii, with carvings of interlaced foliage in the manner of Saintonge, and two angels displaying the Lamb in a nimbus. The outside of the nave has decorated capitals at each window, while the ends of the transepts are plain, as if to emphasise the single arcade round the windows of the apse. The interior is equally restrained – as so often elsewhere the floor level has been raised – and the chapel in the south transept has a very classical arcade at the level of the top of the window, the rest of the wall being plain. Nothing is known of the history of the church; but it is exactly what a Romanesque church in a small village should be, modest, timeless and perfect.

To the north of Lichères a route signed as the *circuit des vallées* leads to Vertheuil, whose church possesses a sixteenth-century Entombment of Christ in polychrome plaster – not to my taste – and where there is a château belonging to the Rochefoucauld family (not open to the public). Here Arthur Young stayed in 1787 and wrote that 'we found everything that travellers could wish in a hospitable mansion', and noted that the Emperor Charles V had praised the hospitality there two and a half centuries before. He went on: 'It is excellently kept; in thorough repair, fully furnished, and all in order, which merits praise . . . If this just attention to the interests of posterity was more general, we should not see the melancholy spectacle of ruined châteaus in so many parts of France.'

Returning down the N 10, take a road to the right after Mansle. It leads to **St Amant de Boixe**, whose spacious abbey commemorates the hermit Amant, who died here in the sixth century. The tradition of a hermitage continued after his death, but in the tenth century the site was seized by the counts of Angoulême. In 988 Guillaume II Taillefer gave it to the Bishop of Angoulême in expiation of his ancestors' misdeeds. It became a Benedictine monastery about 1020, but the building of the abbey was not started until after the discovery of St Amant's body in 1125, and was only completed in 1170. Among the benefactors was Eleanor of Aquitaine. In the Hundred Years' War the abbey was fortified and survived unharmed; but in the wars of religion, between 1562 and 1568, it was plundered several times by the Protestants and never recovered. It now serves as a parish church.

The nave, which retains its original descending staircase from the west door, is flanked by massive pillars, and lit by windows high in the aisles. Above the crossing there is a remarkable cupola, supported on a blind arcade below the dome itself. The Gothic choir is out of line with the nave, perhaps to emphasise the difference between new and old. In the south transept are fourteenth-century frescoes taken from the old crypt and representing the Annunciation, Visitation and Presentation. The façade is later than the body of the church; it is four-square and plain, with the minimum of geometric decoration on the arches and blind oculi to left and right of the upper arcade to break up the flat surfaces. Its proportions are similar to that of Civray, but the sculpture is in very sharp contrast to Civray's rich textures.

A mile to the south of St Amant the castle of Montignac overlooks the Charente valley. Of the twelfth-century keep built by Vulgrim II Taillefer only the massive base survives; there is also a gateway and part of the outer wall on the side nearest to the village.

Further along the D 15, and across the N 10, three small Romanesque churches are to be found along the valley of the river Tardoire. The church at Coulgens was built in the eleventh century and refashioned a hundred years later; it has an unusual, severe façade, and some striking capitals. In the centre of the village green in La Rochette, the small church of St Sebastian offers another example of the figure of Constantine on horseback; but here it has an unusual counterpart, because it is paired by another rider on a strange beast, symbol of vice. Inside, the capitals have lively scenes which have not yet been identified: a man attacked by a monster, another grappling with lions, another carrying a goose. It is possible, though unlikely, that they are simply fantasies. Ste Colombe, across the other side of the valley, owes its name to a martyr of the third century AD. It is a simple, unrestored late-twelfth-century church. To the south of the nave a capital shows Ste Colombe, and she appears again to the left of the central window of the façade, with St Peter on the right, two striking elongated statues in a very archaic style. Round the outside there are lively corbels, and among the little bas-reliefs are several doves (*colombes*).

To the right of the river as we turn south to La Rochefoucauld lies the Forêt de la Braconne, partly used as a military training ground. This is limestone terrain, and in the forest are a number of chasms or sink-holes which have been formed by surface water running into fissures in the limestone. The *grande fosse* is the most spectacular, while the *fosse mobile* is so called because when a local robber tried to throw the body of one of his victims into it, the chasm moved away from him. To the south of the forest are the **Grottes du Queroy,** surrounded by a rather tawdry fairground, while we shall meet the other end of the underground water-courses at the Sources de la Touvre (p. 128).

As one nears **La Rochefoucauld**, the massive presence of its château can be seen towering above the river. But here disappointment is in store, because this once-splendid monument is little better than a ruin, uninhabited for nearly forty years; part of the donjon and inner gateway crumbled in 1960, and the superb *cour d'honneur*, one of the glories of Renaissance France, is in a highly dangerous state. A glimpse into the outer courtyard, with its huge Venetian vase in the antique style and box trees deep in grass, may be possible, despite the formidable notices on the outer door. To the left the ruined donjon gives the façade the air of some cardboard palace; the abruptness of the broken edge against the sky makes one doubt the solidity of the rest. Alas, the only work in hand at the moment is that of securing the foundations, a formidable task in itself. It may well be a decade or more before we can look again on the home of one of France's greatest writers, François de la Rochefoucauld (1613–80), whose witty and bitter *Reflexions ou Sentences et Maximes Morales* are a cool antidote to the glories of the Sun King, Louis XIV, and his court. After an erratic political and military career, including imprisonment and rebellion, the duke spent his later years in the salons of Paris as friend of Madame de la Fayette and Madame de Sévigné. The *Maximes* are the fruit of a career at court and among the seats of power; under the epigraph 'Our virtues are usually only vices in disguise', he paints a cynical picture of human egotism.

Return to the centre of La Rochefoucauld and take the D 6 and
D 110, which lead to **Rancogne**, a delightful little country village,
complete with château, miller's house and a little bridge over a tree-
hung river. Along the river are caves hollowed by the water and used
as shelters in prehistoric times, but not now accessible. Continuing
by Pranzac, with a fine twelfth-century *lanterne des morts*, and
skirting the Forêt de la Braconne again, the N 669 leads to Touvre,
where a turning to the left takes you down to the **Sources de la
Touvre**. Here an underground river emerges from a cavern below a
little fortified church on a vine-clad hill, and from springs along the
bank. An ugly square modern fish-hatchery diminishes the effect of
strangeness and mystery, for this was – not surprisingly – a local
centre of pagan worship. The Gauls, being of Celtic blood, especially
revered hidden pools and dark groves. The Roman poet Lucan,
describing such a grove near Marseilles, says:

> On these boughs . . . birds feared to perch; in those coverts, wild
> beasts would not lie down; no wind ever bore down upon that
> wood, nor thunderbolt hurled from black clouds; the trees, even
> when they spread their leaves to the breeze, rustled among them-
> selves. Water also fell there in abundance from dark springs. The
> images of the gods, grim and rude, were uncouth blocks, formed
> of felled tree-trunks.

Even on a sunlit day a little of the ancient awe still lingers, particularly in the obscurity of the cavern to the right. In prosaic reality,
the water comes from the Tardoire and the Dandiat a few miles
away. There is a *son et lumière* performance each evening in July
and August.

Return by Montbrun on the N 699, where a turning to the right
about three miles to the east of the town offers an attractive detour
through another part of the Tardoire valley to La Tricherie. **Bussière-
Badil**, a spacious village arranged around a lovely Romanesque
church, is four miles or so to the left. Most such churches, unless they
have very fine stained glass, are particularly rewarding in the evening,
when the west door may be wide open to the sun. The charm of this
building lies in its simplicity. Only the transepts stray into Gothic;

its high-aisled nave and earlier, low-arched choir are purest Roman-esque. There are occasional carved capitals of wild men bearing shields, mermaids and a bird-woman harpy. The warm yellow stone of the façade, with its elaborately carved portal (to the left the Annunciation, Visitation and Nativity can be made out) contrasts pleasantly with the plain whitewashed interior. Opposite the church a canary sings outside the village smithy; and a pleasant tree-lined green runs down to the village wash-house and to a group of old houses and farm buildings bordering the river.

The road on which we arrived, the D 90, bears away to the left after two miles and leads, after a sharp descent, to Varaignes. Cross-ing the D 75 just beyond the village, a road (D 92) to the right brings us to another fine Romanesque church at **La Chapelle St Robert,** standing in an open space which was once a priory and cemetery. The four-square tower makes the building seem larger than it is; the pattern of a plain lower tier, then blind arcades and a pierced belfry, is common in this region, but this is a splendidly proportioned example. The portal, with its blind arches on either side, is dignified; dignified, too, are the elephants which wend their unexpected way round the capital to the right. Inside, the stone and plaster are spotted with mildew; but this only heightens the effect of age and of distance from worldly commotions. The capitals, except in the apse, are plain; the priory was never rich, and there was no money for later remodelling. The whole church is of very early twelfth-century date, and survives with barely a detail changed.

The D 93 takes us to **Charras,** where the church was converted into a fortress during the Hundred Years' War, complete with battlements. Much of the warfare of the period consisted of raids into enemy territory, designed to terrorise the inhabitants into changing their allegiance or simply to lay waste the land. Even a simple defensive building like this would serve as a refuge against a passing troop of soldiers, who were unlikely to lay siege to it for more than an hour or two.

Across the N 139 to the south **Villebois-Lavalette** occupies the site of a Roman fort above a road of the same period. It became a fortified village under the Lusignans (see p. 49) in the twelfth century, and in the seventeenth century the château itself was rebuilt inside the medieval walls by the Marshal de Navailles. At Magnac-Lavalette the vast white mass of the Château de la Mercerie looks like some huge public building transported to the countryside. It was in fact built in the last century. Set against a wooded hillside amid a huge park filled with a collection of rare trees, it has a large formal garden as well, and the interior is furnished with seventeenth-century pieces. It is open from Easter until November.

At Torsac, five miles toward Angoulême, the church has a capital showing Orpheus playing his lyre, a very rare example of a twelfth-century use of a subject from classical myth.

South down the main road to Libourne the village of **Puypéroux** is to the right. In this well-wooded and watered countryside, with its sheltered valleys, a number of hermits established themselves in the seventh century, following the example of St Cybard at Angoulême. Puypéroux was the site of one of these hermitages, which became an abbey by the twelfth century. Its great treasure was the body of St Gilles, who had converted the people of the area around Toulouse. According to legend he had just finished the church at La Couronne (p. 132) and did not know where to build his next church. So he threw his hammer in the air, said a prayer, and declared: 'Where the hammer lands, there I will build my next abbey.' He could hardly have found a more romantic site than Puypéroux. From the east end of the church, built on the heights of a long ridge, the land falls away in folds of green, broken by the reflections from a lake.

The church is approached by a flight of steps: the façade collapsed after a thunderstorm in 1836, and was completely rebuilt in the 1840s, when the nave was given a brick vault. Inside. the trefoil arches in the nave echo Moorish architecture – the pilgrim roads again – while to the north is the tomb of St Gilles, much restored also. The focal point of the church is the apse, with seven shallow radiating recesses, barely deep enough to be chapels, which give a feeling of impressive space. Below the cupola which covers the crossing are some lively capitals, mainly of animals. The abbey buildings are now used as a nunnery; from the courtyard the outside of the apse presents an appearance little changed since Carolingian times. The builders of the church left in position the old outer walls, with their uncut stones, and rebuilt the interior only.

Continuing to Blanzac, take the D 7 to Chalais; just outside the town a side-road leads, after about a mile, to the Templar chapel of **Cressac**, isolated on a hillside (key from house next door). The outside is very severe, and architecturally the interior is more like a barn than a church. But it contains some of the most remarkable twelfth-century frescoes to have survived, which were carefully restored in 1967. Their interest is not so much artistic as historical, for these are not saints and madonnas, but the Templars fighting in

Palestine. There is still some doubt as to exactly what the scenes represent, and the loss of half the frescoes early in the twentieth century has not helped solve the mystery. The left-hand wall shows the great fortress of Crac des Chevaliers, while at its far end a body of horsemen make a sortie to drive Nur-ed-Din, the Saracen leader, back into his capital, Damascus. This is the victory of La Bocque in 1183, at which a group of crusaders from Angoulême, led by their count, Guillaume IV Taillefer, were present. The frieze below seems to show the Templars holding a parley with the Saracens and ransoming prisoners. They had begun as a charitable order, looking after pilgrims, and the negotiation of the release of prisoners remained one of their functions for some time. They then became so ferociously warlike that the Saracens refused to take any Templar knight prisoner, but killed such captives on the spot, a compliment which the Templars repaid in kind. On the east-end wall the figures are those of St Michael and St Adhémar, Bishop of Angoulême, while to the right of the west end are two other figures reputed to be of local celebrities, Hugues de Lusignan and Isabella of Angoulême, shown as the protagonists in an allegory of Christianity's triumph over paganism.

Returning to Blanzac, travel some ten miles to the south-west to **Montmoreau,** a peaceful hilltop town crowned by a castle, in the grounds of which are the original gateway of the twelfth century together with its chapel, which were dug out of the nine feet of earth concealing them in the 1950s. The chapel is circular, with three radiating bays, each with a niche designed to hold a reliquary. It formed a kind of spiritual bastion to the castle beside the material and practical defence of the gatehouse, echoing in its shape the Church of the Holy Sepulchre at Jerusalem.

On the slope of the hill, just off the main road, is the spacious church of St Denis, much restored by Abadie in the 1850s. The façade has a richly decorated doorway with a polylobed central arch, a reminder that we are actually on the pilgrim road here. The interior, apart from a clutter of furniture, is almost untouched, preserving the majestic lines of its twelfth-century designers, which are enhanced by a noble flight of steps descending from the west door down into the nave.

Just east of the church we turn left on the main road, toward Angoulême, and then, four miles from Angoulême itself, the D 12 takes us west to **La Couronne,** where the remains of the ruined abbey huddle incongruously in an untidy village next to a cement works: washing hangs in the shelter of the ruins, rather as in a

Piranesi engraving of the humbled glories of eighteenth-century Rome. It was once an early Gothic church on an exceptional scale, but only the choir and transept walls survive of what was the largest abbey in Aquitaine.

Beyond the N 10 toward Angoulême **St Michel d'Entraygues** has a most unusual octagonal church, built in 1137. It seems to have been designed, as the chronicle of the abbey of La Couronne puts it, 'to receive therein the poor followers of Christ', pilgrims making their way to Compostela. Such a church would serve both as a spiritual and physical shelter to a large company of pilgrims, who would otherwise have been difficult to house adequately. The church is in fact made up of eight curved bays crowned by a dome with a lantern above it. This vaulted cupola, a considerable technical feat, may well have been the work of a band of masons whose skills are in evidence elsewhere on the pilgrimage road. It was rebuilt in 1850–1, by the architect Abadie, for once without serious alterations. Above the doorway is a tympanum of St Michael and the dragon, a work of remarkable skill without parallel anywhere in this area. Perhaps it was the work of an artist on pilgrimage himself, but the strength of the design and of its flowing lines, as well as its relatively uncrowded use of the space available, indicate an established master at work. Emile Mâle, the great French art historian, has called this tympanum 'the most vivid image of St Michael created in the twelfth century', no small compliment in view of the popularity of the subject.

On the other bank of the Charente, at Trois-Palis, St Michael reappears in much humbler style on one of the capitals of the church. On the façade, a very early twelfth-century group of Christ and the symbols of the four evangelists are carved in low relief, the flat ornament and swirling draperies strongly reminiscent of contemporary manuscripts.

Turning along the river toward Angoulême, we join the main road at Fléac. Immediately across the road a track leads to a viewpoint overlooking **Angoulême**. Here the town can be seen perched on its cliffs overlooking the Charente, an obvious site for a fortified settlement. Below the cliffs the modern industrial town has spread out, its papermills using the river water as an essential part of their processes. All these are now large commercial factories, though one mill, at Puymoyen, south of the town, still makes hand-made paper in the traditional moulds.

The upper town, known as the Plateau, is on the site of the Roman *Civitas Ecolismensium*, which grew up in the fourth century as a new provincial capital in an area which had previously been governed by

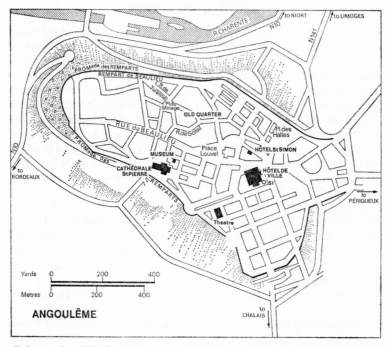

ANGOULÊME

Saintes. In 419 the Romans ceded the area to the Visigoths, but after the first battle of Poitiers in 507 Angoulême became part of Clovis's Frankish kingdom, and the clergy of the area assembled there to thank their new ruler for delivering them from the Arian heresy which the Visigoths supported. In the early Middle Ages Angoulême became the centre of a county; and its counts, the Taillefers, who remained loyal to the dukes of Aquitaine, profited from their faithful service to become lords of considerable domains. The line died out in the thirteenth century with Isabella of Angoulême, wife of King John; she had been betrothed to Hugues de Lusignan, but John carried her off before the marriage could take place. Hugues de Lusignan's subsequent rebellion led to John losing most of his possessions in France. After John's death Isabella married Hugues, and the Lusignans became counts of Angoulême and so remained until the end of the thirteenth century, when the title was taken from them by Philip the Fair, and became one of the titles given to younger sons of the royal family. In 1345, during the Hundred Years' War, Angoulême fell to the English under the Earl of Derby, and remained in their hands until 1373. It was the favourite residence of the Black Prince during his rule in Aquitaine, and his

133

eldest son was christened here in great splendour in 1365. At the end of the fifteenth century the French throne passed to the counts of Angoulême, when Francis I became king. His sister, Marguerite d'Angoulême, was one of the founders of the French Renaissance. Learned and witty, she was a great patron of the arts, and wrote a *Heptameron* in imitation of Boccaccio's famous *Decameron*, probably with contributions from members of her court. She married the King of Navarre (and is often referred to as Marguerite de Navarre); her grandson became King of France as Henri IV. It was he who brought peace to France and ended the wars of religion; Angoulême had suffered severely in them, particularly after it was captured by the Protestants in 1568.

Of the medieval town only the ramparts remain. Starting from the Place des Halles on the north side of the town, it takes about half an hour to walk round them; at the western end there is a tree-lined promenade with a wide view over the Charente valley. From the tower at the north end one of Napoleon's generals experimented with gliding, the idea being to launch men from balloons during the invasion of England. He escaped with a broken leg and the project was abandoned.

The ramparts end at the **cathedral.** This fascinating building seems at first to be a superbly preserved Romanesque church of the twelfth century, built in the gleaming white local stone; but this is far from the real truth.

This cathedral is the fourth to be built on the site, the first going back to the late Roman times. The crypt of the second cathedral of about AD 560 was discovered in the nineteenth century, but was destroyed. A third cathedral, on the same modest scale as its predecessors, replaced the second after a fire in 981. This in turn was pulled down when Girard, bishop from 1101 onwards, decided to rebuild it. Girard was widely travelled, well known as a scholar and diplomat, and the cathedral bears the stamp of his forceful personality in its ambitious size. But today it also bears the stamp of the Victorian architect who rebuilt much of it under the guise of restoration, Paul Abadie.

The façade, on the evidence of old engravings, was the part least affected by Abadie's work, though he invented both the flanking towers and the pediment with its odd rising arcade. Originally it could well have been a screen-façade with horizontal lines dominating, as at Civray, because there was a horizontal frieze level with the top of the central arch, and Abadie lowered the original masonry to insert the towers. He also replaced the damaged heads of several of the figures with copies which are often badly out of scale. This is true of the central figure of Christ in the mandorla. This said, there is much that still gives pleasure to the eye: at the lowest stage knightly life is portrayed in hunting scenes and a battle, perhaps an echo of the campaigns against the Moors in Spain in which knights from Aquitaine took part. These friezes, on the arcades and above the doorway, frame the twelve apostles as they set out on their preaching mission. (The tympanum over the doorway is Abadie's work, as are the two statues of St George and St Martin.) The apostles reappear at the bottom of the main group of sculptures, superbly individual portraits obviously taken from contemporary life. Eleven are shown in the three central bays, the figure to the left at the foot of the central window being that of the Virgin Mary. Their gaze leads us up to the impetuous movements of the angels adoring Christ, who is surrounded by the symbols of the four evangelists. It is not so much the overall composition of the façade as the loving care lavished on each individual figure or scene that makes this one of the glories of Romanesque art.

The interior is much more deeply marked by Abadie's work. Some of his changes were undoubtedly for the good, and repairs were essential. The first bay of the nave was originally left plain, to emphasise the decoration elsewhere and draw the eye on into the body of the church: now the same blind arcading is repeated throughout. But the original windows had been replaced by larger semicircular ones to the south, and these were restored at the same time. The line of domes, in the so-called Angevin style, were probably copied from Fontévrault in the Loire valley, which dates from a few years earlier. Those above the nave are much as they were when first put up; notice the apparent effortlessness of the newly found solution to the problem of basing a circular dome on a square foundation. The cupola over the crossing has gone, replaced in 1638 by an octagonal lantern which Abadie reworked, and which destroys the original subtle lighting of this part of the church. The two transepts are merely links to the great bell-towers of which only the northern one survives, while the choir is still imposing despite the lowering of the ground level – and the resulting scandalous destruction of the sixth-century crypt, Abadie's most serious blunder.

The exterior owes much of its appearance to Abadie; not only the towers of the façade but the great central dome above the lantern are his work, and he took down and rebuilt the northern bell-tower. Although it corresponds to the original very closely, none of the sculptures were re-used, but were broken up as roadstone. The southern bell-tower, reputedly higher than the surviving one, was burnt down by the Huguenots in 1568. On the outside of the central window of the apse the frieze showing a stag hunt balances the carvings on the façade.

Next to the cathedral, on the north side, is a little museum, housed in the old bishop's palace. Among its varied collections are a number of Romanesque capitals, some of which may have come from the cathedral during the restorations, notably a fine lion whose pose is reminiscent of Sicilian sculpture of the same period. Other rooms offer paintings of the seventeenth to nineteenth centuries, and pottery from the region.

Walking east, we come to the **Hôtel de Ville**, built between 1858 and 1865, a largely original work by Abadie in best railway-station Gothic with a dash of Renaissance thrown in. It does incorporate part of the keep of the thirteenth-century castle of the counts of Angoulême (open July to September), and a fifteenth-century tower which is the reputed birthplace of Marguerite d'Angoulême. To the south of the Hôtel de Ville the Place New York is a reminder that the site of New York was first named Angoulême by early French explorers.

The narrow streets of the **old quarter,** reached via the Place Louvel, conceal a number of fine town houses. The rue de Beaulieu has an eighteenth-century example at No 79; in the same street is the Franciscan chapel where the author Guez de Balzac was buried in 1654. His letters, discussing contemporary morals and politics, were written in a clear and elegant French prose which earned him the title 'restorer of the French language'. (He was also a distant ancestor of Honoré de Balzac.) The street behind the chapel leads to the ramparts, where, on the right, in the rue de Turenne, No 15 has a fine early-seventeenth-century gateway. Beyond the attractive little Place du Minage, the rue du Soleil offers a Louis XVI façade in the courtyard at No 17. On the way back to the Hôtel de Ville, the rue de la Cloche-Verte to the north contains the Hôtel de St Simon, with a Renaissance courtyard of 1535–40.

We now retrace our route eastwards, taking the N 135 toward Périgueux and, after five miles, forking left along the D 75 to Nontron. From Nontron the D 85 brings us to Chalus.

## Chapter 9

# Limoges and the Limousin

✣

From the top of **Le Puyconnieux**, three miles west of Chalus, the Limousin countryside spreads out in a scattering of fields amid woodland, with little river valleys hidden in the folds of the gentle hills. The view appears extensive; to the naked eye it seems as though the horizon must extend to its full limit, but the haze in the distance is not more than a dozen miles off. As with most such views it is best on a clear autumn morning, when the morning mist has evaporated into a clear sky, and the patterns of trees and ploughland are a rich palette of varied browns.

For this is not grandiose country. Its churches and châteaux are for the most part modest and delightful. Two of the best examples are within a short distance of Le Puyconnieux. **Montbrun** is a mile to the south, half-surrounded by a moat which could not have been designed to better visual effect. It lies in a hollow ringed beyond the moat by trees; a hopelessly indefensible position from a military point of view, but all the more intimate and domestic for that. One only of its towers is twelfth-century, from Aimeric Brun's original four-square keep; the rest was burnt by the English in 1385. The bishop of Limoges being a Montbrun, it was he who reconstructed it, much in the same form as it appears today, despite a Huguenot siege, revolutionary assaults in the 1790s and a fire in 1917. It is the surviving twelfth-century tower with its original crenellations which dominates the building and gives it its character. It is open every day (though the caretaker, who lives in a cottage up the hill to the right of the castle, may be reluctant to admit one or two visitors only). During the summer, there is a *son et lumière* performance each evening at 21.30.

To the north of Le Puyconnieux the château of **Brie** offers a very different aspect: a Renaissance *maison forte*, with walls in places seven feet thick. Its overall appearance would be domestic and almost intimate, screened from the road by an alley of planes and high white wrought-iron gates, were it not for its severe grey roofs and pale yellow stone. It is only open on summer weekends and

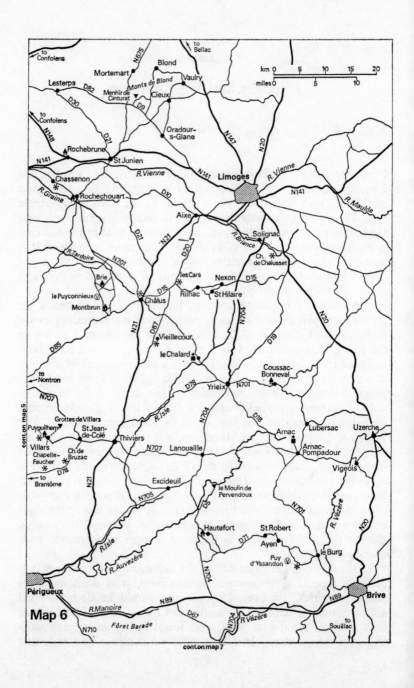

cont. on map 5

cont. on map 7

**Map 6**

holidays from 14.00–18.00; but the interior is rewarding with a fine Renaissance staircase and the painted room called the *chambre des amours*.

From Brie a pleasant drive north along side-roads and then the N 701 brings us to **Rochechouart**, whose château greets us as we approach the town, perched dramatically on a short, sheer cliff, while the town straggles up the hill beside it. The church has a splendid twisted 'witch's hat' spire in slate, echoed by the twisted columns in the courtyard of the château, which we enter over a small bridge. There are remains of the portcullis machinery in the gateway, the earliest part of the building. The Rochechouart family was prominent from the twelfth century onward. Aimery IV was at Jerusalem with the first crusade; Aimery V went on the second crusade in 1147; and under the Plantagenets Bertrand de Born (see p. 154) praised the beauty of Agnès de Rochechouart:

> And now to Rochechouart I'll hasten on my way
> To claim the lock of hair that Lady Agnes promised me.

In the 'salle des chasses' on the ground floor are vivid murals of the château and its surroundings in the late fifteenth century; there is a small archaeological collection on the first floor (open 10–12, 14.00–18.00 in July and August, and Sundays and holidays). The rest of the building is occupied by municipal offices. Leaving the castle, a set of steps to the left leads to a splendid avenue of limes with pleasant views across the valley of the Graine; a road winds down through the old gate of the outer bailey of the castle across a little medieval bridge, and leads eventually back to the D 29 near Chassenon.

Just to the south of **Chassenon** lies an apparently haphazard group of ruins. But excavations carried out since 1958 have revealed an extensive series of subterranean rooms, probably the water reservoir for a luxurious set of baths attached to a country sanctuary. Remains of a group of temples have also been found. The rooms are curious rather than impressive: intended for a purely functional purpose, they have no ornamental detail, and it is only their age and extent that makes them remarkable.

Continuing north to the N 141 we reach **Rochebrune**, where a small château lies just off the junction with the N 148. Its four towers and moat date back to the thirteenth or even to the eleventh century, but the house which joins these massive corners is sixteenth-century, one side being open; at this period it was the home of Blaise de

Monluc, the ferocious Catholic general of the wars of religion. In his old age he wrote his *Commentaires* (see p. 226); his audience was 'the captains, my companions' rather than 'learned young gentlemen', and a bluff self-portrait emerges with an honest concept of duty and not too many moral qualms, rather as he appears in his portrait in the château. A little over two hundred years later Roche-brune came into the hands of the Comte du Pont, one of Napoleon's lieutenants in Italy and Austria, who ended his career as Minister of War under Louis XVIII. A collection of his relics, of variable interest, occupies many of the rooms, though there is also some pleasant early furniture; du Pont's initials decorate a number of later pieces, in the fashion of the Napoleonic era, because the 'new men' of the period could not compete with the old nobility in terms of quarterings on their coats of arms.

The main road (the N 141) takes us east to **St Junien**, a prosperous glove-making town with a fine Romanesque church, whose chief glory is the tomb of the saint of the same name. The church itself, in the centre of the town, has an attractive portal, but is otherwise un-distinguished outside, with no sculpture. Opposite the west door is a thirteenth-century house, built of the same granite as the church. The interior is spacious, even though the first part of the nave is eleventh-century; the choir and crossing have been rebuilt, following the collapse of the central tower in 1922. None the less there is here a sense of endurance and age which the wholesale restorations of the nineteenth century always destroyed; the coarseness of the work (due to the harsh granite in which the church is built) and a relatively dark stone contrast with the blandness of the interiors of Angoulême and Périgueux cathedrals. There are occasional capitals, squatting giants, Samson slaying the lion, and antelopes with their horns entangled in bushes – according to the medieval *Book of Beasts* this was the only way they could be caught.

The **Tomb of St Junien** was originally part of the altar, and has been partly reconstructed after its separation in the nineteenth century. On the end Christ in a mandorla is surrounded by the four evangelical creatures. On one side a noble Virgin and Child are supported by swirling angels, while the twelve elders of the Apocalypse play a variety of instruments. Another twelve elders surround the Lamb. In style the sculpture is partly southern, partly Poitevin, with no particular local characteristics. Its lively details and sharp out-lines were probably the work of a wandering master mason.

Elsewhere in the church a series of polychrome statues of the fifteenth century seem coarse by contrast with the tomb; and there is a much battered brass of Martial Fornier (died 1513) in the south aisle. The remains of twelfth-century wall paintings include a massive St Christopher in lively colours in the north transept, a crawling man perched over the chapel to the right, and, in the vault of the chapel in the south transept, Dives and Lazarus and the apostles. Alas, only fragments, but enough to give us some idea of the vanished glories of design and colour which must have filled the church.

To the south of the town, on the road to Rochechouart, a thirteenth-century bridge spans the Vienne: on it is a fifteenth-century chapel, with elaborate granite pillars supporting its vaults and a thirteenth-century statue of the Virgin.

The D 21 runs north through deserted country to **Lesterps**, where an impressive belfry porch is all that remains of an eleventh-century abbey. Over 120 feet high, it has a vaulted porch, and above, reached by a little staircase tower, a tribune, itself 40 feet high with an octagonal domed roof. From Lesterps the D 82 leads to the edge of the Monts du Blond, granite hills with attractive woods and lakes. (At Mortemart, on the N 675, are the remains of the castle of Madame de Montespan's family.) A turning off the D 9 leads down a rough byroad to the lonely Menhir de Cinturat, about a mile off the road across an open heath. This is the central chamber of a prehistoric barrow, the outside covering of soil having been eroded away. Blond itself has a fortified Romanesque church, and the road via Vaulry and Cieux makes a good circuit of the area.

Back on the main road **Oradour-sur-Glane** appears to our right. The simple words *Souviens Toi* ('Remember') are written below the name on the edge of the village. The starkness of the burnt-out houses of this little village seem to me a more powerful reminder of the horrors of war than the trenches of the Somme or the concentration camps themselves. At Dachau, where the tragedy is no longer on a human scale, it escapes the mind's grasp. Here is a place where people lived and worked, and one day of war was enough to make it their tomb and memorial. On the afternoon of 10 June 1944, in revenge for attacks on German soldiers by local resistance partisans, the entire population was massacred by the SS. Nearly five hundred women and children were burnt to death in the church.

**Limoges** itself has distant echoes of the horrors of a much earlier war. In 1370, the city, which had been in English hands for many years, went over to the French, and the Black Prince swore to revenge himself on their treachery. He was a sick man, and had to be carried in a litter to direct the siege. His engineers succeeded in undermining the town wall, and the English troops poured in through the breach.

'You would then have seen,' writes Froissart,

> pillagers, active to do mischief, running through the town, slaying
> men, women and children, according to their orders. It was a
> most melancholy business; for all ranks, ages and sexes cast them-
> selves on their knees before the prince, begging for mercy; but he
> was so inflamed with passion and revenge that he listened to none,
> but all were put to the sword, wherever they could be found, even
> those who were not guilty; for I know not why the poor were not
> spared, who could not have had any part in this treason ... upwards
> of three thousand men, women and children were put to death
> that day. God have mercy on their souls! for they were true martyrs.

In fact, Froissart is writing propaganda, for nothing like this
massacre took place; what was done on the prince's orders was the
demolition of most of the Cité, the part of the town around the
Cathedral. (The other part, the Château, had not rebelled.)

All this will seem very far off and long ago as we come into the busy
modern industrial city that **Limoges** has become. What little that
remains of the old centre has been overwhelmed by nineteenth- and
twentieth-century rebuilding and is dwarfed by the suburbs. The
Place de la République, in the very heart of the town, has been
rebuilt as a modern precinct, complete with underground car park.
During the excavations for this the crypt of the old abbey of St
Martial was rediscovered, parts of it dating back to the fourth
century AD, surrounded by Roman masonry. St Martial, according
to the legend, came to convert the 'Lemovices', as the Gaulish inhabitants of the town were called, in the middle of the third century
AD. He was given hospitality, and protection from the pagan priests,
by a lady of the city whose daughter Valeria was the governor's
fiancée. Martial converted Valeria, who broke off her engagement,
and was condemned to death. Her heroic end led to the governor's
conversion; and when Martial himself was imprisoned for interrupt-
ing a spectacle at the local amphitheatre his cell was miraculously
lit up, and the astonished crowd who were howling for his blood
released him instead, and were likewise converted. In the crypt
(entrance in the centre of square, the open July to September 9.30–
12, 14.30–19.00; *son et lumière*) the tomb of Valeria is preserved, as
well as a sarcophagus said to be that of her former fiancé, and a
ninth-century mosaic. The centrepiece is the tomb of St Martial
himself, around which in the eleventh century one of the greatest
abbeys in France grew up, famous for its riches, learning and music.

The grandiose abbey fell into ruins in the eighteenth century, and was finally destroyed in 1791 by the revolutionaries. It suffered in earlier centuries, too: it was sacked by Henry the Young King (Henry II's eldest son) just before his death in 1183 (see p. 188), and again in the Hundred Years' War. Its heyday was in the tenth, eleventh and twelfth centuries; manuscripts and the famous Limoges enamels survive to bear witness to its riches. Sadly, the manuscripts can only be seen in Paris, at the Bibliothèque Nationale; none of them has remained here, but the enamels can be seen at the museum (p. 144). In the musical field, St Martial was famous for the use of tropes or embellishments to the plainsong melody; these are said to have influenced the songs of the troubadours in the twelfth century.

In the rue Porte Tourny, off the Place de la République, is the church of St Pierre du Queyroix, with a flamboyant Gothic façade. Inside, massive pillars betray a twelfth-century origin, but the vaulting is Gothic, and there is a vivid, much restored, stained-glass window of 1510 showing the death and coronation of the Virgin. Turn to the right down the busy rue Georges Perin to the Place Wilson (named after the American President), then take the rue Raspail to the **Cathedral**, across the Boulevard de la Cité. Begun in 1273, it incorporates the base of the old Romanesque bell-tower. The choir was completed early in the fourteenth century, but the nave was not begun until a hundred years later, and remained unfinished until 1888. The north doorway, of 1516 to 1530, is the main entrance, a splendid Gothic composition which is a miniature cathedral wall in itself, complete with rose window. The interior is dark, with a low clerestory and seven narrow-arched chapels off the choir. The most interesting details are the tombs in the choir, two fifteenth-century stained-glass windows and a fine rood screen, now placed at the west end of the nave. The rood screen, the work of craftsmen from the Loire valley in 1533-4, is in the most ornamental French Renaissance style, and its decoration shows that its makers were more at home in castles than churches. A low relief of flowers and garlands contrasts with the projecting pendant niches for statues and architectural fantasies in classical style. It is flanked by two delightful winding staircases, and must have looked very out of keeping with the sombre choir when it was in its original position. In the choir is the tomb of the bishop who had the rood screen built, Jean de Langeac, a Renaissance baldaquin of 1544 framed by two Gothic pillars which could scarcely be a less appropriate setting for this composition of Corinthian capitals and weeping cherubs. The barely visible sculptures are freely based on Dürer engravings, his so-called 'Small Passion', published in 1511. Two other tombs are noteworthy: that of Raynaud de la Porte, who built much of the choir. He was one of the papal commissioners in the inquiry of 1309–11 into the order of Knights Templars, which led to the suppression of the order in 1312. Although the commissioners themselves were open-minded enough, Philip the Fair used every possible means to secure the downfall of the Templars, and the outcome was largely due to the work of his agents. The tomb of Bernard Brun, of the same period, has four fine bas-reliefs, one showing the local legend of the martyrdom of Ste Valérie.

To the south of the cathedral, set in a large formal garden, is the former bishop's palace. From the terrace at the end of the garden there is a wide view down the Vienne valley, including two bridges, both thirteenth-century, to right and left. The palace itself houses the **municipal museum**. Here there is an abundant display of Limoges enamels, the art for which the town was famous in the Middle Ages and Renaissance. The products of the Limoges craftsmen were known in England by 1167, when the cathedral at Rochester had a book-cover in 'Limoges work'. A late-twelfth-century pyx, or box for consecrated wafers, has an enamel background with figures in low relief; the heads are in high relief, and seem to have been mass produced by specialist foundries, just as the enamelling and metalwork would have been the work of different studios. The front shows God in Majesty, flanked by the Virgin and St Peter. This is a simple piece of *champlêvé* work, where the raised metal ridges served to hold the powdered enamel in place as it became liquid and fused under heat. Most of the medieval work is of this kind; the casket would have been assembled after each of the sides had been fired. The stem from the processional cross, of about the same period, has a multi-coloured bird on a curved surface, which must have required considerable technical skill.

We shall meet other examples of medieval Limoges enamels, but here the best part of the collection is that devoted to Renaissance painted enamels, which were developed from about 1470. The colours were applied over a white ground, and the dividing bands of metal were no longer needed, as the colour adhered to the prepared base. The first examples are late Gothic, but the art did not come into its own until the early sixteenth century, when Léonard Limousin was appointed chief painter in enamels to Francis I. His work usually derives from contemporary prints, but his mastery of the technical possibilities of enamel painting produced some engaging pieces, which are reworkings of a theme rather than mere copies. His

22. Templar knights ride out to attack the Saracens in Palestine: a frescoe from the little chapel at Cressac (outside Blanzac, near Barbezieux)

23. An example of Limoges porcelain. This **service à café** dates from around 1780

24. A rustic idyll: the marvellously simple twelfth-century church at St Léon-sur-Vézère

enamel portraits are original works, reminiscent of Clouet, though the enamels lack the subtlety of tone of oils. His *Helen* and *Samson* are the finest of the pieces here. At this period a fashion for painting in grisaille developed, and on small pieces such as boxes the effect is perfectly matched to the 'antique' decorative detail beloved of the Renaissance; here the work of three enamellers called Jean Pénicaud stands out, in particular that of Jean II and Jean III Pénicaud. The return of coloured work in the 1560s led to a decline in the artistic quality of the work, which now tended to aim at purely ornamental effect; and only occasional pieces, such as those by the Laudin family, rise above the level of decoration or folk art. Even the Laudins were not far off folk art, as with the droll *Augustus on horseback*, where the horse is quite clearly a carthorse! Modern attempts to revive the craft produced a number of interesting Art Nouveau pieces, though better work was done outside Limoges. Nowadays there is an urgent need for an artist of standing to do for Limoges enamels what Jean Lurçat has done for tapestries. (The modern enamel studios are mostly near the Place Wilson, and can be visited during shopping hours: they offer completed work for sale rather than a demonstration of enamelling techniques.)

Elsewhere in the museum are an archaeological collection, mostly Gallo-Roman, on the first floor, with a second-century fresco found in the rue Vigne-de-Fer, and collections of paintings – including two (rather dull) portraits by Renoir – and Egyptology. The Egyptology section has a reconstruction of the tomb of the princess Nakht, and a number of funerary figures.

From the museum, the rue des Petites-Maisons leads to the Avenue Georges Dumas and the Boulevard Gambetta. On the right of the hillside off the Boulevard Gambetta is the medieval quarter known as 'La Boucherie', literally 'The Shambles' or 'butchers' quarter'. Its narrow streets have been the site of butchers' shops since the tenth century; although only a few medieval houses remain the ground-plan has not changed. Beyond the rue du Consulat the rue Férrerie leads to the church of St Michel des Lions, so called from the two fine granite lions near the south doorway. It is a dark, late Gothic church, begun in 1364; extensive restoration is at present in progress. Among its church plate is a thirteenth-century monstrance (for exhibiting a relic, in this case the hair of the Virgin Mary) crowned by a seated Madonna and Child. The most notable relic of the church today is the head of St Martial, preserved in a gilded wooden chest behind the main altar.

Continuing north along the rue Turgot we reach the Place Winston

Churchill, and the **Musée Adrien-Dubouché** (open 10–12, 13.30–17.00; closed Tuesdays and holidays). Founded in 1867 by the man whose name it bears, it is one of the most wide-ranging collections of china and ceramics in the world. It was intended not only as a great collection but also as an inspiration for local designers, and has an art school attached to it, started a year after the museum. In 1950 it became a national museum; it was thoroughly modernised and the cases were set out in a methodical order. It is a display to make any collector's mouth water; but even if you do not find china particularly exciting it should not be missed.

The sequence begins to the left of the entrance hall, with French porcelain. The earliest experiments in reproducing Chinese porcelain were at Rouen and Saint Cloud from the 1670s on. The products of Saint Cloud which claimed to be 'of the same quality, more beautiful and just as perfect' as the Chinese original were at first either white or blue and white; but other colours were soon in use, as the second case shows. This leads to the work of the Chantilly factory; there is a strikingly original teapot among the pieces from this source, though competition from the royal factory at Vincennes soon led to a decline in the standard of design. In the third case pieces from minor factories of the mid-eighteenth century include a delightful pot-pourri jar on a flower-strewn base with a dog peering round the corner of it. The Vincennes factory, set up in 1745 to compete with the work of Meissen in Saxony, occupies half of the fourth case: its treatment of flowers, particularly in modelled relief, and monopoly of the use of gilding make its products distinctive. In 1756 the factory was transferred to Sèvres, which was to become the centre of the French porcelain industry. Among the Sèvres pieces, mostly made for royalty, is a remarkable anti-slavery medallion of a negro with the inscription 'Am I not a man, a brother?' which was made in April 1789 and at once banned.

All the pieces so far have been in soft-paste porcelain, made without the kaolin, of which only the Chinese and Germans had supplies until the 1770s. The pieces which follow are in hard-paste porcelain, which paradoxically has a less hard and glassy surface. Some are from Sèvres, others from Paris: the Sèvres pieces are of a very high technical standard, and were widely imitated by the other factories, and by the provincial makers represented in case 6. Sèvres continues to dominate the display of nineteenth-century porcelain in the following cases; but the most pleasing pieces are often the products of humbler factories, such as the twin baskets by Jacob Petit in case 9.

The central place in the museum, not unnaturally, is reserved for Limoges pieces. It was at St Yrieix (see p. 150) that kaolin was first found in France, and Limoges porcelain has always been of the hard-paste type. In 1784 the Limoges factory was bought by the king, and became a kind of counterpart to Sèvres. Its products were much more delicate, without the excesses of some Sèvres pieces: see for example the flower-bordered plates (case B 2) and the Empire sugarbowl with an edge of pearls and plain gold (case B 3). However, in the nineteenth century Limoges porcelain became an industrial enterprise, and some of the results are remarkable examples of what popular taste required, whether in the 'Gothic', 'troubadour' or Second Empire manner. Among such items the blanc-de-chine pieces by the Pouyat family stand out as models of restraint (case B 8–9). There are some examples of Art Nouveau in case B 12.

The Chinese wares which were the models for early European experiments in porcelain are displayed in the third section. Most of the major types are included, as are a wide range of pieces from the rest of Europe, though the latter do not form more than a collection of samples, except in the case of Tournai and Meissen (D 3–4).

The first floor presents examples of *faïence*, or glazed earthenware, most of the pieces being either European or French.

South of the town the N 21 runs beside the Vienne for a mile or two: across the bridge at Aixe is a simple country inn, the Auberge des Deux Ponts, which offers a good and relatively cheap meal. At **Châlus** we come to the Tardoire valley, above which rises the round tower of the château. This has been partly restored, having fallen into picturesque decay as a farm. The tower can be ascended on ladders, though this is only for the agile. The other buildings contain a Gallo-Roman cellar with its original cement roof, a fine thirteenth-century *salle d'honneur* overlooking the site of the lower château of Châlus-Chabrol, since the lord of that period liked to oversee his new building. There is a small museum of local objects, including a nostalgic room full of disused farm and country implements.

Every story about the rooms of the château, however, harks back to one theme: the death of Richard Coeur-de-Lion. Richard, newly returned from his German prison, was locked in the political struggle with Philip Augustus of France which was to end with John's loss of the Plantagenet territories in France. The quarrel rarely erupted into serious fighting, and when in Lent 1199 Richard agreed a truce with Philip Augustus, he moved south with his lieutenant Mercadier to chastise his vassal, the Viscount of Limoges, for making common cause with the French king. He probably expected a swift apology and return to former allegiance; but the viscount shut himself up in his castle at Châlus. Ralph of Coggeshall, the English chronicler, describes what ensued:

He [Richard] arrived at Chali-Chaperol [Châlus]; he besieged a tower and attacked it furiously for three days, ordering his miners to undermine the tower and demolish it; which they later did. In the said tower the only soldiers or defenders were men of Viscount's guard who misguidedly helped their lord, not realising that the King was present at the siege, but thinking it was one of his henchmen. While the miners were at work, the King attacked them with crossbowmen so fiercely that they scarcely dared show themselves above the crenellations or to attempt to defend it . . . After dinner on the evening of the third day [26 March] the King, unarmed except for a helmet, boldly approached the tower with his men, and attacked the besieged in the usual way with javelins and arrows. A certain soldier who had stood almost all day before dinner in one of the crenellations of the tower, and had avoided harm by catching all the enemy spears and arrows on his shield, observed the besiegers closely, and suddenly drew his crossbow. He fired a bolt at the King, who saw him and cried out; the bolt struck him in the left shoulder near the vertebra of the neck, the wound curving down towards his left side, because the King had failed to stoop far enough down behind the square shield which was carried in front of him . . . Later, as though nothing had happened, and while many people knew nothing of it, he entered his lodging which was nearby, and in drawing out the wooden shaft, broke it; the iron head remained in his body. So the King lay down in his chamber and a certain surgeon from the household of the impious Mercadier in cutting the King's body wounded him seriously, indeed mortally, as he worked by the light of torches; and he could not easily find the iron head in the over-fat flesh, nor extract it without great violence. Though they applied medicines and plasters diligently, the wounds began to grow worse and turn black, until they threatened to be fatal . . . He freely forgave the man who had fatally wounded him; thus on 7 April, eleven days after he was wounded, he died at the close of day.

A host of local legends surrounds the aftermath. One story says that

Richard actually died at the château of Vieillecour, five miles south-east of Châlus; and others recount the gruesome punishment meted out to Pierre Basile, the 'knight' who was supposed to have fired the fatal shot, despite Richard's pardon on his deathbed. It seems likely that Pierre Basile was not a knight, as the crossbow was regarded as a dishonourable weapon by most knights; he might more probably have been one of the Genoese mercenaries who specialised in the use of crossbows, and his faintly Italian name bears this out. The most extravagant story of all reports that Richard came to claim a vast treasure found by the viscount, consisting of life-size Roman statues in solid gold.

If we want to recapture something of the feeling of the country in Richard's day, the churches offer much more than most castles. Heading east from Châlus along the D 15 we find several minor Romanesque churches, at Les Cars, Rilhac, Nexon and St Hilaire Les Places, as well as several castles. At Les Cars the remains of two fifteenth-century towers survive, while at Nexon the castle was rebuilt in the nineteenth century. St Hilaire retains part of a twelfth-century keep, with a little circular kitchen at the foot. But it is only at **Solignac**, north of Nexon on the N 704, that we find an important survival of the period. The granite church, once belonging to an abbey, is hidden in the folds of the valley of the Briance. The abbey had a long history, dating back to the seventh century, when it was one of the glories of Merovingian France. It was also one of the first centres of Limoges enamels. Sacked by the Vikings, it rose again in the ninth century; the present church was built in the early twelfth century, the porch dating from a century later. The massive vaulting with large pendentives (the device by which the square ground plan becomes a circular cupola) gives a powerful, almost squat appearance; and both the blind arcades in the nave and the clerestory (upper windows) in the choir are unusual. The proportions of Solignac are individual, an original solution to the limits of early technique which none the less follow a normal lay-out. There are a few interesting details, notably some lively capitals, an early Christ in Majesty now in the north transept, and a fifteenth-century mural of St Christopher.

Its contemporary, the château of Châlusset three miles to the east along the D 32, is no more than a ruin, accessible to the adventurous by a private path near the bridge across the Briance. Destroyed by the men of Limoges in the wars of religion, it had been a thorn in their side since the Hundred Years' War, when the English had used it as a base, particularly since it commanded two important routes to the south. Even those châteaux which survived until the Revolution were often destroyed, either by neglect or by private entrepreneurs who sold the stones. This was the fate of the lower château at Châlus, just as many an English abbey became a building quarry during the Reformation.

Between Châlus and St Yrieix is the little church of **Le Chalard,** to the right of the road, perched on a spur of land over the valley of the Isle. The nave was never completed; and the stump of the transept and choir became a fortress in 1417, when the English used it as a stronghold. What its architecture lacks is made up for by its site, with a sunny graveyard full of monks' tombs, surrounded by a rough hedge on one side and a crumbling wall on the other. The interior of the church, never finished, is disproportionately high, and cold and damp into the bargain. There are two or three good capitals, and a strange Gothic carved and painted reliquary cupboard, containing the relics of St Geoffrey, who built this church in 1097–1100, in the face of opposition from the local clergy. The church also possesses a good Limoges enamel *chasse* of the thirteenth century. Beside the church the old priory has some early buildings, later fortified, and a walled garden which is full of wild cyclamen in the autumn.

At **St Yrieix** itself, a large square to the north of the church marks the site of the vanished monastery buildings. The church itself, perched on a hilltop among a maze of narrow streets, is best seen from the road to Châlus, and best approached by the south door, where a damaged Christ in Majesty presides. Guide cards are provided at the west end, on the pillar to the south of the porch. Despite some nineteenth-century restoration by Abadie the simple but powerful interior remains unspoilt. The nave, long as it is, has only two arches. A row of corbel heads peers out below a gallery running right round the church, and the choir is ornately railed. These heads must have been a welcome diversion for the masons, who carved everything from grimaces to pretty girls on them. The reliquary head of St Yrieix, of uncertain age, seems dull by comparison; it is kept behind a grille to the north of the choir. Just outside the church the **Tour du Plô,** part of the town's medieval fortifications, has modern houses built into its base, serenely untroubled by the bushes growing from the upper storeys. To the south of the town **La Tour Blanche** is a pleasant little hotel in an old house.

But the real fame of St Yrieix is as the place where kaolin deposits were found in the 1760s. It is not certain exactly how the precious material, essential to the making of hard-paste porcelain, came to light. One story says that samples were sent from Sèvres to the Archbishop of Bordeaux, who was asked to find out if there were similar soils in his diocese. Another story says that the city apothecary of Bordeaux made inquiries about such a clay, and was told by Darnet, the doctor of St Yrieix, that his wife used it to wash her linen. In 1768, kaolin was certainly sent from St Yrieix to Sèvres, and early in 1769 the first pieces made with it were shown in Paris. Darnet was put in charge of the quarry, and regular production began. Other deposits were found; today a quarry can be seen about two miles east of the town on the N 701.

Further to the east is the château of **Coussac-Bonneval,** a fourteenth century building whose outer wall once defended the whole village. The central part survives (open 14.00–18.00, on Thursdays and Sundays). The west side was rebuilt in the nineteenth century. Inside, there are some fine Aubusson tapestries, Louis XVI furniture, and a collection of prints relating to one of the lords of Bonneval, who, as a soldier of fortune in the early eighteenth century, ended up as a pasha in the service of the Sultan at Constantinople.

**Lubersac,** to the south, is a small, slightly decaying town with an unrestored church. The south door has a polylobed vault, and amid the confused part-Gothic, part-Romanesque interior, with sloping altars and decaying seventeenth-century canvases, there are some lively capitals to be found in the choir. The subjects are all from the New Testament: the Annunciation, Adoration of the Magi, flight into Egypt, and Crucifixion and Deposition are readily distinguished. The two eastern bays of the nave are very early eleventh-century, and other parts of the patchwork fabric date from the early twelfth to the seventeenth century.

We head south again to **Arnac-Pompadour**, home of the Pompadour stud founded by Louis XV in 1761, which is still famous for its stallions. Arthur Young saw the stud in 1787 and noted that 'the horses are not saddled till six years old. They pasture all day, but at night are confined on account of wolves, which are so common as to be a great plague to the people.' The château was given by Louis XV to Jeanne d'Etioles with the title of Marquise de Pompadour when she became his mistress in 1745. She came from a Parisian family, and had no connection with the region: the château was a mere appendage to the title. It is a solid fifteenth-century building, now used as offices for the stud.

The little church at **Arnac** and the much-restored monastery at **Vigeois** both have series of figured capitals in the style of those at Lubersac. Beyond Vigeois, built across the Vézère river on the main road from Limoges to Brive, is **Uzerche**, a large medieval town with many fine houses. If you approach from the south, park where the main road forks to the right: the medieval town is best explored on foot. The road to the left leads to the Porte Bécharie, part of the old fortified outer wall. Uzerche's defences were so strong that it was never captured during the Middle Ages: the motto on the town's coat of arms (to the left of the gate) 'Never defiled', recalls this proud record. In the narrow streets, particularly in the rue Pierre-Chalaud, there are a number of half-timbered medieval houses. An old saying runs 'If you have a house in Uzerche, you have a château in the Limousin'. Indeed, one of the houses is called Château Tayac, complete with fifteenth-century tower and a coat of arms over the doorway. At the top of the hill is the church of **St Pierre.** At the east end a little doorway gives access to the crypt, of the eleventh century or earlier, with an elaborate ground-plan echoing that of the choir above. The early history of the abbey of which this was the church is obscure – the charter-roll of Uzerche was a byword for forgery – and the exact date of the crypt is uncertain. The church itself has a Romanesque choir, with radiating chapels; the foliage capitals are bold in design. The nave is partly eleventh-century, with massive cruciform pillars and a thirteenth-century vaulted roof. In the fourteenth century a massive tower was added on the south-west, and the whole church was fortified. The bell-tower which crowns the skyline of the town is twelfth-century; the transition from a square base to an octagonal upper storey is an early attempt at this arrangement, and the slate roof which has replaced its original stone capping does not improve its rather solid appearance. From the terrace by the church we look over the Vézèré again as it forms a loop round the town: to the left immediately below is another fortified house, the Château Pontier. As you return to the Porte Bécharie notice the twelfth-century tower called the 'Black Prince's Tower', among a group of medieval houses, some rather tumble-down.

From the road (D 3) toward Eymoutiers, on the other side of the valley, there is a good view of the town 'covering a conical hill, rising in the hollow of an amphitheatre of wood, and surrounded at its feet by a noble river', much as Arthur Young described it in 1787. He also admired the country between here and **Brive**:

> a quick succession of landscapes, many of which would be rendered famous in England by the resort of travellers to view them. The country is all hill or valley; the hills are very high, and would be called by us mountains, if waste and covered with

heath ... Add to this, the rich robe with which nature's bounteous hand has dressed the slopes with hanging woods of chestnut. And whether the vales open their verdant bosoms, and admit the sun to illumine the rivers in their comparative repose; or whether they be closed in deep glens, that afford a passage with difficulty to the water rolling over their rocky beds, and dazzling the eye with the lustre of cascades; in every case the features are interesting and characteristic of the scenery.

Brive he found disappointing, but we now find the 'close, ill-built, crooked, dirty, stinking streets' of the old centre much more evocative than the outer 'promenades', now a huge car park. These promenades are on the site of the old ramparts; Brive earned its nickname 'la Gaillarde' (sturdy), because it underwent so many sieges during the Middle Ages. A few medieval houses survive, notably near the church of St Martin (which has some good capitals and a font carved with the symbols of the evangelists). There is an exotic Renaissance house called the 'tour des Echevins' immediately south of the cathedral.

The rue Dr Massenat brings us to the Musée Ernest Rupin (open 10–12, 14.00–18.00; closed on Tuesdays), a varied collection of mainly local interest, though the prehistoric implements are well laid out and show the stages of cultural development clearly. There are plaster casts of the Romanesque capitals from the church, a rare opportunity to study such pieces at close quarters. A collection of coins on the first floor gives an idea of the division of this area between French and English during the Middle Ages, with rival currencies to match. The top floor is devoted to local history and trades; note the striking eighteenth-century penitent's costume, a black version of a Ku Klux Klan habit.

Almost opposite the museum the rue Raynal runs past the Hôtel de Labenche, a sixteenth-century town house in the most magnificent Renaissance style, but of the Toulouse rather than the Loire school. It is not open to the public, except for the courtyard, which has graceful arcades and, above the windows, a series of busts in exaggerated mannerist poses.

In the surrounding countryside, the best place to appreciate Arthur Young's praise of the scenery is at the Puy d'Yssandon, off the N 701 to the north (via the D 5 and D 147). The single ruined tower of a fourteenth-century castle guards the steep approach: on the way up there is a wide view to the south, and at the top a view across to Brive.

A cross-country road via Ayen and St Robert (D 5 and D 71)

twists and turns to **Hautefort,** on a rocky outcrop dominating the Auvézère valley. Here a civilised Renaissance château has replaced the keep from which Bertran de Born launched his defiant songs (the poetic form known as *servientes*) at a hostile Plantagenet world in the twelfth century. Even the round of the seasons was far from peaceful for him:

> Easter again! the time of year that I like best;
> Its flowers and showers and birdsong in the leafy woods
> Rejoice my heart; but better still the gay pavilions,
> The sward bedecked with glistening shields and polished arms,
> The keen-edged swords and lances flashing in the fray!

Bertran de Born sided with the Plantagenets only when they were rebels, and it was he who wrote the moving elegy to Henry II's eldest son, Henry the Young King, when he died at Martel in 1183 (see p. 188).

> . . . All pride in battle, skill in song and rhyme
> Must yield to sorrow's humble threnody,
> For cruel death, that mortal warrior,
> Has harshly taken from us the best of knights:
> Beside him charity itself was mean,
> And in him every noble virtue shone.

Ejected from Hautefort by Henry II in favour of his brother Constantine, he was reinstated in 1185 only to have Constantine seize the castle again the following year, at which he retired to a monastery in the best medieval manner, to make a pious end. Dante did not feel that he had succeeded in this last scheme, for he portrays him in the *Inferno* among those Sowers of Discord who are continually smitten asunder by a demon with a sword:

> . . . Bertran de Born am I, whose fell
> Counsel, warping the mind of the Young King
> Like Absalom with David, made rebel
> Son against father, father against son
> Deadly as the malice of Achitophel . . .

The present château dates from the sixteenth and seventeenth centuries; but it bears the scars of a very recent disaster. On the night of 30/31 August 1968 the main part of the building was destroyed by fire, leaving only the two projecting wings. However, the work of restoration is being energetically pursued (in sharp contrast to La Rochefoucauld) and the damage should be repaired, as far as it can be, within a year or two.

The road winds up through the village of Hautefort, which retains much of its medieval aspect. Just after you have entered the château grounds a large wooded terrace stretches to the right, while around the foot of the château itself a brightly coloured formal garden contrasts with the grey slate roofs of the towers. From the eastern end of the ridge a wide view includes the neighbouring château of Badefols. All that can be shown of the interior (guide, at hours indicated outside main gate) consists of the *cour d'honneur*, with its splendid southern aspect, and the two wings. The east wing contains a fine seventeenth-century chapel, with an inlaid floor and fine furnishings; the west wing has a magnificent oak roof, untouched since it was built in the sixteenth century, and photographs of the fire in 1968. The defences over the drawbridge, with alarming machicolations, are a reminder that a French château in the seventeenth century would still be built with an eye to its military potential: the wars of religion were too recent a memory to allow a calm architecture like that of Elizabethan and Jacobean England to flourish.

A hint of what Hautefort might have looked like in the twelfth century can be gleaned at **Excideuil** (to the north-west, reached along the N 704 and N 705), where two towers of an eleventh-century donjon rise above the town. A gate to the side leads up to a Renaissance entrance. Just beside it is a memorial to Giraut de Borneilh, a contemporary of Bertran de Born, whose verses were devoted to the more orthodox subject of the beauty of ladies and to love-longings of poets.

To the east of Excideuil (by the N 705 and D 4), the mill at Pervendoux occupies a dramatic site. Quite suddenly the road drops down through woods into the Auvézère valley where the mill lies in a ribbon of green meadows; and climbs as sharply again to a viewpoint just short of the crest of the hill opposite. It is a peaceful spot, disturbed only rarely by a car toiling up the steep incline. The deep-sided valley, eaten through the soft limestone by the river's action, is the forerunner of the more dramatic valleys of the Dordogne, but on a tamer and more domestic scale.

From Excideuil, the D 76 leads to Thiviers, the starting point for our exploration of Périgord.

# Chapter 10

# Périgueux and Western Périgord

❧

Just south of Châlus we cross into the Périgord, dropping down from the hills of the Limousin to the river valleys of the Isle and the Dordogne. The patchwork of the Limousin landscape gives way to alternating belts of forest on the chalk uplands and farms on the richer soil of the valleys. Thiviers, astride the N 21, is largely spoilt by the traffic which roars through its centre. It is worth stopping to look at its church, which has a fine set of capitals, whose quality has survived a drastic modern recutting. Most of the scenes illustrate monsters in combat with human beings; here a face peers out between the monster's jaws; another man goes head-first to oblivion; two men stand on the backs of double-bodied stags; a monster in the choir seizes a man by an arm and a leg. But Samson has his revenge on the lion as well, and there is a calm and reassuring Christ in Majesty, flanked by Mary Magdalene and St Peter.

A turning to the right leads to St Jean de Colé, where an old road flanked by half-timbered and stone houses runs beside the present narrow street, leading to a bridge and a mill just above it. On this deserted and peaceful thoroughfare a decayed château faces the little church, once attached to a priory. Its present form betrays a history full of change and chance. Completed in the twelfth century, it was fortified by the English in 1364 and held by them for ten years; ruin and then use by the Protestants in the next century were followed by attempts to revive monasticism as late as 1877. The last canons regular left in 1904. Seen from the north, the church juts out into the countryside, with the little apse chapels sheltering against it but strangely detached from it. Inside, the largest cupola in the region – larger even than those of the cathedrals – gives it a strangely unfamiliar air, as though it were nearer to the Pantheon than to a homely Christian place of worship; and this is not due to the failure of a grandiose scheme for a nave in proportion, but to a deliberate original plan, not far removed from the Templars' circular churches. The hexagonal chapels re-echo the plan of the nave in almost identical proportion: they contain some fine capitals with Old Testament themes, with elongated figures in a very different style from those at Thiviers.

For **Puyguilhem** take a left-hand turn at the edge of St Jean de Colé (the D 98). On the far side of the village of Villars stand a sixteenth-century château and the ruins of an abbey. The château has superb sculptural decorations both inside and outside, particularly on the windows and balconies. Two towers in contrasting shapes, rectangular and elegant flanked by squat and circular, give it an individual air. The style is that of the Loire rather than the more practical and severe local manner; but arrow-slits are still to be seen at the base of the circular tower and by the doorway. To the north-east of Villars the **Grottes de Villars** contain fine crystalline formations and traces of prehistoric murals.

Returning to St Jean de Colé, take the road to Brantôme; it is studded with châteaux, ruined or restored. On the right the ruins of the fifteenth-century Château de Bruzac are just accessible, though large trees growing in the roofless halls bear witness to long neglect. The fine Renaissance château at La Chapelle-Faucher was gutted by fire, though its imposing exterior still dominates the valley from a cliff-top. And just before Brantôme itself the truncated towers of Puymarteau appear above the trees to the right, behind a fine dolmen, fifty yards off the road.

**Brantôme** itself is a delightful town; built on an island in the Dronne, little gardens full of vines and flowers run down from red-roofed houses to the water's edge, where a Renaissance balustrade encompasses both banks. The centre of the town is modern; from the abbey on the opposite bank a dog-leg bridge with a Renaissance pavilion at one end across the junction of the two branches of the river leads to a pretty, formal garden with summerhouses of the same date linked by a cypress alley. A path with a good view of the abbey belfry leads past weeping willows to a bridge back to the town. By bearing left at the end of the next bridge the circuit is completed. The abbey itself is now occupied by the *mairie*, but parts of it, including the dormitory and grand staircase, can be visited; there is a strange little museum of paintings done by a local artist under the influence of a spiritualist medium. More rewarding is the grotto behind the buildings, approached from the left-hand end, where a huge Crucifixion was carved in the sixteenth century. Weathered by water seeping through the cave roof, it has acquired the ritual rigidity of some Aztec carving. The church itself is disappointing; an unbalanced piece of Gothic architecture, it lacks the Gothic lightness. Behind the church arises a splendid Romanesque belfry, which is not open to visitors, but which well repays the trouble of finding a good viewpoint: the far side of the river, toward the south of the town, or the bridge already mentioned, are the best places. Its arcading is very elaborate – the kind of fantasy usually found only in the miniature of an illuminated manuscript – and the total height of over a hundred feet is also unusual.

In the sixteenth century, the abbey became a kind of lay property and was consequently abused. One of its abbots under this system was the chronicler Pierre de Bourdeille, known as Brantôme, whose *Book of the Ladies* is a most unecclesiastical work. His adventurous career as a soldier, including journeys to Scotland, Italy and Malta, and long service at the French court, gave him good sources for gossip; and the 'Gallant Ladies' of the second part are an entertaining balance to the 'Illustrious Ladies' of the first part, who include Mary Queen of Scots and Catherine de Medici. He is a lightweight beside La Rochefoucauld and Montaigne, while something of his delight in scandal may be due to his own disappointed hopes of office; but he often brings a vivid enthusiasm to his work, as in his portrait of Marguerite of Navarre. His other work was the *Lives of the Great Captains*, a collection of portraits of soldiers whom he admired.

Brantôme's family château, at **Bourdeilles** (open June–October, 9–11.30, 14.00–18.30; closed on Tuesdays), is six miles to the south-west along the Dronne valley. If you keep to the right bank along the D 106 you will pass the dramatic Devil's Anvil rock, formed by the river's action on the limestone. The château appears on the left bank, on a spur in front of the town, with a fine Renaissance front. The approach from the town centre leads into the medieval part, an octagonal donjon with massive walls dating from the thirteenth century. The Renaissance part, entered through the Porte des Sénéchaux, contains some good furniture and paintings, including a bed, reputedly that of Charles V, the Spanish Emperor. But the chief glory is the 'gilded salon' on the first floor, decorated about 1565 by Ambroise Le Noble, an artist of the Fontainebleau school which flourished under Francis I and his successors; Francis himself appears with his falconers on one of the tapestries. The ceiling is a riot of those Renaissance fantasies which repeat themselves everywhere on the work of this period, from stone to the title pages of books. On the river below is a medieval bridge with cutwater piers, and a water mill of medieval origin.

Back on the main road there is a fine view north over the Dronne valley at Puy de Fourches, an Italianate landscape of red-roofed farmhouses and poplars, as a last glimpse of the countryside before we reach **Périgueux**.

From the Pont des Barris to the left of the main road the old city stands out clearly, grouped round the startling white silhouette of the cathedral of **St Front**. The rue Daumesnil climbs up past the terraced east end to the entrance on the north side. If St Front looks remarkable today it has had an even more remarkable history. The first church to be built there, the ruins of which can be traced to the west of the present building, was put up in honour of the saint who brought Christianity to the Périgord region, and whose relics belonged to a monastery on this site. They were preserved in a most unusual round tomb below the high altar. Probably as the result of a fire which destroyed much of the monastery and the old church in 1120, a new church was begun to the east of the existing one, centring on the same high altar, and therefore facing west. This new church was the first of the great churches with a line of domes instead of a vaulted roof: these and its Greek-cross plan have suggested an Eastern model, perhaps one of the Byzantine churches which the crusaders had seen a few years earlier. The bell-tower is one of the few surviving original parts, though the detail and the cone which crowns it were reworked during the restorations of the last century. Otherwise, the ravages of the Protestants in 1575 (when the tomb of St Front was destroyed), of the rebels of the *Fronde* in 1652 under the Prince de Condé, and a succession of makeshift attempts to repair the fabric, had all left the cathedral in a perilous state. In 1852 the architect Paul Abadie was called in. His enthusiasm for Romanesque architecture was considerable; but the knowledge and techniques needed for a proper restoration were not to hand. Instead he virtually rebuilt the whole edifice. The result may break the purist's heart, but the new church has a strong character of its own. The exterior, with its multiple spires, pinnacles and domes, is a forerunner of Sacré-Coeur at Montmartre, but it has individual touches, such as the use of *lauzes*, flat stone tiles heaped up to form the pyramidal roofs, and the pillared supports below them, which are rooted in the local style of medieval building. And no one can deny the force of its silhouette when seen from across the river.

The interior is less successful. The proportions may be elegant, but the greyish-white stone and regularity of the work make it monotonous. The west end incorporates parts of the earliest church, including two curious cells, called 'confessionals', to north and south. The cloister, to the south (ring bell outside sacristy), is in sharp contrast to the church. Little restored, it is lined by square columns and a small, formal garden has been made in the centre; here the original top of the bell-tower is preserved. A staircase leads up to a terrace with views to the south, across the river; and for the adventurous there is a walk round Abadie's forest of spires, a fascinating tour – though only for the reasonably agile – with glimpses of the red and grey roofs of the old town with little balustraded verandahs on some of the top storeys.

The streets to the north of the old quarter are full of delightful old houses; the rue Limogeanne, running north–south, has at No 3, the Maison Estiguard, a fine doorway into a small courtyard and a 'corkscrew' staircase; at No 12 there is a doorway with a double vault, and a coat of arms surmounted by a knight's helm, indicating a nobleman's town house. The most impressive is the Maison du Tenant in the rue St Louis, with a corner doorway and the remains of a tower above. In the rue de la Miséricorde the Hôtel de St Astier has a fine Renaissance staircase. Emerging to the north of the maze of streets, we reach the Allées de Tourny; the neo-classical building of the Musée du Perigord (open 10–12, 14.00–17.00; closed on Tuesdays) houses an archaeological collection from prehistoric times to the Middle Ages. Next to it the restaurant Léon is a good place to pause if you want a substantial lunch.

To the west of the Allées de Tourny the Avenue de Paris leads round the outside of the city walls to the Place de Francheville. On the corner of this stands the Tour Mataguerre, part of the old defences. And defences were certainly needed, because just a few hundred yards to the west stood a rival community, built on the site of the old Roman town. The old town that we see today is in fact that of Puy St Front, centred on the cathedral, which grew up from the tenth century on. Its rise was viewed with jealousy by the inhabitants of the Cité; there was occasional warfare, and often the two towns would ally themselves with different sides in the Anglo-French wars – the Cité was usually pro-English, Puy St Front pro-French. Then, in 1251, when the two were united under the French king Puy St Front gained the upper hand.

From the Place de Francheville the Boulevard de Vesone leads to the **Tour de Vesone,** the remains of a circular temple dedicated to the goddess of the city. Périgueux was originally the capital of the Gaulish tribe called '*Petrucorii*', and under Roman occupation was known as '*Vesunna Petrucoriorum*'. Although the Petrucorii had helped Vercingetorix in his rebellion their city soon became an important Romanised centre, and the ruins of this imposing building show that by Hadrian's reign (117–38) it must have been a wealthy

25. **(above)** Low relief carving from the prehistoric site of Fourneau du Diable, now in the Musée des Eyzies

26. **(below)** The hidden treasure of the cave at Lascaux, now sealed off and closed to the public: a scene from the hall of the bulls

27. Rocamadour, a shrine whose very site on the edge of the Alzou
gorge seems an act of faith

place. The plan of the temple – a circular sanctuary with a clerestory (the window spaces can still be seen) and an outer colonnade – was a most unusual one, and excavations are still revealing more of its ramifications. The masonry, seven feet thick, has survived despite the massive breach to the north, traditionally made by St Front with his episcopal crook. The tower was originally clad with marble.

Taking the rue Lafon and crossing the square in front of the church of St Etienne de la Cité, we come to a public garden which has in it the remains of the arena, a bare outline of its ground plan in scattered pieces of surviving masonry. Much of the Roman settlement was torn down after the third century AD, when the inhabitants withdrew from the relatively spacious suburbs and shut themselves in a fortified enclave, using the stone from temples and other public buildings to construct a defensive rampart.

The church of **St Etienne de la Cité**, like St Front, has had a chequered history. Built between the end of the eleventh century and the mid-twelfth century, it was attacked so severely by the Huguenots that three-quarters of the church was destroyed. Attempts to rebuild it from 1615 on failed (the new domes collapsed), and in 1652 it was used as a stable by the rebels of the Fronde. In 1669 the status of cathedral was transferred to St Front, and from 1790 to 1805 the church was abandoned. It was repaired after 1840, when it was declared a *monument historique*.

What remains of a once extensive Romanesque church are the two eastern cupolas of a nave and apse originally twice the length. The first bay is the older of the two; the dome is more squat, the general effect more massive. The choir is lighter and more elegant, with far greater detail. Fortunately, the monstrous altar, a piece of seventeenth-century virtuosity which may delight lovers of the baroque but no one else, has recently been moved to the southwest corner of the nave. To the south of the choir is an interesting inscription carved directly on to the masonry, a table of the dates for Easter from 1163 to 1253. A year or two later than the first date is the tomb of Jean d'Asside, bishop from 1160 to 1169, placed against the north wall of the nave. It has a simple arch carved with elaborate patterning, and – rarity of rarities – an inscription naming the sculptor, Constantine of Jarnac. The style of the sculpture alone would indicate the work of someone from the neighbourhood of Saintes, but it is interesting to have this confirmed.

Due west of St Etienne, just by the railway, another public garden contains the Château Barrière, a medieval fortified house built into the remains of the Roman city wall.

Leave Périgueux on the Angoulême road, and you will find the abbey of **Chancelade** just off the N 710, which forks left for Ribérac a mile outside the town. It lies in the hollow of a valley, its central tower masked by trees until you are close to it. From the twelfth century on it was an important and wealthy abbey although little is left of the original buildings. After the Hundred Years' War much of the church was rebuilt, only to suffer again in the religious wars of the sixteenth century. The result is a mixture of styles, all subdued and plain. The central tower has some Romanesque arcading at the base, and the west door is mainly Romanesque. A descending flight of steps leads into a largely seventeenth-century interior, but in the choir are two striking fourteenth-century frescoes, of St Christopher and of St Thomas à Becket. The former is a large and dramatic figure, very much in the style of English miniatures of the late thirteenth century. St Thomas à Becket is on a smaller scale, and less impressive because less well preserved. To the west of the abbey church and the seventeenth-century abbey buildings is a twelfth-century parish church, set amid trees and gardens. It is on a very small scale, but with a pleasing harmony of geometric decoration and balanced proportions, emphasising the abbey church's loss of these qualities through rebuilding.

Instead of returning to the main road follow the D 1 north-west, through well-wooded country, until a blue-and-white sign indicates the track to the priory of **Merlande,** in a remote valley in the forest. This is a crowded and popular place at weekends, but at other times it can be suitably solitary. Founded in the mid-twelfth century as a priory of the abbey at Chancelade, the church was built in three stages in the last half of that century, but fortifications were added in the sixteenth century. The façade is severe, and on a bright day the interior seems dark and bare. But as you get accustomed to the light, you should be able to make out a very small chancel arch with three rising steps at the east end of the rectangular space which appeared at first to be the entire church. Smaller than the west doorway, this cutting off and raising of the east end reinforces the sense of its being a sanctuary, a special sacred place. On either side of the arch are rich capitals, repeated with variations round the walls of the apse, which is in the form of another rectangle, smaller than that of the nave. The subject is always the same: lions and foliage. But each capital shows them in different attitudes, challenging each other, devouring each other, while some share a single head. (One in particular is strikingly similar to the unicorn on the Horn of Ulf at York Minster, a reminder that Romanesque art had a rich visual tradition from the past on which to draw.) The private ritual of the lions seems to reflect the atmosphere of secluded ceremonies which pervades the church as a whole. As more and more visitors have sought it out, it has lost something of its remoteness, but on a weekday it may still be as deserted as ever.

The D 1 continues to Lisle (where the church has a Romanesque choir) and then across the river Dronne to **Grand Brassac,** in the hills to the north of the river valley. This powerfully fortified church is in fact a simple twelfth-century building (note the cupolas of the original roof) with a superstructure which almost doubles its size until it looks like a small château. The battlements and defences date from the thirteenth to the sixteenth centuries, and the closing stages of the work are marked by a late Gothic doorway with sculptures of the fourteenth to sixteenth centuries. It is interesting to compare this church with Charras, fifteen miles to the north, and with examples further afield like St Jean de Colé and St Amand de Coly: there are some similarities, but by and large each village seems to have built by experiment to its own design rather than following a precise and widely accepted pattern such as can be found in the plans of the original church buildings themselves. By contrast with the church, the two châteaux near Grand Brassac – Marouatte to the north and Montardit to the west – have both been given nineteenth-century silhouettes, though Montardit has escaped the 'troubadour style' treatment of Marouatte.

Back in the Dronne valley there is a good view of the landscape from the church at Montagrier, though the foreground is ruined by a new row of bungalows which deprive the scene of its feeling of space and solitude. The main road runs along the south bank of the river to Ribérac, a plain little market town, remarkable only as the birthplace of the twelfth-century troubadour Arnaut Daniel, of whom Dante said:

> Love-rhyme or prose in language of Romaunt
> He topped them all . . .

His greatest poetry was in the obscure, allusive style known as *trobar ric.* He wryly hints at its artificiality when he says of himself:

> I am Arnaut, who gathers the air into sacks
> Who uses oxen from the yoke to hunt the hare
> Who swims in swift rivers against the current.

The complexity and richness of Provençal culture of this period – in poetry, art (the Romanesque churches) and in sheer ostentation – was partly its downfall. The poets reached a *ne plus ultra* of obscurity, the churches were built on too large a scale to be replaced in the new Gothic style, and the country's wealth attracted the land-hungry knights of northern France. To the south of Ribérac lies the **Forêt de la Double,** once a malaria-ridden terrain of marshy lakes, where a handful of inhabitants eked out an unhealthy existence as foresters and fishers. Now that malaria has been controlled, the area is increasingly being cleared, and farmland and woodland are mixed in equal proportions with the occasional small lake. In 768, when this was a remote and impenetrable wilderness, the last of the independent dukes of Aquitaine, Waifre, was pursued into its depths and killed by the troops of Pépin the Short, Charlemagne's father.

From Ribérac take the D 5 toward St Aulaye, turning off to St Privat-des-Prés, where there are the remains of a twelfth-century castle and a plain well-proportioned church of the same period, distinguished by the use of elegant blind arcades on the façade and on the north and south walls which recall the pillars of a Greek temple.

Four miles to the north, back in the Dronne valley, **Aubeterre sur Dronne** has a very remarkable church indeed, that of St Jean. In the twelfth century the lord of Aubeterre went on crusade, and, like so many pilgrims to the Holy Land, returned with various holy relics. To house these a cavern below the castle was hewn out and made into a church, which was placed under the care of the Knights Templars. At the Revolution it was turned into a gunpowder factory, and then became the local cemetery, until in 1865 it was classified as a historic monument. Its use as a cemetery was curious, because recent excavations have shown that it was in use for this purpose in the sixth and seventh centuries. Just by the main entrance the same excavations have brought to light an unusual baptismal font of much the same period. Designed for baptism by immersion, it has a large cross cut into the rock at the bottom. The twelfth-century work consisted of cutting away the roof of the cavern, forming the great pillars, cutting the staircase to the gallery on the far side of the church, and sculpting the elaborate octagonal reliquary-altar at the east end. The relative darkness makes all this seem on an immense scale, though it is in fact no larger than many Gothic churches of moderate size. The old entrance used to be to the west, the site of the early cemetery, while the present entrance was once a transept, with a vaulted roof continuing outward from the top of the opening. Below the transept was a small chapel, perhaps used for funerals, which has also been excavated recently. From the gallery a staircase led to the castle itself: below, the church seems mysterious and awesome, more a temple to some exotic earth-goddess than a Christian building, and a far cry from the sunlit façades of Saintonge away to the west.

By way of contrast, higher up the hill, is the ruin of St Jacques, with just such a façade, with three sculptured doorways at ground level, topped by an elaborate arcade. The subjects of the carving include the labours of the months and the signs of the zodiac. We shall not see such rich stonework again for many miles, as we turn south-west into 'Périgord vert', retracing the D 20 and N 710 to Périgueux, and taking the N 89 east of the town.

## Chapter 11

# Les Eyzies and the Vézère valley

❧

From Périgueux the road to Brive follows the valley of the river Manoire for a couple of miles before the N 710 to Les Eyzies forks to the right. After a further two miles a minor road to the left leads into the Barrade forest, and to the remote ruin of **Château de l'Herm**. The walls and a staircase tower of this early-sixteenth-century château still stand, ivy-covered and decaying. Inside, three monumental fireplaces tower bleakly one above the other. This, a real late Gothic ruin, was the scene of equally 'Gothick' crimes: murders and assassinations among a family whose history rivals that of the house of Atreus in Greek myth. A locally famous nineteenth-century novel, *Jacquou Lou Croquant* by Eugène le Roy, has this castle as its setting. The story tells of the peasants' revolt at the end of the sixteenth century.

**Les Eyzies** lies on the far side of the Vézère valley, along which the road runs for a short while before crossing the river into the town. On the left as you come into the town is **Les Glycines,** still a delightful and fairly simple country hotel. The front has a huge wistaria (hence the hotel's name); and there is a peaceful garden at the back. A side-road to the left leads to the fortified church of Tayac, while on the road is the Hôtel du Cro-Magnon, more expensive, with good food, and a pleasant interior. The modern Hôtel Centenaire also provides good cuisine.

You are now in the heart of prehistoric territory, with its vast time-scale and tiny fragments of early civilisation. Before you look at any of the caves or shelters the **Musée nationale de préhistoire** (9–12, 14.00–18.00 (winter 10–12, 14.00–16.00); closed on Tuesdays) is an essential guide to the subject. It is housed in a sixteenth-century fortress overlooking the village, reached by a turning to the left just by the little square. Here the first room is given over to a clear chart of the different periods of prehistory. This is followed by a room dealing with prehistoric art in general, drawing on reproductions from elsewhere in France and from Altamira in Spain, as well as plaster-casts of reliefs, statuettes and engraved bone. The emphasis

166

is at first on technique, as with so much of prehistory, but the artistic power of much of the work is soon apparent. On the same floor are reconstructions of a number of burials found in the region, and an upper storey (in process of rearrangement) contains a more general collection of prehistoric finds.

Also essential to the enjoyment of the different sites is a knowledge of the history of the discovery of the meaning of prehistoric remains. In the middle of the nineteenth century the gradual acceptance of Darwin's theory of evolution overturned all the accepted views of the distant past, including the delightfully precise dating worked out by Archbishop Ussher in the seventeenth century which insisted that the Creation began in 4004 BC, and which often appears in seventeenth- and eighteenth-century bibles. Geologists had already outlined the principle of stratification – that unless subject to violent change rocks lay in the order in which they were formed, and could be a guide to the relative age of a landscape. But in the early nineteenth century the time-scale was far from established, and it was possible to believe that the oldest rocks were no more than 6,000 years old. As to the fossil and other remains found in the different strata, they were regarded as freaks or natural curiosities, while since, according to prevailing belief, man had always existed, any man-made remains belonged to a backward race which had vanished within historical, or at least Biblical, times. Darwin's theory provided an explanation for the fossils, and interest centred almost entirely on this branch of geology at first, which soon acquired the name of 'palaeontology'. A time-scale was gradually worked out on the basis that the rate of natural change had always been the same: if it takes a river ten years to silt up by one foot today, the same will be true, in general terms, for the formation of a silt deposit at any geological period. Geologists found their time-scale multiplied a hundred thousandfold and more; but we need not worry about such incomprehensible figures. Here in the Dordogne everything – in geological terms – comes within the most recent, or Pleistocene, age.

It was gradually realised that these new ideas had implications for the early history of man. Progress was slower in this sphere because Darwin's idea that mankind was descended from ape-like creatures was still the least readily acceptable part of *The Origin of Species*. Here and there archaeologists began to push back man's own time-scale: Boucher de Perthes at Abbéville in northern France studied what he called 'ante-diluvian man' from 1830 on, publishing the first results in 1847. It was not until 1859 that his work was vindicated with the support of Joseph Prestwich, later professor of geology

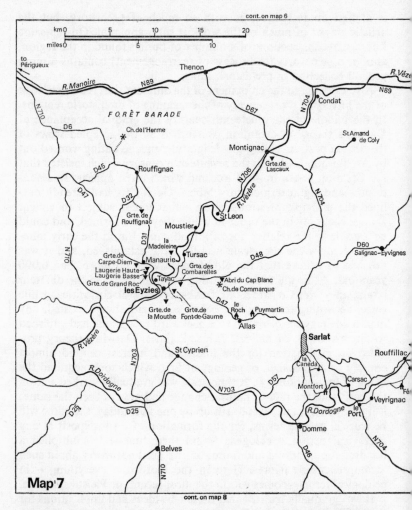

cont. on map 6

cont. on map 8

Map 7

at Oxford. Soon after another Englishman, the banker Henry Christy, helped a French enthusiast named Edouard Lartet to carry out excavations: Lartet had been investigating the caves of south-west France, and had been sent a box of fragments from Les Eyzies. Realising that there were rich possibilities in the sample material, he concentrated on this neighbourhood and from 1863 carried out a series of excavations. Two years later the results of these were published in London under the title *Reliquiae Aquitanicae* (*Remains*

168

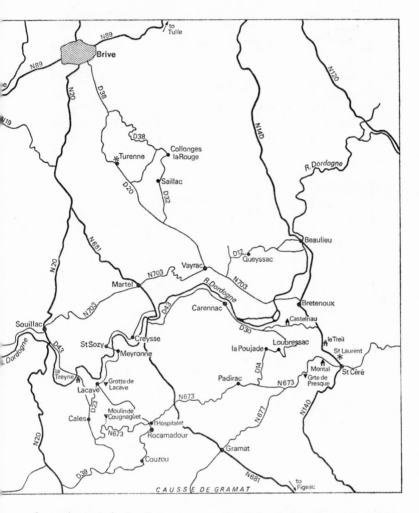

*from Aquitaine*); in the same year Sir John Lubbock produced his
*Prehistoric Times,* and what had been an occasional study for
amateurs quickly became an important science.

The early finds were largely casual, the remains left by human
occupants of caves and shelters. In 1868, during road-building, an
early Stone Age burial was found behind what is now the Hôtel
Cro-Magnon. The three skeletons were carefully studied by a
physical anthropologist, who was able to reconstruct from them the

# Prehistoric Cultures of South–West France

| Period | Cultures of W. Europe | Characteristics | Types of man | Years B.C. |
|---|---|---|---|---|
| LOWER PALAEOLITHIC<br><br>(Old Stone Age) | Clactonian | Earliest tools – chipped pebbles simple flint tools | East African man<br>Early Java man<br>Pekin man | 450,000 |
| MIDDLE PALAEOLITHIC | Abbevillian ↓<br>Acheulian<br><br>Tayacian  Levalloisian | Chipped on two surfaces<br><br><br>Irregular flakes for cutting, scraping and sawing | Swanscombe man<br>Neanderthal man | 150,000 |
| UPPER PALAEOLITHIC | Mousterian ↓ ↓ ↓ ↓<br><br><br>Aurignacian<br>Solutrean<br>Magdalenian | Regular flakes according to purpose<br><br><br>Bone implements<br>Highest development of flint flakes<br>Elaborate bone harpoons, needles, arrowheads | Cro–Magnon man | 30,000<br><br>10,000 |

so-called Cro-Magnon man, who lived during the Upper Palaeo-lithic period or New Stone Age (see table).

The next series of discoveries was of a very different kind. The first traces of Stone Age art had been found in the 1830s, and in 1880 the dramatic paintings at Altamira in Spain had been published. But the experts were sceptical, and there was no way of dating them which could stand up to scientific proof. In 1895 a cave at La Mouthe, just south of Les Eyzies, was excavated; only after much Stone Age débris had been removed were the paintings discovered, the implication being that the paintings must be older than the other finds. Even so this and further discoveries – at the cave of Pair-non-Pair, where engraved figures of animals were found under Stone Age strata levels – were still regarded with doubt. More finds were made in 1901 at Combarelles and Font de Gaume. The champions of the new discoveries were the Abbé Henri Breuil and Émile Rivière; and in 1902 they were eventually able to persuade members of the French Association for the Advancement of Sciences by bringing them on a field visit to Les Eyzies. Prehistoric art now took its rightful place at the beginning of man's creative history instead of being dismissed as a hoax or the work of idle scribblers of later ages. In 1911, at Cap Blanc, north of Les Eyzies, its range was further extended by the finding of sculptures in high relief. But the most famous event of all was the opening of Lascaux (p. 174), only to disappear from sight again in 1963.

Visiting the caves, particularly out of season, needs patience, as it is difficult to know exactly when a party will be taken round: if there are only two or three people waiting for admittance the guide may need some persuading! On the road to Le Bugue a turning to the right at the edge of the village leads to a farm, where a guide can be found (no set hours) to take you to the **Grotte de la Mouthe**. The cave has no electric light and its slippery rock can make progress difficult. The first engraving is about a hundred yards inside the cave, and shows oxen; this is followed by bison, reindeer and deer, both engraved and painted. As with many such works it takes some practice to decipher the faint markings of the engravings in the darkness, or the tones of the paintings as they blend with the rock colour. There are also pictures of a hut and of ibex and woolly rhinoceros (a prehistoric forerunner of the modern rhinoceros, but with a fleece instead of a smooth hide).

On the other side of the Vézère, toward Périgueux, to the left of the road are a line of the natural limestone cliff shelters which first attracted prehistoric man to the area. The first two sites are of no interest: the Gorge d'Enfer is a zoo, and the famous rock carving of a fish in the Abri du Poisson there is no longer accessible. The Musée de Spéléologie is installed in the rock fort of Tayac, just before the Grotte du Grand Roc; it is chiefly of interest to the enthusiast, but has some good photographs and models showing why caves are so numerous in the Périgord. The fort itself was known as a haunt of brigands in 1408; there is a bizarre Edwardian photograph showing it converted into a bar! The Grotte du Grand Roc is a collection of miniature stalactites and stalagmites mostly about a yard high, with coloured lighting in an artificially dug-out cave, each formation being given highly imaginative names: a visit best avoided. Beyond this are the sites known as **Laugerie Haute** and **Laugerie Basse**. The **Laugerie Haute** is mainly interesting as the site of extended excavations, from 1863 to 1939, the first explorers being Lartet and Christy. A sign indicates where the guide is to be found. All that actually remains on the site is the clearly marked strata of the excavations, with a scale beside it explaining the different periods. The **Laugerie Basse** has a similar excavation, but the remains are of much more recent date: only during the Magdalenian period were both shelters occupied, and thereafter, down to the Iron Age, Laugerie Basse alone was inhabited. A small museum houses the finds, which include some engravings on bone as well as the usual flint tools from the earlier period, and pottery from the later period. Beyond Manaurie, on the D 31 to the left, is the Grotte du Carpe-Diem, much advertised, but only of interest for its stalactites and stalagmites. More rewarding is the **Grotte de Rouffignac** (La Grotte aux Cent Mammouthes), again on the D 31; turn right at Manaurie and take the D 32 in Rouffignac. This cave has been a favourite place for excursions for centuries: it is recorded as early as the fifteenth century, and innumerable graffiti have been left by visitors from the seventeenth century on. It is now equipped with an electric train, which covers about a mile and a half of the five miles of caves. In 1956 Professor Nougier discovered that the cave also had some fine examples of prehistoric art, some actually defaced by later graffiti. The earliest occupants of the caves seem to have been bears: their paw marks and pits are side by side with curious holes leading down, and unexplained, apparently man-made, markings. Near these holes are found the groups of paintings and sculpture, the most remarkable being a frieze showing two bull bison challenging each other; elsewhere there is a huge mammoth, nicknamed 'the patriarch', and a number of lesser drawings. A tentative theory suggests that primitive man worshipped an earth force, which would explain why paintings are found at the furthest ends of caves, as near to the earth's heart as possible, and why the holes, from which the force might have seemed to emanate, were also particularly sacred. The man-made markings are perhaps ritual scribblings done in the ecstasy of some ceremony, or perhaps a kind of visible prayer: but all this is guesswork.

To the north of Les Eyzies the N 706 follows the Vézère valley, with steep cliffs to either side; but everything is on a pastoral scale, unlike the grandiose scenery of the Dordogne itself. **Tursac** has a simple Romanesque church with domes typical of this area. On the overhanging cliffs to the right after Tursac is **La Roque St Christophe**, inhabited from prehistoric times until the sixteenth century. Steep staircases lead up to a terrace with a fine view over the river valley; small wonder that such a commanding site was fortified in the tenth century. Across the river are two famous sites, the **Abri du Moustier**, in the village of Le Moustier, and the **Gisement de la Madeleine**, opposite Tursac, which have given their names to two periods of prehistory, Mousterian and Magdalenian. At La Madeleine a guide is available in summer every three-quarters of an hour; most of the finds are either at Les Eyzies or elsewhere, but the rock shelters can still be seen.

Further up the valley, beyond Le Moustier, **St Léon-sur-Vézère** lies on a loop of the river. It has a small sixteenth-century château, which is little more than a glorified manor house, and a sober but very lovely Romanesque church amid the willows and poplars on the riverbank, reached through very narrow streets. The church, damaged by flooding in 1961, has recently been restored in the austere style favoured by the *Service des Monuments Historiques* nowadays. Here it is most effective. The exterior has very four-square lines, but this only serves to throw into relief the elegant bell-tower. Inside, the nave roof has always been a simple flat timber structure, which explains the height of the side walls. The large windows are, surprisingly, very early, of the eleventh century or before (notice the height of their sills and also the small masonry), while the crossing and apse are twelfth-century. The passages round the western piers of the crossing, which give a variety of perspectives as you walk round the church, are common in Berry, to the north-east, but rare here. The fragments of frescoes on the domed vault of the apse are fourteenth- and fifteenth-century. On the edge of the village the fortified Manoir de la Salle has a great four-square battlemented tower. Continuing north we come to the little town of Montignac, where we cross the river again toward Sarlat. Just outside Sarlat is the **Grotte de Lascaux**, with the most famous prehistoric paintings in Europe. The story of their discovery alone is dramatic enough. On 12 September 1940 three local boys and two refugees from occupied France – the Périgord was under the Vichy government – went out rabbit-shooting on the hillside south of Montignac. Their dog Robot disappeared down a large hole left by a fir tree which had blown down many years before, and which had never filled in, leaving a kind of pot-hole. The dog's owner decided to try and rescue it, and the others followed him. They found themselves in a large cave, and when they lit matches saw that it was decorated with superb rock-paintings. They recognised these as prehistoric because their school-master had taken them to the caves near Les Eyzies. A week later the great expert on such paintings, the Abbé Breuil, was called in, and the following month a preliminary report was prepared, in which Breuil described the cave as 'the Versailles of prehistory'. It was closed for the remainder of the war, and only after elaborate equipment to light it had been installed was it opened, in 1948. Un-like most other caves it was easily accessible, being only a small distance into the hillside. The size and spaciousness as well as the scale of the paintings made it a striking contrast to the other caves, and it quickly became world-famous. Alas, the film of carbonate of lime which had acted as a varnish on the paintings and so preserved them began to dissolve with the change of atmosphere, being par-ticularly susceptible to the carbon dioxide which visitors breathed out. It was therefore decided that the caves should be sealed off again until a solution to the problem could be found, and so the famous images can only be seen in reproduction. During the summer (1 July–13 September) an exhibition of colour slides is presented in the entrance to the cave; otherwise it is a matter of reading either the guide to Lascaux by Jean Taralon, or, better still, the Abbé Breuil's *Four Hundred Centuries of Cave Art*.

To the east of Les Eyzies are the two caves where the foundations of the study of prehistoric art were laid. The **Grotte de Font de Gaume** lies a good distance from the parking place on the road; allow a quarter of an hour for the walk up a long path to the actual entrance. The cave itself is not for anyone prone to claustrophobia: it starts as a very narrow rift about a hundred yards long, and the guide firmly shuts the iron door behind you as you go in. Despite this narrow entrance, the cave was known in the eighteenth century, and some of the paintings are damaged by graffiti from that period. A very narrow part leads to a wider hall, and here a mass of confused, often super-imposed paintings appears. As elsewhere, the beasts of the chase predominate: bison, mammoths, deer and reindeer, horses. Most of the drawings are in colour, though one or two of the earlier ones are monochrome: the woolly rhinoceros in red line, an ox and a pair of reindeer are particularly memorable. There are also handprints and curious geometrical symbols whose meaning is still obscure. Not all the paintings are easy to decipher. At the extreme end is a small grotto with very early paintings, including one of a human figure, a great rarity in prehistoric art; but this is very difficult to reach and therefore is not open to the public.

At **Combarelles**, a mile or so further along the road, the cave is only dimly lit, and the guide will show the various figures with his torch. Here the work is all engraved, not painted, and is perhaps the most difficult of all to make out. The engravings were discovered by two local men who broke through a wall of stalactites and stalag-mites into the inner cavern in 1901. The evidence of the age of this slowly-formed barrier was crucial in proving that the engravings were authentic. There are vast numbers of them, over 400; some show interesting aspects of technique, particularly where mistakes have occurred because the artist could barely see what he was doing. One fascinating group shows a herd of reindeer crossing a river, from the bed of which a javelin projects, perhaps representing the hunter lying in wait in a bed of rushes to stab them from below as they passed. There is also a scene from nature, a lion attacking an antelope; and another rarity is a drawing of a giraffe. The visit is a slow one, because the path winds past stalactites and each engraving needs to be looked at for a moment or two before it becomes clear.

A little beyond Combarelles the D 48 leads off to the left and to the **Abri du Cap Blanc**. This is not easy to enter: a notice says 'sound your horn for the guide', but as he is a local farmer he is not always free to come. I have never succeeded in summoning him, but in high season you may find him at the cave itself. It is a pity that visitors should find this cave difficult to visit, because it represents a third aspect of prehistoric art which is scarce elsewhere: sculptures in relief. These were discovered in 1911, together with remains of two hearths and a burial, from the Magdalenian period. The sculptures form a frieze, and portray two bison and a herd of horses. The scale is large: the biggest horse measures over six feet in length. As the figures are today, they seem from photographs very concentrated, showing line and form but little detail: but they are eroded and the colouring (of which traces can be seen) has also disappeared, so it is perhaps unwise to hail them as the first Cubist sculptures! The forms use the natural shape of the rock as much as possible, because the sculptor was limited by his very simple tools. From a rock shelter a little further along the road (behind the motley fifteenth-century roofs of the château of Laussel) there came the most famous of the prehistoric sculptures of the Périgord, the fertility Goddess known as the Venus de Laussel, now at Bordeaux (p. 111).

Across the valley are the lonely ruins of the **Château de Commarque**, with a double donjon, one Romanesque, the other Gothic. It stands in the depths of a large wood. The adventurous explorer can reach it on foot, from a byroad on the other side of the valley beyond Sireuil: a track leads into the woods and the path is then marked by coloured bands on the trees, but a good sense of direction is needed. The ruins, although classified as a *monument historique*, are in a dangerous state, but the remains of a large defensive system and the general plan of the building, including a twelfth-century chapel, can still be made out. Like Laussel, the castle is on a prehistoric site, though a cave containing rock-engravings is no longer accessible. The site, after thousands of years of human habitation, was only abandoned in the seventeenth century.

There are a number of other castles near Les Eyzies, though none is open to the public. On the road to Sarlat, Le Roc at Allas dominates the road from a spur of the hillside. Its name comes from the limestone cliff on which it stands, but despite the prominent site it is a dull eighteenth-century building. A mile or two beyond, the towers of Puymartin appear behind a screen of trees. This is a more interesting, fifteenth-century building, much restored about sixty years ago, but most of its original interior and furnishings are intact, including seventeenth-century murals.

Along the Vézère valley are the two châteaux on opposite sides of the river at Marzac, near Tursac; both can be seen in the distance when visiting the site of La Madeleine (p. 173). Marzac proper, on the south bank, is fifteenth-century, with seventeenth-century additions, a harmonious and well-proportioned small castle, with Renaissance dovecote and elegant formal gardens. Petit Marzac is a ruin of the twelfth and thirteenth centuries, just off the road to La Madeleine.

Away from the Vézère valley, down a turning off the N 704 east of Montignac, is one of the best-preserved and most dramatic of the fortified churches of the area, at **St Amand-de-Coly**. Its tower, built by monks in the twelfth century, rises like a great monolith against the hillside beyond a wooded vale. Unlike most other dual-purpose churches its fortifications seem to have been part of the original plan. If this were indeed the case the monks were remarkably prescient, because the abbey suffered severely during the Hundred Years' War and in 1575 underwent a siege by 2,000 cavalry and a bombardment lasting six days.

The façade, with the high arch set into the otherwise plain tower, gives the church a completely individual and original character. From the upper chamber the defenders of the church could beat off attacks on the main door; if this failed the inner arrangements provided a gallery from which enemies inside the building could be attacked. The interior is equally imposing, its details ranging from an early-twelfth-century cupola to the late-twelfth-century square east end, with a flat ribbed vault and a simple but striking east wall, well-lit by the ten windows. The apse of the north transept has a small inscription commemorating the founder, Abbot William, dated 1130, and fragments of a fifteenth-century pietà in the local golden limestone. The rising slope of the stone floor lends emphasis to the sanctuary. There is virtually no other decoration; yet this is one of the most memorable places of the region, its towering, silent spaces echoing with the conflicting ghosts of war and worship.

From St Amand-de-Coly return to the N 704, and then take the N 84 to Brive-la-Gaillarde.

# Chapter 12

# The Dordogne Valley: Beaulieu to Sarlat

❧

South of Brive (p. 153) the D 38 climbs sharply from the town and runs along the side of a ridge of hills, with wide views to the southwest. Just south of the road, fifteen miles from Brive, and on the lower slopes of the hillside, stands the village of **Collonges la Rouge**.

Collonges is not a place for a hurried visit: an afternoon is needed to enjoy its atmosphere. Only then will you be able to persuade yourself that the last old man you passed had the true Gaulish droop to his moustache, and the last girl a face fresh from a medieval corbel. It has a faint air of being washed up by time, left as the flotsam of some great medieval flood which swept up the valley. The red sandstone houses which line your way as you walk down from the car park on the main road are loosely grouped within old fortifications, which have disappeared to the north, though the name 'rue de la Barrière' (the street leading from the car park) recalls them. The warm colour of the stone and the gardens and glimpses of countryside between the houses, as well as the absence of cars, give an air of ease, almost of lethargy, as the village basks in the sunshine. Until recently it was decayed and underpopulated; now it is cared for by 'Les amis de Collonges la Rouge', whose attentions have so far been in the best tradition of careful restoration and repair without altering its character. On the right of the rue de la Barrière is the Maison de la Sirène, which has just been repaired: on the corner gable, below the roof of grey *lauzes*, is a carving of a siren holding a lute, a suitable symbol for such an enchanted, timeless place. Further on, the Porte du Prieuré leads through the stone pillars of the open market hall into the heart of the village, which was once a fortified quarter centred on the church. The church itself acquired fortifications during the wars of religion in the sixteenth century. The interior, much altered, is a jumble and interesting only if you enjoy piecing together the various stages of alterations; but the outside retains a very early belfry with elaborate upper storeys, ending in an octagon and an unfinished spire. Above the entrance, the tympanum is a powerful early-twelfth-century work, by an artist whose style has

178

something cosmopolitan about it. The lively figures of the apostles and noble figure of Christ hint at the style both of Souillac and Moissac as well as the later portals of the Ile de France. On the extreme right a capital shows a man driving a bear.

The street to the north of the church winds past delightful old houses with loggias: nothing new seems to have been built here since the early nineteenth century, and the wistaria draped round the houses looks as if it had grown up and aged with them. The street emerges at the castel de Maussac, a nobleman's town house with a square tower. Continue downhill and turn right into the rue de la Garde, where the castel de Vassignac appears on the southern edge of the village. It was built in 1583 by the lord of Collonges, Gideon de Vassignac, and is a typical small castle of the region, a manor house which bristles with towers in the hope of frightening off would-be assailants. Its equivalent in England would be a half-timbered house or some Elizabethan manor with large windows; here there are arrow-slits and crenellations instead. Walk back past the church to where the Porte Plate bridges the road (so called because it lacks its towers) and on the right is the excellent Relais de St Jacques de Compostelle where you can eat under the trellis on the terrace; and the food is worthy of the setting. The road winds downhill out of the village into the valley past more fortified houses, the last with a pepper-pot tower.

**Saillac**, down a byroad to the south of Collonges, has a surprising Romanesque portal inside the church, above a flat lintel supported on a pillar with twisted bands of hounds chasing up it, alternating with bands of foliage. The tympanum shows the Adoration of the Magi and a local saint with a monster, but has been repainted in enthusiastic and garish colours.

From Saillac the castle at **Turenne** towers over the landscape, built on an outcrop of rock rising steeply from the valley floor. The approach from the south gives a good view of the whole group of buildings, with the medieval buildings of the little town perched on the cliffs below the castle itself, whose two towers form the peaks. The road up to the castle is narrow, but can be managed in a car; otherwise the climb is a steep one, taking about twenty minutes.

Turenne was one of the most important of the lordships of south-west France in the Middle Ages, and the scale of the castle reflected its grandeur. All that is left is the outer ring of defences and two of the towers. Where most of the buildings stood there is now a garden which is a blaze of colour in the summer. This alone, with the spectacular views from the walls across to the Dordogne valley to the south and to the Massif Central in the east, make it well worth a visit. The thirteenth-century 'Caesar's Tower' has an even more astonishing panorama from the top of its stone staircase, the steps worn to the point where they are almost dangerous. In the Tour d'Horloge the main room contains late medieval armour and a chair reputedly used to hide salt from the tax-collectors. The *gabelle* or salt-tax was a major source of the French Crown's revenue. It was a much-resented burden on the poor, and evasion was common.

In the sixteenth century one of the viscounts of Turenne was a staunch supporter of Henri IV of Navarre, and when the latter came to the throne he rewarded his lieutenant by marrying him to the heiress to the duchy of Bouillon. So his grandson, who became Marshal Turenne, was brought up at Sédan in the Ardennes, and had little to do with the castle from which he got his name. His military career spanned over fifty years, and included the campaigns which brought the Thirty Years' War to an end in 1648, the conquest of the Spanish Netherlands, and the wars with Austria. He and the Prince de Condé were the two generals who made France a major military power under Louis XIV: but these great exploits did not help the family fortunes, and in the eighteenth century the estate was sold to the Crown to pay off debts.

From Turenne the D 20 leads south to Vayrac. On the right of the road is the **Puy d'Issolud**, scene of the last Gaulish resistance to Caesar in 51 BC. This steep limestone cliff was fortified by the Gauls, and as it had its own source of water it seemed impregnable. But the Roman engineers were equal to the task: they tunnelled into the rock and diverted the spring, and built a siege-terrace and wooden tower from which to bombard the defenders. All this is described by one of Caesar's lieutenants, and a tunnel which seems to correspond to that made to direct the spring has been found at Puy d'Issolud, along with other remains now kept in the little museum at Martel (p. 188). Roman technology triumphed, the defenders capitulated, and the conquest of Gaul was completed.

At Vayrac we join the N 703 and then turn left down the D 113 to **Queyssac les Vignes**, where the tower of the old castle offers a wide circular panorama taking in Turenne and the Dordogne valley which form a half circle to the south-east. The other part of the castle buildings is occupied by a little restaurant, *Au vin paillé*; in its spacious dining room with huge twisted pillars and vast carved fireplace you will get as pleasant and reasonably-priced a meal as any hungry traveller could wish for out of a down-to-earth kitchen full of gleaming copper pans. The local speciality, *pets-de-nonnes* ('nuns' coifs'), are a kind of delicious light doughnut. *Vin de paille*, a sweet wine made from grapes dried in the sun on a bed of straw, from which the restaurant takes its name, is also sometimes available.

A narrow side-road leads on to **Beaulieu sur Dordogne**, where the Hôtel Central continues a long tradition of excellent food. In the centre of the old quarter stands the abbey church of St Pierre, all that remains of an abbey founded about 840 and suppressed in 1790. The church was built in the twelfth century after the monastic life at the abbey had recovered from the disorders of the tenth and eleventh centuries. Although Beaulieu is away from the main roads, and particularly from the pilgrimage roads to Spain, it none the less used to attract many travellers, and is another example of a church designed for large crowds and solemn occasions.

The interior is spacious and lofty, but dark, with narrow windows and no clerestory. The grey sandstone, which looks well in a strong light, here adds to the gloom. But the proportions are well-balanced, with relatively wide side-aisles and carefully modelled pillars. The vault is a plain barrel shape, surprising in a building that otherwise is relatively forward-looking. A curious feature is the presence of a gallery, or tribune, running right round the church. In the nave the size of the aisle means that it is a small and rather insignificant feature; but it comes into its own at the east end, where it forms an important part of the balanced tiers of arcading. The fluted pillars of the choir are also surprising, an unusual reminder that the Romanesque style derives directly from classical architecture. The lighting of the choir and transept chapels is much reduced by seventeenth-century woodwork. This disguises the original intention of creating a light and airy east end as the focal point of the darker nave, so that the ceremonies took place on a naturally bright stage. There is very little decoration: two primitive bas-reliefs over doorways in the transepts, a number of simple capitals in the nave.

The plainness of the interior – this is a church where it would be good to see the later furniture removed – is in sharp opposition to the exterior. The same harmony and skilful handling of mass and volume reappears, particularly at the east end, with its grouped chapels, two-tiered apse roof and staircase turrets; and there is the same use of modelled detail in the blind arcades. But the south door possesses a wealth of rich sculpture; it is as if the rest of the building had been designed as a plain setting to show off this elaborate work. Even the arcades of the doorway are left plain, for fear of distracting the eye from the huge tympanum, which fills the whole curve of the arch and even runs down the side pillars. The theme is the Last Judgment: in the centre is the majestic figure of Christ, with an expression and gesture which suggests a demonstration of the divine power rather than either anger or mercy, as he extends his arms to summon the living and the dead. Two angels beside him blow oliphants, while behind him the cross is borne up by two more angels, and the apostles sit engaged in lively conversation. At his feet men come to judgment: the dead rise from their tombs at the left, while to the right pagans in peaked caps point with awe at the figure of Christ. On the frieze below monsters make sport with the damned: there are seven of them, including a bear, a man-headed dragon, and the seven-headed Beast of the Apocalypse itself. On the pillars Saints Peter and Paul guard the doorway, while the central support is a baroque, irregular mass of giants holding up the world of life above. To left and right of the archway panels show the story of Daniel and the temptation of Christ. These lower figures are the most lively of all, moving in flowing curves instead of the hieratic poses of the tympanum, but they are badly weathered. Part of the reason for the stiffness of the upper part of the composition is the nature of the stone, coarse-grained and difficult to work; but all the same this doorway ranks with the related sculptures at Moissac and Souillac as one of the masterpieces of the southern Romanesque.

The main road crosses the Dordogne and turns south across the Céré to Brétenoux, the first of the medieval *bastides* or fortified villages (see p. 203) that we have reached; founded in 1277 by the local lord, it still retains many of its original features. The grid plan of the streets is still clear, there are traces of ramparts, and the market-place has some of its covered arcades. Next to the bridge, a walk has been made along the bank of the Dordogne: the river here flows through level, wooded country, its course broken by little willow-grown islands.

On the south bank beyond Brétenoux the château of **Castelnau** rises on a steep bluff. Its red-sandstone walls brood over a peaceful landscape of which it is the focal point. The original castle was built in the eleventh century by barons who were rivals of the lords of Turenne. Early in the thirteenth century they were forced to become vassals of Turenne, but the payment due was a single egg, which was solemnly taken to Turenne once a year in a special bullock-cart. New fortifications were added in the fourteenth century and again in the wars of religion in the sixteenth century; but the huge ancient building was not to the taste of later lords, and it became a ruin, gutted by fire in 1851. However, it was bought by a successful opera singer, who spent nearly forty years restoring one wing, and gave it to the State in 1932. It is now classified as the second most important military castle (château-fort) in France (open 9–12, 14.00–18.00 except on Tuesdays; ring for admittance), the finest being at Pierrefonds near Compiègne. A walk round the ramparts gives a good idea of the different periods of the buildings and of their size (at full strength the garrison was said to be 1,500 men); the eleventh-century keep is a ruin, but the south wing is being restored. The interior is unexpected: housed in a series of rather dimly lit rooms are a fine collection of art treasures, including a number of fourteenth- and fifteenth-century altarpieces by Aragonese and Italian masters, among them a delicate Sienese school Madonna and Child. The furnishings are mainly sixteenth- and seventeenth-century; some pieces are of outstanding quality, and two rooms still have their original painted ceilings from the same period. Another room, where the parliament of the province used to meet, has large Romanesque windows. The south wing and stables are being refurbished to house the collections properly.

The D 43 winds its way back to the main road; after the château of Le Treil and that of St Laurent les Tours high on the hillside, both to the left, we come to the little town of **St Céré**. In the centre of the town the Place du Mercadial has two or three fine old houses, one with a striking angled roof, and both here and in the neighbouring streets there is a good deal of half-timbered work. On the boulevard round the old quarter the Hôtel Miramon has a Renaissance loggia. In the casino, on the eastern edge of the town, there is a permanent exhibition of work designed by the artist Jean Lurçat (who lived and worked at St Laurent les Tours) for the weavers of Aubusson; his striking use of colour has led to a considerable revival of the art of tapestry, which until recently was chiefly used for lifeless reproductions of seventeenth- and eighteenth-century cartoons. St Laurent les Tours can be reached by a byroad off the N 673 to Sousceyrac; the château is not open, but the exterior can be seen, with its twelfth- and fifteenth-century keeps linked by a curtain wall. Lurçat bought the château because its vast rooms were ideal for work on tapestry cartoons.

Along the road to Gramat the little château of **Montal** appears down a byroad to the right, in a green hollow below the hills of the Causse de Gramat. Here we are a world away from the feudal pride of Castelnau. Montal was built between 1523 and 1534, a gem of the French Renaissance which can stand beside the far more famous

Loire châteaux. It has had a sad history. Jeanne de Montal had it built for her eldest son Robert, whose life as a courtier and soldier kept him elsewhere until his death, and he never saw the château. His mother engraved the motto '*Plus d'espoir*' ('No more hope') below the window where she had awaited his return; the work in progress was brought to a finish, but more grandiose plans were laid aside. At the Revolution it was confiscated, and its fabric badly damaged: as a result it was sold to a speculator for demolition in 1879. The stonework was dismantled, and some of the sculptures sold to the Louvre, only the main staircase and the four walls remaining. But, just in time, a local art-lover and industrialist, M. Fenaille, came to the rescue. He bought the ruins and laboriously set about buying back the pieces which had been dispersed, and the main part of the restoration was achieved in 1908. However, the sculptures which were in the Louvre were State property and therefore impossible to purchase. This impasse was resolved in 1913, when M. Fenaille presented the château to the State, retaining the right of his family to live there; the sculptures were returned on loan. In 1955 the last chimneypiece was bought back, and only one of the gable windows is a copy, the original being in the Metropolitan Museum, New York.

The château (open 9–12, 14.00–18.00, except when the family are there) was planned as a square, with a central courtyard; but only two wings were built. The exterior is sombre, grey-roofed, not far from its fortress predecessors; but inside the courtyard all is light and delicate. A plain, squat lower storey gives way to an elaborate frieze where a cornucopia of all the favourite designs of Renaissance ornament is interspersed between the initials of Jeanne de Montal and her two sons, Robert and Dorde. Between the first-floor windows the seven busts in niches are a marvellously realistic set of portraits of members of the family. On the wing to the left Jeanne herself is shown with her husband Amaury and her son Dorde; on the wing to the right are Robert, Jeanne's parents, and a cousin. Above these rise the gable windows, crowned by elaborate sculptures commemorating the death of Robert: death as a skeleton bearing a scythe, a young knight holding a scroll with the motto '*Plus d'espoir*'.

The doorway in the corner of the two wings is relatively simple, but it leads to the splendours of the Renaissance staircase, whose walls are covered in pillared niches, and whose steps are decorated on the under-surface, forming a dazzling spiral ceiling of ornamented stone. The rooms, with monumental chimneys in the same style, have been suitably furnished; the château is enhanced by still being lived in, and there is none of the frozen atmosphere of a museum, though the tapestries and furniture are worthy of any collection.

Beyond Montal, the road climbs up the edge of the Causse. On the hillside is the **Grotte de Presque**, with some well-formed stalagmites; it is relatively easily accessible, but pales beside the splendours of the **Gouffre de Padirac** five miles to the west. At Padirac, there are wonders enough to convert the most sceptical cave visitor. The 'gouffre' itself is an enormous crater, caused by the collapse of the roof of an underground river-cavern. It measures 300 feet across and just over 300 deep. Lifts, with a dramatic view of the sides, go down to the bottom of this chasm, which was used by local inhabitants as a place of safety during the Hundred Years' War. A long path through a high corridor leads to the edge of the underground river. This was first explored from 1889 to 1900, and in 1898 staircases were installed for visitors. In 1947 experiments showed that the river re-emerges into the Dordogne some seven miles away, but so far only three miles of its length have been explored, the rest being too dangerous. Half of the known galleries are open.

At the edge of the river is a landing stage, from which boats leave at frequent intervals. It is an extraordinary voyage, between huge cliffs of limestone rising as much as 200 feet above the river, whose dark water is none the less very clear. At the end of the river a huge stalactite descends from the roof, amid a mass of lesser concretions still being formed by the 'rain' which seeps through the rock into the river. Leaving the boat we continue on foot into the largest cavern of all, a narrower version of the chasm at the beginning, where a vault 300 feet high is covered by only 27 feet of rock above, a space as large as the dome of St Paul's.

Not surprisingly Padirac is often crowded during the season, but it is also a sight not to be missed. If the throngs are too much for you it is easy to escape: return to the N 673 and turn left, the next road to the left leading through lonely country down toward the Dordogne, with wide views on the way. At La Poujade take the road along the hill to **Loubressac.** The medieval village clusters below the castle, and its narrow streets make an attractive approach to the castle gateway. Little survives of the medieval fort which was unsuccessfully besieged by a company of English 'free-booters' under Sir Robert Knolles in 1352. The site of the present castle was first built on in 1363, and the building was remodelled in the fifteenth and seventeenth centuries. In 1909 the writer Henri de Lavedan bought it;

185

it now houses, besides some unremarkable furniture, a collection of mementoes of the Revolution, including rare *toiles de Jouy*, prints of the period, furniture and china with revolutionary symbols and a copy of the revolutionary calendar with its ten-day week. From the terrace beside a well-tended garden there is a vast view to the north, best seen in the long shadows of the evening light. On a clear day Turenne, St Laurent les Tours, Montal, and the Dordogne valley can all be made out, while the hills of the Causse rise behind the castle to the south. A little fifteenth-century watch-tower broods over this peaceful expanse, a reminder of the days when it was the battleground of French and English armies.

The lanes from Loubressac drop steeply down to the valley floor, where the D 30 takes us to **Carennac**. The inn here is the Hostellerie Fénelon, perched on the edge of the Dordogne, which provides good, unambitious food in a dining room overlooking the river. Its name commemorates the most famous inhabitant of this peaceful village, the seventeenth-century writer and orator François de la Mothe-Fénelon, Archbishop of Cambrai, renowned for his gentle and persuasive style. Tradition has it that he wrote his romance *Télémaque* here, the adventures of Telemachus in search of his father Odysseus designed as a moral allegory on statesmanship; when it was written, Fénelon was tutor to Louis XIV's grandson, the Duke of Burgundy. As hereditary Prior of Carennac, Fénelon certainly spent much time here as a retreat from Versailles. The priory church stands beside the road; its entrance is through an archway and up a flight of steps. It is little changed from Fénelon's day. Above the doorway is a richly carved tympanum, where Christ blesses the worshipper as he enters the church; he is shown in a mandorla, with the apostles ranged neatly in two rows. Round him are the symbols of the evangelists, while two adoring angels make awestruck, fluttering obeisance, their lively movements breaking the arc of the outer frieze. In the lower corners two curious, solemn figures hold books and look straight ahead, unmoved by the surrounding glory. A bear, a lion, a peacock and other creatures along the lintel are framed in a kind of double Greek key frieze.

A small porch leads into the church – notice the four capitals on the inner door, two of them with the curious inscription 'Gerbert the Mason made this porch, blessed be his soul'. The interior has a nave and aisles of almost equal height, though the arches are relatively low, giving an interplay of shade and light from the spacious windows. The north aisle is Gothic, with a late-fifteenth-century deposition group in the north transept, much admired by connoisseurs of this style, which seems weak and effeminate beside the sculpture of the entrance door. The painted ceiling, of the same period, is more vigorous, a rustic interpretation of the symbols of the four evangelists. In the main aisle a series of simple capitals, twenty-four in all, are decorated with crude images of men, animals and monsters. To the south the cloister seems to belong to an intro-spective, vanished world of its own; only the ravages of the revo-lutionaries in the 1790s and the decay of time bear witness that we are no longer in the Middle Ages.

West of Carennac a lane follows the wooded banks of the Dordogne to the **Cirque de Montvalent**, an arc of limestone cliffs where the river cuts through the **Causse**, or limestone uplands. Crossing to the north bank, you will get a good view of the cliffs. The hamlet of **Creysse**, reached by a dramatic corniche road to the left, is most attractive, with a stream running through the centre and a twelfth-century castle on the hill above. A cobbled street over-grown with grass climbs to the castle chapel, now the parish church, an odd building with two apses side by side, one of coarse primitive masonry, perhaps tenth-century, the other of the twelfth century. Its whole atmosphere is one of rustic simplicity: no hint of the greater world outside, except in the seventeenth-century addition to the porch. A marvellously slow-ticking clock heightens the effect of remoteness in time.

Inland from Creysse lies **Martel**, now a sleepy little market town. Reputedly founded by Charles Martel after his victory over the Saracens at Poitiers in 732, it was a place of some importance in the early Middle Ages, and the scene of the dramatic death of the eldest son of Henry II, also called Henry. Henry was crowned during his father's lifetime, and was usually known as 'the Young King'. But his father refused to relinquish his hold on the reins of power, and in 1173 the Young King's discontent became open rebellion. His father crushed this revolt, and an uneasy peace lasted until 1183, during which the Young King amused himself at tournaments in France. His tutor and companion-in-arms, William Marshal, wrote of him later:

It was the Young King who revived chivalry, for she was dead, or almost so. He was the door through which she entered, her standard-bearer. In those days the magnates did nothing for young men; he set an example and kept men of worth about him. And when the men of high rank saw how he assembled all men of worth they were astonished at his wisdom, and copied his example. The Count of Flanders did likewise, and so horses and arms, lands and money were distributed to young men of valour. Nowadays the great have put chivalry and largesse in prison once more; the life of knights-errant and tourneys is abandoned in favour of lawsuits.

But this love of chivalry reflected the Young King's lack of a temperament suited to the real business of statesmanship. In the New Year of 1183 a quarrel arose between him and his brother Richard, and fighting broke out. The elder Henry at first supported the Young King, but he decided to wage war on his own account with a view to seizing Poitou for himself, and Henry hastened south to help Richard. He blockaded the Young King in Limoges, but at the end of May his son managed to escape from the town by pretending to have decided to go on crusade. He made his way south to raise another army, but at Uzerche he fell ill; however, he soon recovered, and went on to pillage Rocamadour (p. 189), in order to pay the mercenary soldiers he had hired. He crossed the Dordogne to Martel, where the sickness returned, hailed by his opponents as a divine retribution for his sacrilege. He sent for his father, but the latter suspected a trick and refused to come; on 7 June he made his confession, and on 11 June he died, lying on a bed of ashes and clothed in a crusader's cloak. By his side stood William Marshal, who went on crusade in fulfilment of his master's vow.

The house where the Young King died is still said to exist, the Maison Fabri near the market-place, but this seems to be a fourteenth-century building with a sixteenth-century tower. (The inscription wrongly calls the Young King 'Curtmantle' ('short cloak'); this was his father's nickname.) In the main square is a massive eighteenth-century market hall with an elaborate wood roof. Nearby is the fourteenth-century Hôtel de la Raymondie, with a pleasing courtyard below its crenellated bell-tower. A little museum houses relics from Uxellodunum (see p. 180). Beyond the medieval streets are the remains of the fortifications of the Middle Ages, and the church, to the east of the town, has a huge defensive belfry-porch with an oculus in the centre of the vault and arrow-slits around it. The apse wall has watch-towers and there are battlements on the roof. In more peaceful vein, there is a Romanesque tympanum over the main door, somewhat restored, of a Christ in Majesty at the Last Judgment. The sixteenth-century glass in the east window is similar to the work of Arnaud de Moles at the cathedral at Auch (p. 241).

There is a main road from Martel to Souillac across the **Causse**, but a better route is to return to the Dordogne valley and take the narrow road to St Sozy, crossing to Meyronne on the other bank; from here turn west to **Lacave**. The Grottes de Lacave is another limestone cave, similar to Padirac. The entrance is via a long, dark tunnel through which a little train runs, and there is about a mile of caves, with formations on an impressive scale, though nothing to rival Padirac – except perhaps a section lit entirely by ultra-violet light, a surprisingly beautiful effect.

A byroad to the south from Lacave climbs up the edge of the *causse* to Cales, where we take the road to **Rocamadour**. A track to the left leads to the isolated fortified mill of Cougnaguet. Rocamadour appears below the ridge after seven miles of winding roads, but it is worth driving on to L'Hospitalet, and approaching from below – or even better, approaching from the D 32 from Couzon, though this means a long detour across the *causse*. The town is built on the side of a gorge formed by the river Alzou, the side of which rises 300 feet, almost sheer, with buildings precariously perched on it.

It is an extraordinary site, with an extraordinary history. In 1166, according to a local chronicler of the period, a miraculously preserved corpse was found in the little chapel dedicated to the Virgin. It was identified as that of St Amadour, a name probably invented on the spur of the moment. Its fame grew rapidly, in an amazing fashion: Henry II visited the shrine at Michaelmas 1170, to give thanks for his recovery from an illness which had almost proved fatal. The shrine survived being plundered by Henry the Young King just before his death in 1183; by then it was already known as a very rich church, and possessed relics such as a sword called 'Durendal', said to have belonged to the Frankish hero Roland, whose story is told in the eleventh-century epic poem, the *Chanson de Roland*. The Young King replaced it with his own sword; but we have seen how his sacrilege was punished. In the following centuries, the sovereigns of France were the shrine's chief patrons: St Louis and his wife Blanche of Castille came in 1244, Philip the Fair in 1303, Philip VI in 1323 and Louis XI in 1443 and 1463. The object of veneration was not St Amadour, but the image of the Virgin in the chapel where the saint's body was found, the so-called 'Black Virgin'. Churches in her honour are to be found as far afield as Lisbon and Sicily.

But as with so many of the religious centres of this area, the fourteenth and fifteenth centuries saw the beginning of Rocamadour's decline, plundered again by soldiers, the roads no longer safe for the pilgrims who had once flocked there in thousands. In the wars of religion the shrine was virtually destroyed, though the image of the

Virgin survived: and it was not until the late nineteenth century that the Bishop of Cahors revived the pilgrimages.

So Rocamadour is not a place for the lover of art and architecture. It has a number of thirteenth- and fourteenth-century buildings, mostly well restored: but most of it is less than a hundred years old. Arriving from L'Hospitalet, park at the top of the town near the Porte de Figuier and walk down the main street. (An easier way is to park at the château and walk to the shrines: there is a lift in the main street which takes you back up to the top of the main stairway.) The Porte de Figuier is medieval, and among the souvenir shops and waxwork museums occasional ancient buildings survive, increasing in number as you go down the hill. The town hall is a much-rebuilt fifteenth-century house. Beyond this, the road widens into the Place de la Carreta, which is the starting point of the main stairway. Pilgrims sometimes mount this on their knees – a slow process, for there are 141 steps to the first level, and 75 beyond this. Off the Place des Senhals, at the first level, is the rue de la Mercerie, with old houses and gardens, ending in a thirteenth-century gate. The next staircase leads to the religious centre of Rocamadour, the *enceinte sacrée*. On the right is the old palace of the bishops on the cliff face, while around the little Place St Amadour seven chapels are grouped. Only two are of any great age, the basilica of St Sauveur and the Chapelle St Michel, and neither is of any real architectural interest. The Chapelle St Michel does have two well-preserved Romanesque frescoes in bright colours on the exterior, and frescoes in the choir. To see these and the other chapels, apply at the shop on the square. The rebuilt chapel of Our Lady of Rocamadour contains the famous 'Black Virgin', a twelfth-century black wooden image, surrounded by innumerable offerings from grateful pilgrims. The ancient iron bell hanging from the ceiling is said to ring of its own accord when a miracle is about to take place. Above the doorway is an iron sword embedded in the rock, said to be the famous sword Durendal. In the museum on the square is a varied collection of church plate and other pieces, including some minor Limoges enamels from the Middle Ages and fifteenth-century stained glass.

From the square a tunnel leads to the foot of the castle. A steep path meanders up the hillside to the castle buildings, constructed in the nineteenth century on the site of fourteenth-century chaplains' houses. From the battlements there is a sheer view down over Rocamadour into the gorge below and across to the sparse greenery of the hills of the Causse de Gramat. Though not a place to be by-passed, Rocamadour is, all in all, disappointing; with so much history, and such an aura attached to it, perhaps it is best left to the pilgrims and the curious sub-culture that pilgrimages produce. (It is remarkable how similar Rocamadour is to the shrine of Montserrat in Catalonia: another Virgin, another spectacular site – but much the same uneasy mixture of religion and commerce.)

Retracing our steps to Cales on the N 673, we take a byroad down to **La Treyne,** where, just before the bridge across the Dordogne, to the left, is the entrance to a charming seventeenth-century château in a garden which is for once worthy of the building. The central tower is fourteenth-century, and the entrance façade belies the relaxed seventeenth-century interior. After the wars of religion, which left the castle a ruin, extensive rebuilding took place, but the castle remained unaltered and decaying until the present century. It has now been carefully restored. The furniture includes some Renaissance pieces, but is mostly Louis XIII (early seventeenth-century) which seems to be the usual furnishing for châteaux on the Dordogne, though here it is of good quality. There is a salon of very pleasing proportions, and one room in eighteenth-century style. It is the kind of place which is a house – and not necessarily a very stately one – and which is all the more attractive because it is obviously designed to be lived in. The terrace overhangs the Dordogne in an almost alarming fashion, and the river completes a perfect cameo of house, garden and setting.

A narrow bridge across the river brings us to **Souillac.** The church of the abbey of Ste Marie is to the left of the main road, toward Sarlat. Founded in the tenth century, the church was built in the twelfth century, when the abbots were lords of the town of Souillac and much of the surrounding country. The abbey had a chequered career in the later Middle Ages; the town was taken by English troops and bought back by the Pope, while the countryside's inhabitants suffered from the Plague and from the depredations of the 'Free Companies', bands of mercenary soldiers who owed allegiance only to the highest bidder. A breathing space of a century was followed by the disasters of the wars of religion, when the abbey buildings were burnt, and the church pillaged. Only in the late seventeenth century did the abbey regain something of its old glory. The rebuilding was just completed before the French Revolution; and once again disaster struck, though the church itself suffered only from neglect. Since 1841, when it was classified as a *monument historique,* a continuing programme of restoration has been put in hand, and the latest series of works has just been completed in the apse.

The cupolas of the roof appear on the skyline of the narrow streets, but the entrance is plain, almost fortress-like, as we enter below the ninth-century west tower. An unexpected seventeenth-century porch bears on its ironwork the Benedictine motto 'Peace', a reminder of the period when the abbey was part of the congregation of St Maur (see p. 51). The interior is spacious, with a simple ground plan and little decoration: the removal of the nineteenth-century furniture has revealed the impressive proportions of the nave, with its three cupolas, and has emphasised the plain harmony of the arcading. The apse, with three radiating chapels, has an unusual series of windows, between the chapels and forming a clerestory below the dome, with traces of seventeenth-century frescoes.

But the great glory of Souillac is the former entrance doorway, reconstructed inside the church as the west wall in the seventeenth century. The rich movement of the sculptures is set off by the plain setting of the interior, and they have been protected from the weathering which has caused such damage at Beaulieu. What we see today is a doorway-screen rebuilt from the remains of the old outer doorway after its destruction by the Huguenots. Above the door, from left to right, are St Benedict, holding the manuscript of his monastic rules, a bas-relief, and St Peter. The bas-relief shows one of the more curious episodes of the popular stories of the miracles of the Virgin. Theophilus, a deacon in a Near Eastern church, swears homage to the Devil to regain his post (right), which he has lost with the arrival of a new bishop. Once he is safely installed again he implores the Virgin for aid: she appears from the heavens (centre) and snatches back the scroll recording Theophilus's pact with the Devil. All this is depicted in a hubbub of movement, with a robust portrait of the Devil and little architectural sketches as a background. Even the lobes of the arches above are affected by the swirl of activity.

To the left of the doorway part of a pillar shows a lion and lioness attacking a ram, a theme which reappears at Moissac. A complete pillar to the right has on its outer face a young man and an old man embracing, their figures repeated three times. Facing you as you look into the church is a confusion of birds and beasts, in which the birds' bodies, with their strong diagonal lines, give a pattern to the whole, surmounted by a ferocious vulture attacking a naked man. On the inside a stiffly-clad angel descends with a ram to save Isaac from being sacrificed by his father Abraham: their faces express vividly the situation – Isaac's eyes are closed, and he bows his head in

28. **(previous page)** The prophet Isaiah,, from the portal at Souillac: late romanesque work where the curving ecstatic lines traced by the sculptor seem to make the stone itself flow and vibra

29 & 30 Two views of the ca of Beynac; from the air, showing the rolling hinterland to the north, and from the river Dordogne at the foot of the castle

resignation, while Abraham stares mindlessly into the distance as he carries out Jehovah's command.

In all this there is much fine detail; but for the masterpiece of the Souillac sculptor we must turn to the figure of Isaiah at the foot of the pillar, a graceful dancing image expressing the prophet's joy at the foretelling of the birth of Christ. The sweep of his richly fringed robe balances the curved tension of his body; even the mutilated head is eloquent. It is perhaps the most powerful single composition of the Romanesque sculpture of the south-west, and suggests that had the Souillac carvings survived intact they might well have outshone the glories of Moissac.

From Souillac the road follows the Dordogne valley toward Sarlat. At Rouffiac the D 61 crosses the river to St Julien; a road to the right leads to the castle of **Fénelon** on the edge of the rising ground south of the river. This, the birthplace of Fénelon (see p. 186), is a medieval *château-fort* whose outer walls now enclose a seventeenth-century country house. This is approached by a terrace, and there is a double staircase up to the *cour d'honneur*, which takes the form of a cloister. A little fourteenth-century chapel to the left is matched by a fifteenth-century tower to the right, known locally as the Tour de Confiture or 'Jam Tower' – the improbable explanation given is that during a siege the supplies of boiling oil ran out and boiling jam was poured on the besiegers instead. This tower has a fine *lauze* roof, and the way in which these massive coverings were built can be seen clearly. The room said to be Fénelon's has seventeenth-century furniture, among it a State bed, while the salon is eighteenth-century. There are lovely views from the ramparts.

Just down the road, at **Veyrignac,** is a very different eighteenth-century house (burnt by the Germans in 1944 and recently rebuilt): a single-storey central wing links two-storeyed pavilions. Both plan and decoration are very restrained.

At Le Port we cross back to the north bank of the Dordogne. In **Carsac** the road to Montfort branches off to the left, passing a little Romanesque church surrounded by lime trees. Inside, there are some surprises: beside the primitive Romanesque capitals there is Gothic vaulting and modern stained glass at the east end, both pleasing in their way. From the corniche outside the village there is a view over the loop in the river called the 'Cingle de Montfort', with high cliffs rising behind, and the castle of **Montfort** strategically placed overlooking the valley. It was a key fortress for any military operations in the area, and suffered frequently as a result. It was first destroyed by Simon de Montfort (father of Edward I's opponent, but not connected with the château) in 1214, during his campaign against the Cathar heretics of Languedoc. The present building is the fifth on the site, dating from the sixteenth century; earlier fortresses were rased during the Hundred Years' War, at the end of the fifteenth century and in the wars of religion. One wing was restored in the nineteenth century. The interiors are pleasant, with early furniture, but at every turn it is the wide view of the Dordogne, framed in the windows or spread out in the sunlight on the terrace, that catches the eye. In the garden, the old ramparts and guardhouse survive, as well as a Renaissance staircase flanked by statues.

From Montfort a byroad through La Canéda brings us to the edge of Sarlat.

# Chapter 13

# The Dordogne Valley: Sarlat to Bergerac

✤

**Sarlat** is the main town of southern Périgord, and a good centre from which to explore the most popular part of the Dordogne valley, with castles and villages perched high on the limestone cliffs overlooking the river. This is the area usually meant by the loose term 'Dordogne', well colonised nowadays by English and Dutch owners of holiday homes, and famous for its many good and attractive inns as well as its scenery. Sarlat is a medieval town lying in the hollow of a valley, with a nineteenth-century boulevard driven straight through the old centre, as with so many French towns. Down this road the traffic roars, but to the west the old streets are almost free of cars and full of treasures; many buildings are being lovingly restored.

From the Place du Quatorze Juillet at the southern end of the town, with the eighteenth-century garden, La Grande Rigaudie, on the right, the first turning right off the main street leads to the old bishop's palace, now a theatre, with a delightful loggia on the top storey beside the cathedral doorway, probably built by a sixteenth-century Italian who was bishop here. The cathedral itself is a re-markable mixture. All that remains of the twelfth-century Roman-esque church is the belfry-porch; the rest, already in bad repair in 1321, was demolished in 1504. Attempts to rebuild it, after some initial progress, dragged on until the end of the seventeenth century. The porch was replaced by a massive classical doorway in 1706, and the lantern at the top is also eighteenth-century. Inside, the choir and its radiating chapels are sixteenth-century: the nave was completed in 1683, another example of very late Gothic, with curious pro-portions. Low arches are surmounted by a vast expanse of wall, with small clerestory lights just under the roof. There are one or two good examples of seventeenth-century woodwork to be made out amid the gloom.

Walking round the outside of the cathedral, you will see early tomb niches outside the apse, and, to the south, a quiet little court-yard, once the site of a ninth-century Benedictine monastery. A small Romanesque chapel dedicated to St Benedict has recently been

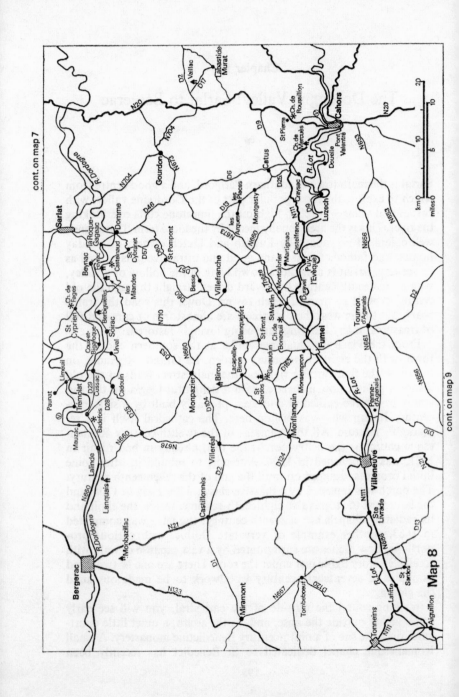

cont. on map 7

cont. on map 9

Map 8

restored, a sanctuary of golden stone and sunlight and dahlias on the altar. Beyond the chapel the canons' buildings form another courtyard round a fountain, once the only source of water in the town.

From the Place du Peyron north of the cathedral a narrow lane, the rue de Montaigne, climbs the hill. To the right is the twelfth-century *lanterne des morts*: this is an unusual example because of its size, and was probably a chapel rather than simply a place of safe-keeping for the coffin. It was certainly dedicated (or re-dedicated) as such in 1693. Local legend avers that it was built to commemorate a miracle performed by St Bernard in 1147, on his return from the cruelties of the crusade against Albigensian heretics. At Sarlat he is said to have consecrated some bread which cured all those who partook of it. There is no means of access to the upper part except by ladder, and even then the apertures are too narrow for a man to enter; but there is room to place a lamp in the four windows.

The alley opposite the *lanterne des morts* leads past a local art gallery to the Présidial, the law court from the sixteenth to the eighteenth century and now a private house. It has a delightful double-arched front with a little ceremonial staircase and delicate ironwork, with a staircase tower to the left and a squat lantern which must once have housed a bell.

Back in the Place du Peyron, the house of Étienne de la Boëtie in the north-west corner is the finest of Sarlat's Renaissance buildings. It was built by Antoine de la Boëtie between 1520 and 1525, and has been thoroughly but carefully restored. Its richly carved façade belongs to the same school as the courtyard at Montal, though here the main gable is relatively plain and only the smaller roof window has a real flourish to it. Otherwise the decoration is mainly on the flat surfaces of the window frames, textured in a variety of patterns. Medallions flanking the main first-floor window include portraits, said to be of the La Boëtie family. Etienne de la Boëtie, born here in 1530 followed a political career, and was also known as a poet and translator of the classics; but he is chiefly remembered as a close friend of the essayist Michel de Montaigne. His premature death at the age of 33 inspired Montaigne's famous essay on friendship. They had met when practising law at Bordeaux; Montaigne had read his work, 'thus preparing the way for that friendship which we preserved as long as God willed, a friendship so complete and perfect that its like has seldom been read of, and nothing comparable is to be seen among the men of our day'.

Next to the Maison de la Boëtie runs the rue de la Liberté. It has a number of half-timbered houses, mostly with modern shop-fronts below: these five-storeyed houses are often only fifteen feet wide. Round the corner the Hôtel de Maleville is occupied by the Syndicat d'Initiative. It was remodelled in the sixteenth century from two or three earlier houses. A formal doorway has portrait medallions of Henri IV and Marie de Medici. From the courtyard (entry on application to the Syndicat d'Initiative) a spiral stone staircase with carvings of angels and shells leads up to the State room, with a monumental chimney with a crest of a stag and two hands against a background of fruit trees and fluted pillars. From the top storey there is a view over Sarlat's varied roofscape of red tiles and moss-grown stone *lauzes*.

Crossing the Place de la Liberté with a pleasant seventeenth-century Hôtel de Ville, past the old church of Ste Marie, now the meat market, the rue des Consuls has more early houses, of which the best is the newly restored Hôtel du Plamon. While work was in progress it was a particular pleasure to watch the tracery of the Gothic windows being pieced together again, replacing dull nine-teenth-century frames. In the next house, which has a marvellous scallop-shell ornament below the balcony on the corner, a vast walnut staircase fills the entire courtyard.

Crossing the rue de la République you come to the eastern half of the town. It has fewer imposing buildings, though much of it is fifteenth- and sixteenth-century, and is slowly being restored. Off the rue des Cordils, about half-way down the rue de la République on the right, is a fifteenth-century watch-tower, in a decaying but attractive group of houses.

Back in the Dordogne valley south of Sarlat, **La Roque-Gageac** is built on the cliff-side, its streets little more than alleys. From the church at the top of the village there is another of the dramatic views which are the hallmark of this part of the river. On the roadside by the river is the Hôtel Belle Étoile, a delightful, fairly simple hotel with a vine-hung terrace on the first floor which is an ideal place for a leisurely lunch on a hot day. Round the next bend in the river is the even more attractive Hôtel Bonnet at **Beynac**, justifiably a favourite haunt of English visitors and usually very busy. On the hill behind it, reached by a long detour by road inland, or by a steep direct foot-path, the castle of Beynac (guided tours every hour on the half-hour; in summer 9.30–11.30, 14.30–18.30; in winter 9.30–11.30, 14.30–16.30) hangs on the edge of the most sheer of all the cliffs of the valley. This eyrie was notorious in the twelfth century, when Mercadier, a famous mercenary soldier-bandit who was one of

Richard the Lionheart's lieutenants, used it as a base; and in 1214 Simon de Montfort the elder burnt it, just as he had done at Montfort further up the river. The castle was rebuilt soon after, and remained in the same family for another 700 years. It was sold, in a ruinous state, in 1960, since when £100,000 has been spent on excellent restorations which are expected to continue for the rest of this century.

The central building is the thirteenth-century keep, perched on the cliff-edge. The entrance gate is of the same period, but there are also sixteenth- and seventeenth-century alterations and additions designed to make the castle more habitable, in contrast with the powerful double defences on the landward side. Some of the rooms have their original woodwork and painted ceilings, while in the vast guardroom, sometimes called the 'salle des Etats' because it was used for the local parliament, a little oratory has a lively set of sixteenth-century frescoes. From the top of the keep there is a dizzying view down into the depths of the river valley nearly 400 feet below.

After Beynac the valley widens out, and the road runs through open country to **St Cyprien,** a little market town huddled below the huge church of its vanished priory, with a Romanesque belfry-porch and Gothic nave. Near the church is the Hôtel de l'Abbaye, modern and fairly expensive. Behind the town the D 48 and a byroad wind up the hillside to the ruins of the **Château de Fages,** once an elegant Renaissance building but now shorn of much of its ornaments. Its interior is now being restored. The windows and chimneypieces show what it must once have been, though the flourishes of the gable-windows have almost entirely vanished. Attempts are being made to preserve the painted walls and gilded ceilings inside, but anything more than partial restoration seems out of the question.

The Dordogne curves broadly to the south, with steep hillsides rising from the narrow roads along the riverbank until Limeuil, where the Vézère flows in from the north-east. **Limeuil** is a delightful backwater of a village, from the broad grassy spaces by the water's edge up through the narrow streets to the church at the top. A mile up the Vézère valley is the isolated church of St Martin, also dedicated to Thomas à Becket, founded in 1194; among the names listed on the foundation inscription is that of Richard the Lionheart. It survives as a simple almost untouched Romanesque building, with stags and a lion pursuing a goat carved on the main doorway, but little other decoration.

In the next valley after Limeuil a byroad runs north to **Paunat,** with an abbey founded in the eighth century. Destroyed by the Northmen in the ninth century, it was rebuilt in the twelfth century; of this building the belfry and east end remain, with a nave of nondescript date and appearance. At the base of the west tower is a simple four-doored porch with a cupola roof and worn paving that lies in uneven waves. Above is a series of defensive rooms, for this was a refuge as well as a place of worship; and the east end has similar defensive spaces above it, as its massive silhouette indicates. The walls, with narrow windows, are as thick as those of a castle. Tucked away in the hollow of a quiet valley full of trees, it seems an unlikely spot for warfare; but nowhere was safe from raiding soldiers in those lawless times.

The road climbs inland, cutting across a loop in the river, before dropping down to **Trémolat**. In the main square a dingy-looking façade conceals a church with a fine row of four cupolas and fortifications. As at Paunat, this is a church with a dual purpose. The nave is eleventh-century, the narrow doorway at the west end (also designed for defence) and the east end are twelfth-century. The inside is fairly spartan, but its simplicity is attractive; the outside is purposefully bare of all detail except the defensive works just below the roofline, which conceal a space of 350 square yards, sufficient for the whole population of the village, above the nave and in the belfry. Arrow-slits give both internal and external firing points: they can be seen in the cupola above the crossing, designed so that any marauders who broke into the church below could be fired at.

On the right as you leave the village heading north is the admirable Hôtel Périgord, which will feed you simply but very well.

Below Trémolat the Dordogne flows more slowly, at first meandering in another great loop round the **Cingle de Trémolat**, used by dinghy sailors and water-skiers. From a water-tower at the head of the loop (off the road up an unmade track) there is a panorama which takes in not only this but much of the hinterland to the north. Beyond Mauzac (with another good inn) the road widens out, as does the valley, and a dull straight stretch brings us to **Bergerac**, a commercial town whose only attraction is a little museum devoted to the tobacco industry (in the rue Neuve d'Argenson).

There is little of interest on the south bank of the Dordogne between Bergerac and Lalinde. Crossing at Lalinde, you find a little road to the left leading to the ruins of the castle of **Lanquais** on the edge of the little village of the same name. A tree-lined avenue leads up to a fifteenth-century tower; behind this massive front is a largely Renaissance courtyard of the late sixteenth century with many delicate details. Another wing was planned but never progressed beyond the foundations. Inside, bare interiors are relieved mainly by the massive ornamental chimneys; the furnishings are indifferent.

A short detour to the south-west brings us to the château of **Monbazillac** on the crest of the line of hills south of the Dordogne valley. This is the most famous of the Bergerac vineyards. Unlike the majority, which produce a full-bodied red wine, Monbazillac is a sweet white wine, often of a very high quality, certainly equal to the sweet white wines of the Loire, and with more character than the honey-smooth wine of Château Yquem, which I personally find too bland. Monbazillac tends to become slightly *madérisé* with age, but in a way which adds to rather than detracts from the wine.

The castle is open to the public (9–12, 13.30–18.30 in summer). Although the exterior has been well restored and is an interesting survival of the feudal military style into the Renaissance, the interior is empty and dull; a bored guide using a tape-recorded commentary does not help. From the terrace there is a wide view over the vineyard, whose products are for sale by the castle gate.

We return to Lanquais, where the D 8 along the south bank leads east to the ruins of the château of Badefols, and at Cales we turn inland to **Cadouin**. The massive façade of the abbey broods over the village square, as if dreaming regretfully of its past glories. Founded by Cistercian monks (who were opposed to the use of ornament – hence its plain appearance) in the early twelfth century, the abbey was consecrated in 1154. It quickly became a place of pilgrimage, because at its foundation it had been given a precious relic, the 'sudary' or 'sindon' in which Christ's head was wrapped when he was laid in the tomb, said to have been found at Antioch by Adhémar of Le Puy, the Pope's legate on the First Crusade. Crowds flocked from all over Europe to venerate the relic; among the pilgrims were Eleanor of Aquitaine and St Louis. The presence of the relic to some extent protected the abbey during the Hundred Years' War, though its removal to Toulouse led to a decline in the monks' fortunes. On its return in the 1450s the rebuilding of the cloisters was put in hand. Despite the fact that the monastery again grew moribund in the sixteenth century the pilgrimages continued; even during the Revolution there was only a short break, and they began again in 1797. Only the cold hand of twentieth-century science brought them to an end: in 1933, when the number of pilgrims was still very considerable, the church authorities called in specialists to examine the sindon. Their report was devastating: it was unquestionably woven in the eleventh century, and the gold Arabic writing in kufic script round the border named an 'emir Musta Ali' and called on the name of Allah! The pilgrimages were suppressed, and Cadouin stands empty save for occasional visitors.

The severe façade is the most impressive of this type to be found in the region, though the real home of this style is Saintonge. The nave and aisles being of equal height, it is four-square, with strong vertical buttresses, relieved only by the arcading at the top. Inside only the very simplest geometrical decoration relieves the simplicity of the barrel vault and plain pillars.

Next door to the church is the cloister (open 8–12, 14.00–19.00), greatly mutilated since its fifteenth-century reconstruction. Something of its former late Gothic glory still comes through the damaged carvings. In the gallery that runs at right angles to the church (the *galerie royale*) notice the Crucifixion doorway on the left. There are four well-preserved capitals, illustrating the story of Lazarus and one of the trials of Job. Above, a series of carved bosses in the vaulting portray Biblical scenes. A more unusual theme is the subject of the carvings near the door of the chapterhouse, the common thread being the trickery of women. Here we find Virgil suspended in mid-air in a basket by his mistress, Aristotle being ridden by a courtesan, Samson betrayed by Delilah.

The next side (the *galerie abbatiale*) has in the centre the abbot's stone chair, with two bas-reliefs on the walls, one showing Christ carrying the cross, the other a procession of monks. Elsewhere, little vignettes show minor and major sins, such as anger (half-man, half-animal, hair on end and shaking its fists) or envy (two peasants quarrelling over a goose). The remaining sides are of little interest; the south side was entirely rebuilt in 1908.

The nearby church of **St Avit-Sénieur** is a witness to the devastation of the Hundred Years' War. Its vast fortified bulk broods over the landscape, with the ruins of the monastery for which it was built beside it. It was the work of the Benedictines in the twelfth century but was given to Augustinian canons in the thirteenth. Despite its defences the war put an end to its prosperity, and the mouldering interior with its Angevin vault looks as though it has scarcely been touched since then. South of St Avit-Sénieur the village of **Montferrand** is built on a steep hillside, with half-timbered houses and an old market hall; one house has a galleried front. Isolated in open rolling hills a mile or two to the west, the church of **Ste Croix** has a simple charm; its apse is covered with *lauzes*, and there is a simple squared dome over the crossing. Its soft silhouette blends into the landscape.

*

We now come to a group of small towns with a very distinct character, the **bastides**. The countryside is studded with these medieval new towns, instantly recognisable by their grid-iron plan, the surrounding fortifications with gates on each side of the square, the central position of the church, and a market-place with covered arcades. Later development may have destroyed a number of these features, but enough of them usually remain to point to a thirteenth-century origin.

The purpose of the *bastides* is still much discussed. Some writers see them simply as strongholds founded to secure the frontier between English and French territory in the middle years of the thirteenth century: but this oversimplifies the picture. For one thing, Montauban near Toulouse is often called an early *bastide*, having been founded in 1144; but it lacks the distinguishing town plan and is almost certainly a simple 'new town'. On the other hand, it was founded because the local inhabitants appealed to their overlord for protection against an oppressive abbot; and this seems to have been a key factor in many *bastides*. The English dukes of Aquitaine and French counts of Poitou encouraged such appeals, because it gave them an opportunity to establish a direct interest where they had previously had only general claims. A *bastide* was often established by *pareage*, an agreement by which rights were divided between the local lord or bishop and the more distant duke or count, to the benefit of the local community. The duke could offer his powerful protection to the new community, while the other party provided the land and organised the building. There seems little doubt that the original purpose of the *bastides* was economic, to encourage settlement and the exploitation of the land, in a period when the region was only sparsely populated. Only as a result of continued warfare in the area did the *bastides* come to have a defensive aspect. This has survived, while the system of agricultural holdings has vanished, and the market-places have lost their importance.

The great period of *bastide* foundations was from 1250 to 1300. On the French side, Alphonse of Poitiers, Count of Poitou, built Villeneuve-sur-Lot, Monflanquin, Castillonnès, Villefranche-de-Périgord and Villeréal. English *bastides* included Sauveterre, Monpazier, Beaumont, and over a hundred more, mostly built by the royal seneschals who administered Aquitaine for Edward I.

West of Montferrand, **Beaumont**, the first *bastide* we reach, was founded in 1272. It has only its western rampart and parts of the original plan. The Gothic church was the core of the defensive system, and its four towers still bear witness to this, despite drastic

203

nineteenth-century restoration. The façade is decorative, with an ornamental gallery above the doorway, but the interior is plain. The market-place, which stands in the usual relationship to the church for a *bastide* plan, still has two sides of its arcades, and the Porte du Luzier, in the stretch of ramparts to the west, is also thirteenth-century; but to the east the grid-plan vanishes into modern streets.

**Villeréal**, to the south, was a French *bastide* founded by Alphonse de Poitiers in 1269, but came into English hands soon after. Its plan is lozenge-shaped rather than square; a number of its original steep-roofed, overhanging houses are preserved. The unusual building on oak pillars in the middle of the market-place, both market hall and town hall at the same time, is sixteenth- and seventeenth-century. The church is thirteenth-century, with a defensive front, its twin towers provided with arrow-slits. The tympanum has an unusual subject: Salome holding the head of John the Baptist. In 1572 the church was besieged by the Huguenots, and its vault was destroyed; what was adequate against medieval methods of warfare was little protection against artillery.

South again from Villeréal, on an abrupt outcrop, rising 300 feet above the Lède valley, is the *bastide* of **Monflanquin**, founded by Alphonse of Poitiers in 1269. It has been spoilt by recent development to the north, but the steep streets radiating from the market-place are little changed, and there is a fortified church similar to that at Beaumont. The vault is of brick, and there is a general change from stone to brick as one moves further away from the Dordogne valley. From the end of the church there is a wide panorama including the castle of **Biron** to the north-east.

We return to Villeréal and take the D 104 along the valley of the river Dropt toward Monpazier, which brings us to the castle of Biron. From below it seems a magnificent building, astride a rocky outcrop. But once you go inside the many vicissitudes of its history are clear. The family of Gontaut-Biron owned it for fourteen generations, and it has only recently passed out of their hands. Originally a feudal fortress, as the twelfth-century gatehouse tower and thirteenth-century lower ramparts indicate, it was remodelled in the sixteenth century by Armand and Pons de Gontaut. The decoration of the gatehouse and much other detail, including the arcade in the main court with its theatrical view over the Dropt valley, are of this period, as is the chapel. This has two storeys; the lower one, for the serfs of the village, is entered from outside the walls, while the castle chapel proper is on a level with the outer courtyard. It contains the splendid tombs of the brothers Gontaut, but the late Gothic retable from the altar is now in New York.

The beginning of the family's misfortunes was the fall from grace and execution as a traitor of Charles de Gontaut in 1602. Only in the eighteenth century were they able to think of restoring the castle to its former glory, and this time the work was barely completed when the revolution of 1789 broke out. Some work was done in the nineteenth century, notably the re-roofing of the chapel, but a fire made the castle uninhabitable. Some restoration work is now in hand; many of the buildings are little more than ruins.

The upper courtyard typifies the curious mixture which this eventful history has produced: twelfth-century keep, seventeenth-century wing (with a fine chestnut roof and a contemporary parquet floor that may just be saved in time), an eighteenth-century pseudo-Renaissance building – all are grouped together. The north side, with the countryside framed in its elegant arcade, is the only part to attract the eye.

Monpazier is the classic example of a *bastide*. Here much of the outer wall and three of the six gates remain, and the ground plan is virtually unchanged. The grid pattern is clear, and as many of the houses still occupy the exact thirteenth-century sites, the system of narrow spaces, called '*androns*', which separated the buildings, can still be seen. These *androns* prevented the spread of fire, always a hazard in medieval towns. A few of the original buildings survive, including the market-place with its arcades, and at No 39 rue Notre-Dame (the main North/South axis) a house with a perfect thirteenth-century façade. In the (much later) wooden market hall the local set of weights and measures is still kept, a reminder of the days when each community had its own, often very different standards. (Those of Troyes in north-east France, 'troy' weights, are still the norm for weighing precious metals.)

Despite its relatively unchanged appearance Monpazier had a troubled existence, both soon after its foundation in 1284 by Edward I and in the sixteenth century. This has left its mark: the church is not the original one, but a largely Gothic building of about 1550. Later disasters included the capture of the town in 1574 by the Huguenots; there was a great assembly of rebellious peasants here in 1594 and again in 1637; and the Revolution left its mark as well, in the form of an inscription over the church door dedicating it to 'L'Être Suprême', focus of the revolutionary cult.

Taking the D 53 and N 710, we return to the south bank of the

Dordogne. Just before the river is the village of **Siorac**, where the Hôtel Scholly should content the hungriest gourmet, at a reasonable price, in a pleasantly old-fashioned dining room. Across the main road the D 50 passes the four-square mass of the **Château de Berbiguières**, a mixture of thirteenth-century keep (with Gothic windows), sixteenth-century wings and a central seventeenth-century building. **Les Milandes**, down by the river, is famous as the home of the music-hall star Josephine Baker, who devoted her earnings on stage to her 'family' of many adopted children of all races (the 'village du monde'). It was built as a 'château de plaisir' in 1489 by the lord of nearby Castelnaud. Heavily restored in the last century, with a number of new carvings added, it offers a mixed bag of contents, from a Boucher portrait of the philosopher Jean-Jacques Rousseau dressed as a musician, to Josephine Baker's bathrooms with gold-plated taps. The formal gardens and terraces are enhanced by their lovely position on the slope of the valley.

Further east the château of Fayrac (not open to the public), a mixture of everything from the thirteenth to the seventeenth century, lurks above the road. At Castelnaud, on the cliff-side, are the crumbling ruins of the château of **Castelnaud**, once one of the most powerful in the region. It was battle-scarred in the Hundred Years' War and the wars of religion, and is said to have been demolished and rebuilt ten times, though the age of the ruins – twelfth- to fifteenth-century – implies that the demolition was only partial. In the evening sun, its huge red ruin glows above the grey-green valley. Much of the masonry is dangerous, but it is still well worth the steep climb, not least for the wide view to the east, across to Beynac and La Roque-Gageac.

Still further east, reached via St Cybranet and a series of hairpin bends, is a very different kind of fortress from the period of the Hundred Years' War. This is Domme, built on a hilltop overlooking the Dordogne, with one of the widest panoramas of all the viewpoints along the river. But before we climb the hill, the church at **Cénac** is worth turning aside to see. All that survives of the twelfth-century church is the apse and the transept chapels. The elegant proportions of these imply that the building must have been an outstanding one: what has survived, however, is a series of over thirty figured capitals. These are difficult to see with the naked eye: binoculars are a great help. Most of them show animals and monsters, some friendly, some hostile, stylised and naturalistic, as if the sculptor was showing his versatility. In the north chapel, a damaged capital may be of Noah and the ark; here also is Daniel in the lions' den, while on either side of the apse arch are the Adoration (damaged) and the Resurrection of Lazarus. Outside, the corbels below the moulding have some equally lively figures.

**Domme** is an exception to the general plan of *bastides* in two respects. It is unquestionably a fortified town, its site being chosen for its military value rather than agricultural reasons; and the hilltop on which it is built forced its planners to adapt the grid-iron pattern to fit the contours. The road from Cénac offers a good view of the surviving fortifications, adapted by the Huguenots during the wars of religion in the sixteenth century. Enter the town by the Porte au Bos; immediately opposite is the house of a thirteenth-century moneyer, responsible for the local coinage. The market square is on the far side of the town: it has lost its arcades, and the only market building is nineteenth-century. This contains the entry to a series of caves, used as a refuge by the inhabitants in the fourteenth- and sixteenth-century wars. Just beyond the market-place stands the church, as is usual in *bastide* plans: this was rebuilt in the seventeenth century. From the edge of the square, a famous and popular view over the Dordogne unfolds. To the west are Beynac and Roque-Gageac, while to the east is Montfort; and behind these are the wooded hills surrounding Sarlat. A path leads along the edge of the cliffs, scene of a dramatic episode in the wars of religion when thirty Huguenots succeeded in taking the town by climbing the sheer rock-face at night and opening the gates to their comrades before the sleeping inhabitants realised what was happening.

On the east of the town, the Porte des Tours is well-preserved, and there is a walk along the ramparts to the south from the Porte de la Combe; here the view is south-east, into Quercy and the country-side round Gourdon.

But before you turn to Quercy, there is one more detour to make, to Besse. To reach this isolated village, take the D 46 and then the D 60 to Villefranche. At St Pompont a byroad forks left, through deep forest, to the hamlet of **Besse**. The history of the church here is lost in the mists of time: it was reputedly part of a very early Benedictine priory. Tucked away above the sparse buildings of the hamlet, the church is best approached from below, where an arch and stairway frame the portal which is its treasure. Dating from the very end of the eleventh century it is an exceptional piece of work in a region where the churches are usually plain and practical; though even here the church is fortified, with a defensive chamber in the roof.

A lozenge-shaped false pediment emphasises the importance of the carvings on the vault of the doorway, and the golden stone stands out richly against an azure sky and the dark-green forests. The sculpture is archaic, almost innocent. The outer band shows, from left to right, Isaiah offered a burning coal by an angel; Eve, the serpent and Adam being questioned by God, followed by the eating of the apple, in which they are shown clothed. The stag hunt which follows is the legend of St Hubert, to whom Christ on the Cross appeared between the horns of a stag. The right-hand side is completed by a Madonna and Child and St Michael and the dragon. Inside the vault a pattern of chains ends in the angel releasing St Peter from prison, while the inner band is a luxuriant growth of palms, with the Lamb as the keystone. All this is carved in a style which seems amateur beside the sculpture of Saintonge; but though it lacks elegance there is a directness about the images which evokes a much deeper past, echoing the figures of Carolingian manuscripts, and even, in the emphasis on the heads, the style of Celtic art. The interior of the church is disappointing, though there are remains of a Gothic fresco of the Crucifixion in the south transept; the figures of two men at arms can be made out above the south door.

From Besse we can either return to Domme or cut across country westward to Salviac, and then along the N 673 to Gourdon.

31. The arcades surrounding the market square at the fourteenth-century **bastide** of Monpazier, south of the Dordogne valley

32. The interior of the castle of Montal at St Jean-Lespinasse near St Céré

33. Cahors: an aerial view showing the fortified bridge (pont Valentré)

34. Cahors: the north doorway of the cathedral, a formal, decorated composition, a very different variety of Romanesque to that at Moissac

# Chapter 14

# Quercy

※

From Domme the D 46 takes us from Périgord back into Quercy, whose northern corner we have already explored in the chapter on the Dordogne valley from Beaulieu to Sarlat. **Gourdon** is a small provincial town; it has a few medieval buildings in the centre, notably just inside the Porte Majou, which leads uphill (past the rue Zig-Zag) to the church of St Pierre, which once stood in the shadow of the castle. Now there is only an open space and a view-point with a plan showing the chief landmarks in the surrounding country. The church is Gothic, with a rose window rather imprac-tically surmounted by battlements. Inside it is spacious and airy, though seventeenth-century woodwork verging on the baroque com-bines uneasily with the soaring lines of the architecture.

On the edge of the town, to the south, the Hostellerie de la Bouriane (called after the local name for this area on the borders of Quercy and Périgord) is a welcoming inn; the building is modern, the food and service in the best old-fashioned style.

Continuing south-east across the N 21, lovers of wild country will find the Causse de Gramat much to their taste. The D 2 to Livernon crosses the heart of the Causse, the same chalky upland with sparse scrublike vegetation that was the background to Rocamadour. Here it is even more remote and empty of life. A detour down the D 17 passes the castle of Vaillac, with five towers dating from the four-teenth and sixteenth centuries, and leads to **Labastide-Murat**, famous as the birthplace of Joachim Murat, the most colourful of Napoleon's lieutenants: a small museum honours his memory. He was the son of the local innkeeper, and was at first intended for the priesthood, but in his early twenties he joined a cavalry regiment instead. After a chequered career of six or seven years he met Napoleon, and helped him to put down the rebellion of 1795 in Paris. He became his aide-de-camp in Italy, where he quickly distinguished himself. By the end of the Egyptian campaign of 1798 his bravery as a cavalry commander had led to a generalship, and in 1800 he married Napoleon's sister. In 1808 he was made King of Naples by Napoleon, but soon began to pursue an independent course. His diplomatic skill was not on a par with his powers of leadership in the field, and although the allied powers were ready to recognise him as king after the fall of Napoleon his mishandling of the situation led to his exile in 1815. A desperate attempt – with a mere thirty men – to regain his throne ended in his capture and execution in southern Italy later that year.

The main road soon becomes a series of steep descents, the approach to **Cahors**. A turning to the left at St Pierre (D 22) leads to a view of the ruined castle of Roussillon. Founded in the twelfth century, the surviving parts are mostly fourteenth-century. It was not remodelled after the fifteenth century, and the lack of comfortable living quarters led to its abandonment; but it is being made habitable once again by its present owner. What remains is very similar to Bonaguil (see p. 215) thirty miles to the west: the end of a line of feudal fortresses, with little hint of the softer style of the Renaissance.

Nearer to Cahors, another turning to the left (V 10) gives a view over Cahors itself, built on a neck of land round which the river Lot forms a horse-shoe bend, with steep cliffs surrounding it – a secure site which in the Middle Ages commanded both road and river. In Roman times it was the site of a local temple to the goddess of the spring, now called the 'Fontaine des Chartreux', on the west bank of the river, and was the capital of the tribe of *Cadurci*, to whom it owes its name. Like all Roman cities it fell into decay after the Frankish invasions, but was rebuilt under the leadership of the bishop, Didier, in the seventh century. Its bishops remained lords of the city throughout most of the Middle Ages, including its golden age in the thirteenth century, though after 1316 their power was shared by the king. In 1159–60 the city was briefly in English hands; Henry II turned aside from his great expedition to Toulouse to take Cahors, and appointed Thomas à Becket, then chancellor, its governor. When Henry returned to England Becket stayed behind to capture the castles of rebellious local barons. Cahors's trade was originally in wine and cloth, but as business expanded it became an important banking centre in the thirteenth century. Branches of the Cahors banks were represented in the Mediterranean ports and at all the great trading fairs, and bankers from Cahors figure frequently in the records of medieval London and 'cahorsin' came to mean 'banker' or 'money-lender'. In 1360, by the Treaty of Brétigny the town was surrendered to the English, although the English commanders had been unable to capture it. It remained in English hands until 1428, but warfare did not help the trade on which its prosperity depended, and by the middle of the fifteenth century it was half-ruined and empty of people. Worse was to come in the sixteenth century: a rebellion against Henry of Navarre, its lord, led to a siege which ended in his taking the town in 1580. After he became king, in 1589, he removed Cahors's privileges as a wine-market, and it sank to the level of a minor provincial town.

The entrance to the town is guarded by the remains of a line of fortifications which in the Middle Ages cut off the narrow point of the loop of the river. All that remains are a gatehouse and a tower on the riverbank, to the left of the road. A little further down, on the left, are the church of St Barthélemy and the one remaining tower of the bishop's palace. St Barthélemy is a gloomy Gothic building and the tower is impressive only because of its height; but they are both connected with one of Cahors's most famous inhabitants, Jacques Duèze, later Pope John XXII. As adviser to Pope Clement V he recommended the suppression of the Templars in 1310; it is interesting that, like the Cahorsins, the Templars were also international bankers, but in the end it was the northern Italian bankers who took over the Templars' role. On Clement V's death Jacques Duèze was elected pope after a conclave lasting over three months. He proved an ardent champion of papal rights, and did much to restore both the finances and the prestige of the Church, though his reign was marred by a long quarrel with the Franciscans over the rule of poverty. The new taxes which he imposed on Christians everywhere were also unpopular, though, unlike many medieval popes, he did not make any personal fortune from them. He founded a university at Cahors in 1331, which survived until 1751. His brother, Pierre Duèze, Bishop of Cahors, was the builder of the palace next to St Barthélemy, though it is usually called after the pope.

Across the other side of the Place Thiers, behind a modern school building, is a second-century Roman arch, known as the '*porte de Diane*'.

Another famous citizen of Cahors is commemorated in the name of the busy boulevard which divides the old town in two: Léon Gambetta, who was largely responsible for the political recovery of France after the disasters of the Franco-Prussian war and the fall of Napoleon III. To the right, behind the Palais de Justice, the Musée Municipale is largely devoted to mementoes of John XXII and Gambetta, a bearded, swashbuckling figure, as also of Clément Marot, one of the circle of Marguerite de Navarre and the greatest poet of the time. His translations of the psalms and his witty secular verse are the first reflection in French literature of the Reformation and the Renaissance respectively. Most of his career was spent in Paris, with periods of exile in Italy and Geneva.

To the east of the Boulevard Gambetta is the **Cathedral**. Despite the ravages of the troops of Henry of Navarre in 1580 and of the revolutionaries in the 1790s, much of the medieval fabric, dating back to the eleventh century, survives. It is a massive building, almost as much castle as cathedral, just as its bishop was also a secular lord of substance. It stands behind the narrow alleys of the old town; there is no impressive approach or distant view, but the sudden presence of the cliff-like west façade, a Gothic structure deliberately built as a protective screen around the earlier nave. The earlier façade was transferred to the north doorway, where it survives almost undamaged, a marvel of Romanesque sculpture. Above it looms one of the domes of the roof, then a nondescript band of half-bricked-up windows, until the eye is led down to the delicate stripes of rosettes which flank the (rebuilt) vault of the arch. Apart from a curious frieze of struggling, fighting men round the outer arch only the tympanum is decorated, though it seems unlikely that this was the original scheme. The composition is formal, divided into arcaded panels; but it is the figures that catch the eye, moving in an ecstatic frenzy or in stately groups. There is not a single still point among them: even the central figure of Christ seems about to step forward out of the central mandorla. Around him the angels perform a kind of dervishes' dance of worship. To left and right are scenes from the legend of St Stephen, to whom the cathedral is dedicated: the lower right panel shows his martyrdom by stoning. Beneath the lower arcade, with its Moorish arches and battlements, the apostles and the Virgin are grouped in animated conversation. The style of the sculptor owes something to Moissac, something to the tympanum at Carennac; but in the last analysis this is an individual masterpiece which needs no pedigree.

Inside the cathedral the architecture becomes a jigsaw puzzle of different periods, the differences glossed over by a heavy-handed restoration in 1870. Even so the domes of the roof, built in the late eleventh or early twelfth century, survive to dominate the whole; their scale and elegance is all the more surprising when we learn that they are probably the earliest examples of this kind of vault in Western architecture, and only the dome of Hagia Sophia in Constantinople surpassed them in size. The paintings are sixteenth-century, but, in spite of their late date, very striking. The apse roof was rebuilt in the thirteenth century but retains its early-twelfth-century walls with simple capitals on the pillars. A door to the south opens into the Gothic cloister, which sadly lacks much of its tracery and almost all its carvings, destroyed by the Huguenots in 1580. Above it broods the incongruous yet highly individual roofscape of the cathedral, the slate-covered domes shimmering like steel in the sun.

In the cloisters and in the Gothic work in the cathedral the themes of sunbursts, roses and lopped trees appear: and they recur in the **Maison de Roaldes,** to the south of the cathedral on the riverbank. This late-fourteenth-century house (now an antique shop) has a stone north façade of *circa* 1500, and an earlier courtyard front, galleried and half-timbered. It belonged to the Roaldes family until the 1870s; ruined by the destruction of their vineyards by the dreaded phylloxera disease, they emigrated to New Orleans, but one of the family returned in 1912 and bought the house back. It has two of its original chimneypieces, two from elsewhere, and a spiral staircase with an architectural curiosity: three immediately adjoining doors on the wall of the spiral.

A leisurely walk of about a mile round the curve of the river brings us to the most spectacular of Cahors's monuments, the **Pont Valentré,** built between 1308 and about 1360. It is reputed never to have been taken by storm, even in the siege of 1580. Its three towers rise 120 feet above the river, and it is the finest surviving example of the fortified bridges which were once common in medieval cities. Restoration in 1879 deprived it of the barbican which defended it from attack from inside the town; and there was a similar defensive work on the far bank, making it a kind of castle perched above the river. The gates and portcullises have also disappeared. The central part is little changed, however; the height of the towers made them excellent look-out points, as can be seen from the top of the central one.

From the far side of the Pont Valentré the D 8 to the right runs along the valley of the Lot, below the Château de Mercuès on the north bank, now a luxury hotel, to Douelle and **Luzech.** Luzech's castle is ruined, and restoration work aimed at making the walls safe is in progress. It is on the neck of a horse-shoe bend in the river, like Cahors; but at Cahors the whole isthmus is built on, while here the town fades into deep meadows. A track leads to the little chapel of Notre Dame de l'Isle, in a marvellously isolated site in the shadow of a ring of cliffs, its flamboyant Gothic doorway a jewel of artifice in a setting of purely natural beauty.

From Luzech a detour to the north, along the D 9 to Creyssac, leads to the little town of **Catus,** in the hills behind the river valley. Behind the church is the old chapterhouse of a vanished Benedictine priory, with an elaborate central pillar hidden by a cage of scaffolding which supports the sagging vault. The details of the capitals can just be made out, a calling of St Peter shown in two scenes: to the south, Christ gives him the keys, while on the west side a group of apostles watches the scene with lively interest. The decorative carving is also of fine quality. I hope restoration and repair will soon reveal this attractive, quiet place in its true glory.

North of Catus the D 13 and a byroad lead to **Les Arques,** where in a decaying village the little Romanesque church has been carefully resurrected from the débris. The interior is bare, with lovely proportions, simple detail, and warm stone; but appealing though it may be to a modern eye its medieval builders would have lamented the absence of colour and rich altar furnishings. Nearby, on the south side of the church at Goujournac, there is a magnificent Christ with the four evangelists in rustic style, carved from a dark-orange stone.

Retracing our steps to the valley of the Lot, we find **Puy l'Evêque,** perched on the edge of a cliff above the river, its steep streets often no more than flights of steps between the houses. Above the town is a Gothic church with a huge belfry-porch, like that at Martel. The Hôtel Bellevue lives up to its name, with as wide an expanse of plain and river spread out before the bedroom window as you could wish to find. In the hills behind Puy l'Evêque Martignac has a church with fifteenth-century frescoes, discovered in 1938 (closed for restoration 1973). At Montcabrier the church has a good flamboyant doorway. The narrow roads curve round the hillsides through forests and little hilltop villages asleep in the sun, a world away from the industry and intensive farming down by the river.

Back on the main road **Duravel** has a Romanesque church with a remarkable crypt. It is worth seeking out the curé and getting the key to see this (though the search may be an elaborate business – start at the nearby post office, which may be able to help). The Abbot of Moissac founded a monastery at Duravel in the late eleventh century, and sent the relics of three minor saints, early Christian hermits in Egypt, to enhance the new priory. It was these that formed the focal point of the crypt. Around the priory grew up a settlement which by the fourteenth century had become an important town. It was besieged in 1369 by Sir John Chandos and Sir Robert Knolles, but its stout fortifications (including a defensive belfry-porch on the church, demolished in 1884) resisted the English onslaughts. In 1616, after much damage had been caused by Huguenots in the wars of religion, the priory was disbanded, and the church became a simple parish church.

The upper church has been much restored, and only the south transept has frescoes, with a sequence of scenes showing demons lurking in wait for sinners and torturing those who fall into their clutches. At the end of the apse is a sarcophagus which still contains the remains of the three saints. The crypt, below the crossing, is barely twelve feet square, with four central pillars and a niche in which the relics rested until the press of pilgrims grew too great. The capitals are almost all simple: crude reworkings of classical themes, they belong to the beginning of Romanesque art. One has the early Christian emblem of the peacock, symbol of the soul, standing by a palm tree. The base of the same pillar shows a coiled snake. The whole scene is an interior that has remained unchanged for nearly a thousand years.

Below Duravel a byroad climbs over the crest of the hill and descends steeply to the valley of the river Thèze. At St Martin le Redon, a road turns north-west to the castle of **Bonaguil** (guided tours in June, July, August at 10, 11, 15.00, 16.00, 17.00, 18.00; in April, May, September at 10.30, 14.30, 15.30, 16.30) which appears through the trees to the right of the road, an image so unexpected in a peaceful valley that it seems like the fantasy of some cinema mogul. Its builder was a late-fifteenth-century lord, Berenger de Roquefeuil, who, in an age when his fellow-nobles were more interested in creating pleasure-palaces, expressed his own violent and reactionary character by building a model feudal fortress. He is said to have been threatened by the king, Louis XI, with confiscation of all his lands, and to have built Bonaguil so that he could resist an assault by the royal army itself. The result, which took forty years to build, starting in 1477, would have needed an assault by ten thousand men to capture it. It incorporated all the latest and most ingenious thinking in military engineering. The site was chosen because the outcrop of rock is impossible to undermine, while artillery of the period, if brought up to sites on the surrounding hills, had not got sufficient range to do any damage. There is even provision against such stratagems as the poisoning of the castle well by the enemy, in the shape of reserve water supplies in cisterns.

The entrance is at the point where the spur of land joins the hillside nearest to the castle. This, potentially the weakest spot in the defences, is guarded by a massive barbican, large enough to be a fortress in its own right, and with immensely thick walls. It was in fact designed to be separately garrisoned and supplied, and has an escape passage to the inner keep in case of disaster. An internal moat protected the central group of buildings, parts of which were pulled down at the Revolution. However, the main military buildings were too massive to be demolished, and all that was lost were the living quarters to the west and east. The keep is a curious narrow diamond-shape, designed so as to offer as small a target as possible to enemy artillery, the long sides being screened by the now vanished buildings. Also to the west is the enormous 'great tower', a hundred feet high, with walls as massive as those of the barbican. Everywhere in the doorways and passages are concealed openings so that invaders could be held at bay by a mere handful of men. Only a commander prepared to sacrifice thousands of men could have seized the castle, even if it had been defended by a force a tenth the size of the attackers. The doorways are also deliberately narrow, so that only one or two men can enter at a time. Round the outside walls are elaborate arrangements for raking fire which could cover all possible angles of attack. Not surprisingly, no one ever tried to attack Bonaguil: it is one man's folly, a fastness-retreat, rather than a fortress which guards an essential strategic route. Indeed, in terms of military theory, it was already out of date when it was built, in an age when warfare was more and more a question of mobility. Berenger de Roquefeuil might be proof against any military action at Bonaguil; but he would never have defeated his enemy. In a sense, this was all he hoped for – freedom from the king's interference was his purpose, rather than aggressive action against the king.

It is a rude shock to come away from Bonaguil to the industrial chaos of Fumel and an unattractive stretch of road to **Monsempron**. Above the road, however, the church of Monsempron brings back a more peaceful atmosphere. It is not prepossessing from outside; but the interior recalls the almost theatrical atmosphere of St Hilaire at Poitiers. A line of massive pillars support a simple ribbed barrel vault in the nave, whose narrow sight-line focuses on the raised sanctuary and crossing, where the pillars rise to the base of the roof vault, as a setting for the inner shrine. Alas, in the fourteenth century the Romanesque apse was remodelled as a light and airy Gothic east end, and the real power of the earlier architect's ideas can only be found by turning one's back on the altar and looking west down the nave. (The nave is a seventeenth-century reconstruction, but to all appearances a faithful one.) Better still, turn to the chapel in the south transept; three pillars, two windows, a ribbed vault – simplicity itself, but made into a thing of beauty by the delicate use of carved patterns (round the windows and the arch of the opening) which glow in the slanting sunlight. The few figured capitals here and elsewhere are crude beside the elegant formality of the bands of geo-metrical patterns. The outside of the apse, despite the Gothic rebuilding, retains something of the effect of rising tiers of curved roofs designed by the original builders.

North of Monsempron a country road climbs over a ridge of hills and curves down into the Lède valley, where there is a group of interesting villages. At **Gavaudun,** on a rock spur above the road, is the keep of a medieval castle. The entrance is by a narrow path near the school which threads its way up the rock face, ending in a staircase cut through the rock. The keep, which dates from the twelfth to fourteenth centuries, has been excellently restored, with two or three complete rooms: seen through the simple stone window-tracery, the river winds lazily along the valley below. Apart from the keep, some of the defensive works to the north-west also survive. At St Sardos de Laurenque the west door of the church has a very simple and pleasing frieze of fishes and monsters, and the church is set in a little cemetery surrounded by neat box hedges. We rejoin the N 701 along the Lemance valley near St Front-sur-Lemance. At St Front the church has its original Romanesque apse, with blind arcades below and matching arcading around the small windows. Outside the apse wall has three plain buttresses, and presents a sober, almost severe aspect: a fourteenth-century defensive tower beside it almost enhances this fortress-like east end.

At **Blanquefort-sur-Briolance,** to the north, the early-twelfth-century church has a simple plan – a small choir and broader nave – with one remarkable feature: two massive projections by the chancel arch which supported a belfry. They are hollowed out to provide two side-altars, each contained in its own little vault. This arrangement made the provision of transepts less necessary; but it was only used in early Romanesque churches, and very few examples have survived, because the addition of transepts was an obvious way of enlarging a church in succeeding centuries.

Returning down the N 710 to Fumel, you take a dull main road along the Lot valley to **Villeneuve-sur-Lot.** This was once a *bastide* commanding the crossing of the river, which flows through the town between high walls. The old bridge, built in the thirteenth century, can be seen from its modern replacement upstream. The old post of the town watchmen, the medieval Viguerie, survives, though it has been badly altered on the ground floor, and there are also two of the original brick-built gates. A modern brick church dedicated to St Catherine has a series of stained-glass windows of the school of Auch (see p. 241). The main road continues to Ste Livrade, whose church has an apse with an arcade on the outside, much in the style of those of the Médoc.

Down the D 13, to the left, is the village of St Sardos, originally a monastic settlement. Here in 1323 Charles IV of France authorised the building of a *bastide*. The English seneschal of Gascony challenged his right to do this, as it lay within the Gascon lordship. St Sardos was attacked and burnt in November of that year (with the help of the Lord of Monpezat), and Charles, relying on his authority as overlord, hauled those responsible before his court. Edward II, unwilling to go to war, was ready to patch up the quarrel, but seems to have been unable to control affairs in Gascony. As a result, war broke out in August 1324. It ended a year later with the surrender of the region round Agen to the French, and Prince Edward's (later Edward III) installation as Duke of Gascony. If Charles IV had really so wished he could easily have driven out the English altogether, and ended the English presence in France before the Hundred Years War had even begun.

The church at St Sardos is the only relic of the priory around which the new *bastide* was built. It has a fine north doorway, with a frieze of monsters and serpents over the door. Inside, a huge Romanesque capital, carved with a scene of Daniel in the lions' den, has been hollowed out for use as a font.

Back on the N 666, we come to Aiguillon, on the junction of the river Lot and the river Garonne, whose only monument of note is a château rebuilt in 1765.

# Chapter 15

# The Pays d'Albret, Agen and Moissac

❧

We now follow the Garonne valley, with a brief excursion to the edge of the forest of the Landes, eastwards, back into the hills of Lower Quercy, a countryside of deep, rounded valleys and hilltop towns looking across wide expanses of landscape.

But first, at Aiguillon, we cross to the south bank of the Garonne and take the D 8 to Damazan. To the left of the road beyond Damazan (D 108), just before Villefranche de Queyran, are the ruins of the **Chapelle St Savin**. Its apse still has its roof, sheltering what is left of a Romanesque church of high quality. Round the choir and apse is a blind arcade of powerful squat pillars with worn but elaborate capitals: among the subjects are the Temptation of Eve and the Flight into Egypt. The spacious windows are walled up but the sunlight floods the interior as effectively from the ruined west end. Outside is the usual amazing French cemetery, whose own strange art-forms owe nothing to Romanesque restraint.

South of Damazan, near Buzet-sur-Baise, the village of **St Pierre de Buzet** has an almost unaltered twelfth-century church, whose severe lines reflect the Cistercian ideal of a church without decoration. The interior is marred by a nineteenth-century painted pattern of stonework, which will distract all but the most expert eye from the original lines of the building. The outline of the west end is pleasing in its simplicity.

The N 642 leads to **Vianne**, an English *bastide* founded in 1284 and set, unusually, by the riverside. There is a magnificently-preserved outer wall, complete with two of its five towers, to north-west and south-west, and four gates in the centre of each side of the square of ramparts, probably the finest example of *bastide* defences to have survived. The inside plan is also partly preserved, but most of the houses have been rebuilt. The church has the usual fortifications, and a restrained theme of foliage as the only decorative carving.

West of Vianne is **Xaintrailles**, whose twelfth-century castle was

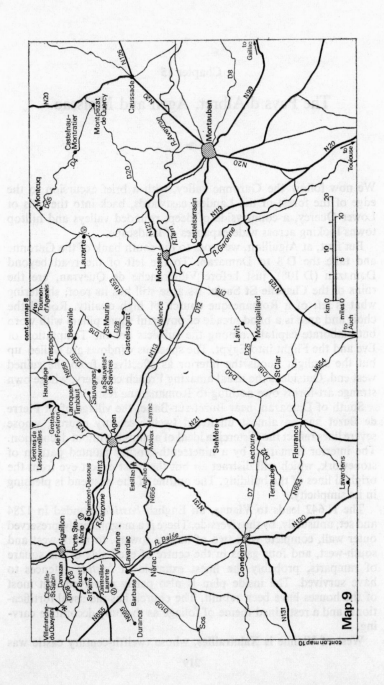

cont. on map 8

cont. on map 10

**Map 9**

Caussade

Montauban

to Gaillac

to Auch

to Toulouse

N20

N126

D8

N99

N113

N127

R. Tarn

R. Aveyron

R. A. Aveyron

Castelsarrasin

Moissac

R. Garonne

N20

D20

Castelnau-Montratier

Montpezat de Quercy

Montcuq

D4

D65

D7

Lauzerte

to Tournon d'Agenais

N653

St Maurin

Beauville

Frespech

Hautefage

D656

Grottes de Lestournelles

Grottes-de-Fontiron

N21

Laroque-Timbaut

Sauvagnas

La Sauvetat-de-Savères

D25

D28

D18

Castelsagrat

Valence

D12

Lavit

Montgaillard

D25

St Clair

D18

D40

Lectoure

D7

SteMère

Fleurance

Terraube

Lavardens

N654

N21

Moirax

Layrac

Astaffort

Aubiac

Estillac

Clermont-Dessous

N113

N656

Agen

Marie

Porte Ste.

R. Garonne

Aiguillon

Vianne

Lavardac

Nérac

Barbaste

R. Baïse

Condom

Durance

Sos

Buzet

St Pierre

Xaintrailles-Lauerte

N655

N665

Chapelle-St Sabin

Damazan

Villefranche-du-Queyran

D108

D3

D109

N130

N131

N238

km

miles

20

10

5

0

rebuilt in the mid-fifteenth century by Pothon de Xaintrailles, replacing the original keep by a still practical but much more elegant piece of architecture. From here there is a view across the huge forest of the Landes, and a detour down a byroad takes us to **Durance**, on the edge of this new landscape. This was once a *bastide*, but little is left of it; nor is there much more of the castle where Henri IV used to come and hunt. A local story tells how he once lost his way at the end of a day's hunting, and found himself at a charcoal-burner's hut. In return for his night's lodging he offered to take the charcoal-burner to Durance to see the king. As they rode into the courtyard, the charcoal-burner riding pillion with his arms round the king's waist, there were peals of laughter as well as the peals of the royal trumpets. Henri turned to the charcoal-burner and said, 'Now you know who the king is!' 'Yes,' said the charcoal-burner, 'it's either you or me.'

There is an excellent inn at Durance, La Palombière, which will make up for any archaeological disappointments.

There are more traces of Henri IV at **Barbaste**, for this is the **Pays d'Albret**, which he inherited from his mother, Jeanne d'Albret. The mill here is an extraordinary fortified building, not improved by being used as a factory. Built in the fourteenth century, it was a favourite residence of Henry's when he visited this part of the world. It certainly deserves to be rescued from its present fate, before its four towers and elaborate system of arrow-slits are completely beyond repair. Downstream from the mill is a thirteenth-century bridge, once equipped with a drawbridge at either end, so that the road could quickly be barred to an approaching enemy from either direction. This was the real reason for the fortification of the mill which acted as a defensive position against any serious attack on the bridge.

Across the river is **Lavardac**, a French *bastide*, founded in 1268 as a rival to Vianne; but nothing of its old aspect remains. We turn right for **Nérac**, the capital of the pays d'Albret, a charming small market town with a number of relics of its brief period of glory as one of the centres of the court of Navarre. It was acquired by the lords of Albret when a Benedictine monastery turned to them for protection in the twelfth century. But the monks found that they had only made matters worse, and in 1306 abandoned their claims to Nérac to their erstwhile protectors. In the sixteenth century a splendid castle and park were Nérac's chief attraction; but of this only a wing of the castle and a long walk beside the river remain. The remainder of the castle was demolished during the Revolution, and the park was sold off at the same time. The surviving wing, with an arcaded Renaissance front with twisted pillars, is now a museum of local history. The interiors have a little of their former glory: those on the ground floor have fine vaulted ceilings. As you walk down from the château to the river the 'promenade de la Garenne' is to the right. This is said to be the setting Shakespeare had in mind when writing *Love's Labours Lost*, described in the First Folio as 'Navarre. A Park, with a palace in it.' The play is clearly intended to be in French rather than Spanish Navarre, and Marguerite d'Angoulême's court at Nérac was one of the literary centres of Renaissance France. Here she, helped perhaps by one or two of the courtiers, wrote her *Heptameron*, a collection of stories modelled on Boccaccio's *Decameron*. She inclined to Protestantism and welcomed Calvin to Nérac; her daughter, Jeanne d'Albret, declared openly for the Protestant cause in 1562. But beside this more severe tradition that of a gay and often licentious court continued, and the court of Henry IV's day could indeed have furnished details for *Love's Labours Lost*. The shady walk by the river with its little fountains set into the hillside seems a fitting spiritual home for Ferdinand, Biron and the 'fantastical Spaniard', Don Armado. On the other bank an octagonal pavilion marks the site of the royal baths.

Opposite the château, on the slopes of the river, a maze of old streets with overhanging houses is known as Petit-Nérac, in contrast to the spacious but dull modern town. Below it is the old humpbacked bridge, all much as it was at the end of the sixteenth century. There is a good view of this from the terrace by the church of St Nicolas, behind the château. The church itself, a severe classical building, was designed by Louis, the eighteenth-century architect responsible for the theatre at Bordeaux. As a Protestant stronghold, Nérac was badly affected by the revocation of the Edict of Nantes in 1687, which sent many Protestants into exile. It has never recovered its past importance.

From Nérac, we take the N 130 to Port Ste-Marie, which has some fine half-timbered houses. To the left of the road beyond Port Ste-Marie we come to the first of the hilltop strongholds of Lower Quercy: its name, **Clermont-Dessous** (Lower Clermont) belies its position, but the 'lower' means downstream of Agen. The site, approached by a steep and narrow road, is indeed spectacular; but the village itself has been too actively restored, and although visitors now provide a new source of livelihood for the villagers it feels more like a museum of folklore than a living community. None the less, the old citadel and its fortifications are largely intact, and the old village street, with low medieval houses on either side, is delightful.

A fast, dull road leads to **Agen**, which at first sight seems to be no more than a busy commercial town, centre of one of the chief fruit-growing areas of France. Its particular speciality is prunes; these are delicious, quite unlike those usually to be found in England, with a much richer and sweeter taste. But Agen has more to offer the visitor than culinary souvenirs. The museum, in two sixteenth-century town houses, is very well laid out, the attractive interiors used as the

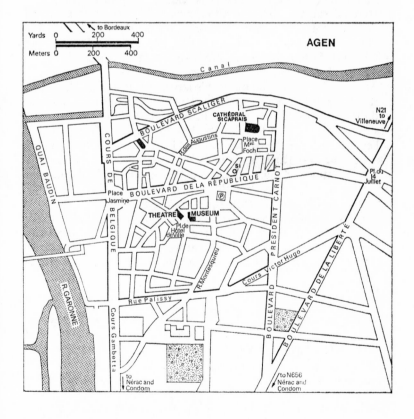

setting for a spacious display. In the old cellars are prehistoric exhibits, but the choicest pieces are those in the Roman section on the ground floor, like the famous Venus de Mas, found at Le Mas d'Agenais south of Marmande in 1876. It is a glorious figure, balancing sensuality against divinity, despite its surprisingly small scale. There is also a well-characterised statue of Silenus, the companion of Bacchus. Also on the ground floor is the medieval collection, including the tomb of Etienne de Durfort, a sixteenth-century monument with curious bas-reliefs of saints round the base which seem to be in pure twelfth-century style – either an extreme example of traditional style surviving in a country district or perhaps a re-use of earlier sculptures. On the first floor is the earliest part of the picture collection, including an outstanding group of Goyas: a self-portrait, a subject from Los Caprichos, and a scene of a hot-air balloon ascent. The pictures continue on the third floor with Impressionist and post-Impressionist works. There are two Boudins and a delightful Sisley, *September Morning*. From the tower there is a view over the old quarter of the town.

At ground level the old quarter is largely commercialised, though parts of the old arcades remain in the streets between the museum and the cathedral of St Caprais. The old cathedral of St Étienne was destroyed during the Revolution, but St Caprais, founded as a collegiate church in the twelfth century, has almost as long a history. The exterior of the apse is the work of a master sure of the style in which he was working, achieving a perfect ensemble despite the difference in volume between the chapels and the main body of the building. Inside, the Romanesque sculptures are obscured by a remarkable set of nineteenth-century wall paintings. Anathema to the purists, who would dearly love to remove them, they have their own sense of colour and majesty, and are worth keeping not merely as curiosities, but as one of the better attempts to revive the Romanesque skills.

Agen is a good base from which to explore both Lower Quercy and the north of the Gers. South of Agen, across the Garonne, the road to Auch skirts **Layrac,** whose centre lies in the fork of the junction of two main roads. At the Auberge La Terrasse, which has very basic rooms but an excellent restaurant, there is no hint of the passing traffic, merely a panorama north across the Garonne. Nearby is the church, whose deep entrance doorway and massive walls contain a simple barrel-vaulted interior on an unusually large scale, a kind of magnified village church. Its exceptional dimensions are explained by its origin as part of a Cluniac priory. The architecture reaches its climax in the nine-bayed apse; on the apse floor are the remains of a rare and splendid eleventh-century mosaic, showing Samson killing the lion. All this has been well restored, though the huge seventeenth-century baldachino in the crossing strikes an incongruous note.

For pure twelfth-century simplicity, even better cared for than at Layrac, and without any such distractions, we must go to **Moirax**, five miles to the north-east, high up in the hills. Again, this is a Cluniac priory. The nave, sober and restrained, is that of the original church. Early in the twelfth century an ambitious new east end was planned, with a gallery round the transepts. This was abandoned for a simpler design, though parts of the incomplete work show below the Gothic vaults of the present crossing, which seem to have been inserted beneath the level of the Romanesque roof, actually decreasing the height of the building. The most unusual dome above the choir has a (rebuilt) lantern and two curious oculi to east and west, perhaps also traces of a more elaborate scheme. Today the building appeals to the eye by its perfect symmetry, the harmony of its proportions and the warmth of the newly-cleaned stone. The details include some engaging, primitive capitals: in the north transept, a family of toy-like lions peers inquisitively down from one pillar. The only decoration is the seventeenth-century choir stalls by a sculptor from Gourdon in Quercy, now mounted on the nave walls.

A little lane just south of Moirax plunges off to the right across the valley to **Aubiac,** whose church presents a severe façade to the world. Its three towers and mixture of styles are in strong contrast to the unity of Moirax. The western and central towers and the nondescript nave are of little appeal, but the choir and the lantern-tower above it are of quite a different order. Although the simplicity of the arcades and vault of the lantern look very early, they are probably twelfth-century, in a very archaic style for the period which harks back to the churches of Charlemagne's day. Three equal chapels open out below the lantern, lit partly from the tower windows and partly by their own narrow openings. The homely figures in the vault of the tower are seventeenth-century, but enhance rather than detract from this rustic yet ambitious architecture.

On the road back to Agen the castle of **Estillac** appears to the left, its silhouette deprived of the defences which protected it in the days of its most famous owner, the general and writer Blaise de Monluc. However, the bulk of these plain buildings are as they were in the sixteenth century. The lower stages of the towers have sloping stone-work as protection against artillery fire and are windowless, for this was very much a fortress. Outside the walls, in the park, a marble effigy of Monluc in armour lies between two cypresses. Both effigy and château underline their owner's military fame. Born into a poor but noble Gascon family, Monluc recorded his own exploits in his *Memoirs*, telling how after an apprenticeship in the Italian wars he won recognition in the French campaign in Piedmont in 1544. Soon after he besieged the English at Boulogne and Calais, and was put in charge of coastal defence against English attacks. His career reached its apogee in 1554 with his stubborn resistance at Siena in face of a six-month siege, but the wars which followed in the next decade were civil, not foreign: after toying with the Huguenot party for a time Monluc became the Catholic commander in the south-west. His severe and often brutal methods served only to stiffen Huguenot resistance, and after five years even his own allies grew weary of him; he was dismissed and a commission of inquiry set up. It was in answer to these charges that he wrote his *Memoirs*, empha-sising his past services to France, and he was not only cleared but died in 1574 a Marshal of France. Bridging the age of chivalry and the harsher times of early modern warfare, Monluc is a contradictory figure; but his Gascon eloquence and colourful career make the *Memoirs* well worth reading.

To the north of Agen the borders of the old provinces of Guyenne and Quercy may lack spectacular monuments, but offer instead the charm of unexpected delights, chiefly unspoilt medieval villages and some of the loveliest and least-known scenery in south-west France. Off the N 21, between Agen and Villeneuve, there are also two caves containing limestone formations, at Fontiron and Lestournelles. But, for the villages, take the N 656 toward Tournon d'Agenais. Five miles out of Agen a small side-road to the right climbs to Sauvagnas, whose church is that of a commandery of the Knights Hospitallers. Laroque-Timbault, across the main road on the D 103, has old houses and the remains of a castle, to the left as you enter the town. Hautefage, on the same road, is grouped round a hexagonal tower which was originally designed as a residence for the bishops of Agen, built by two Italian holders of that see between 1487–1538. It was never finished, and is now the belfry of the nearby church.

North of Hautefage the road drops down into the valley of the little river Lartigue, and a turning to the right leads to **Frespech**. This appears as a tightly-knit group of houses to the left of the road; in fact, it occupies the site of a medieval castle, whose barbican and outer walls survive to the north and have recently been well restored, as have the remaining buildings within the castle enclosure. Next to the little church is a delightful little fifteenth-century half-timbered house, which looks as if it might have belonged to the same family ever since it was built. The barbican frames a perfect view across the Lartigue valley, an almost deserted yet far from inhospitable country-side of sloping woods and rich valleys. The church, at first glance severe, has one of those warm stone roofs on the apse, formed of half-round stones like scales: the interior is simple, with four primitive capitals at the crossing, and has hardly changed since it was first built as the castle chapel in the twelfth century. Altogether this is a quiet and unspoilt corner, not yet overwhelmed by visitors; a world away from Clermont-Dessous despite the active signs of restoration.

Returning to the Hautefage road, turn right to **Penne d'Agenais,** standing high above the plain with a commanding position over the River Lot. A natural fortress, it still retains its outer wall and three gateways. One of these has part of its battlements and crenellations (Porte de Ferracap) while the town gate is flanked by a thirteenth-century house with Gothic windows. Inside the walls is a late-fifteenth-century fortified house, which tradition has made much older, pushing it back a mere thousand years to the period of Alaric the Visigoth! Repeated sieges – in 1212 by Simon de Montfort the elder, in 1372 by the French (when it was an English stronghold) and in 1562 by Blaise de Monluc (see p. 226) – have left only a few fragments of the much-rebuilt castle. Yet despite these medieval riches it is a modern building which stands out sharply at the first sight of the town from the valley below, the basilica of Notre Dame de Peyragude at the foot of the castle, built between 1897 and 1948 on the site of a traditional shrine; it is a frank imitation of Sacré-Coeur at Montmartre, with a gleaming metal-covered dome in place of Sacré-Coeur's whiteness. From a side-road north of the town there is a vista over the Lot valley, heavy with modern development along the N 111, and not particularly beautiful.

We turn east to **Tournon d'Agenais,** a hilltop *bastide* founded by the French. When it fell into English hands Edward III ordered it to be fortified, paying for the gates out of the royal treasury but leaving the inhabitants to build the ramparts. Little of the medieval buildings survived the wars of religion. Ten miles south of Tournon, to the right of the road to Agen, is the much better preserved town of **Beauville,** occupying a promontory on a high ridge of hills above the valley along which the road runs. Hairpin bends bring us to the town ramparts, behind which are a number of medieval houses and a market-place which has part of its arcades. At the furthest point of the promontory is the castle, rebuilt in the sixteenth century with a decorative Renaissance staircase inside but warlike battlements outside; it is now used as a police barracks.

To the south-east of Beauville the twelfth-century church at **La Sauvetat de Savères** has an unusual plan, with semi-circular chapels instead of transepts, a device which avoided the problems of vaulting the crossing by simply opening two arches in the walls of the nave. The church has been recently restored, which is more than can be said for the ruins of the abbey at **St Maurin**, due south of Beauville toward Valence. St Maurin is like a scene from an early-nineteenth-century engraving, when the Revolution had done its worst, and Mérimée and the Beaux-Arts had not yet set to work to retrieve what could be saved. A whole village lives in the ruins of the abbey, and visitors are regarded suspiciously, because the inhabitants evidently dread the possibility of a day when restoration might begin. The abbey was built in the late eleventh century, and the inscription recording the dedication of the church on 5 January 1097 still survives below the belfry. By the fourteenth century it was very rich, but it suffered severely in the Hundred Years' War, being pillaged in 1346 and 1356 by the English. Its renaissance came in the sixteenth century, when the abbot's palace was built and the abbey itself restored: but the wars of religion saw it turned into a fortress, a scene of combat from 1568 to 1580. Restored in the seventeenth century, it was still intact in 1796, and the local council tried to save it: but it was sold and used as a stone quarry. Now half the church has vanished: the *mairie* occupies part of the abbot's palace, while the public lavatories have been tacked on to a corner of it. The chapter-house is a wood-store, while the transept of the church is occupied by private houses, except for the tower which marks the south transept. The nave has disappeared. Around the base of the tower are a number of excellent capitals, including the execution of St Maurin and the saint carrying his severed head.

Heading east, through the *bastide* of Castelsagrat, founded in 1270, we join the N 653, which follows the river Barguelonne to **Lauzerte**, on a knoll above the confluence of two rivers. From its old walls – yet another *bastide*, this time with a variety of houses from the twelfth to the sixteenth centuries – there are views over an attractive landscape to north and south. The valleys are rich and heavily farmed, the uplands dotted with cypresses. Continuing on the same road we come to **Montcuq**, where there is a similarly pleasant site, beneath a keep which is all that survives of the medieval castle. Slow but often delightful side-roads meander east to Castelnau-Montratier, distinguished by three windmills: its streets also contain old houses. But the most spectacular spot of all is **Montpezat de Quercy**, built on a hill facing south, just off the N 20. Below the village itself (which has an excellent small old-fashioned inn, the *Trois Terrasses*) is the collegiate church of St Martin, built by Pierre des Pres, a member of a local family who rose to become Cardinal of Palestrina. His monument is to the right of the choir. The church itself is relatively simple, the work of an architect from Avignon. Its furnishings were given by later members of the family, three of whom were bishops of Montauban. The most imposing pieces are the five specially-made tapestries woven in northern France in the early sixteenth century: their sixteen scenes show episodes from the life of St Martin. The church treasure includes three English alabasters of the fifteenth century, whose subjects are the Birth of Christ, the Resurrection and the Ascension.

Everything we have seen since Agen belongs to the leisured traveller with time for the minor pleasures of life. But **Moissac** will be on everyone's itinerary. However, for this very reason, it is best to time one's visit carefully; perhaps the best method of all is to stay at Moissac overnight (though the hotels are little more than adequate) and to see the church early in the morning, before the peace of the cloister is disturbed by too many groups of visitors. Some places can be appreciated just as well with a throng of people around, but here, where everything is designed for calm and meditation, only peace and quiet will bring out the true spirit of one of the great works of art of the twelfth century.

But let us begin with the south doorway of the church, facing on to a busy street. This is the outward-looking face of the abbey, and its bold designs would hold our attention anywhere. Beneath a nondescript tower and battlements which proclaim the abbey's troubled past, the doorway is sheltered by a deep broken-arched vault, which explains its excellent state of preservation.

That this is an outstanding masterpiece is at once obvious. But why should it be here, in a relatively humble and out-of-the-way place? The history of the abbey soon makes this clear. Founded in the early seventh century, it was given wide lands in Languedoc and Gascony in 680, and in the early ninth century enjoyed the patronage of Charlemagne and his son Louis. In the eleventh and early twelfth century four great abbots made it one of the greatest religious centres in south-west France, and this south doorway was built under the last two of these, Ansquitil and Roger. The figures on the two engaged columns flanking the doorway may be portraits of them; the tall Ansquitil to the left, in monastic habit, while Roger is dressed in the episcopal robes he wore by papal privilege.

It was Ansquitil who 'ordered the construction of the most beautiful doorway', '*fecit fieri pulcherrimum portale*', as the abbey's chronicle records. We do not know from where the sculptors came; but their knowledge of art was wide, their repertory of form and style rich, and they were almost certainly one of the travelling 'studios' who would work on commissions together and then move on as a group. Two of them are represented here on the doorway, to left and right of the tympanum between the capitals of the first and second vaults. One has his tools in his hands, while the other merely gazes up at his work.

The central figure of the tympanum is Christ in Majesty, a stern yet humane figure, handled with the greatest skill and subtlety of perspective and detail: notice how the head is emphasised by a slightly oval tau cross and a suggestion of the traditional mandorla, which disappears behind the body, giving a freedom to the composition which would normally be contained within it. Around the figure of Christ the symbols of the four evangelists move in ecstatic adoration; the enthusiastic impetus of the eagle of St John takes him across the line of the mandorla, while the winged lion and ox strain yearningly toward Christ. This same movement is repeated by the ranks of the elders of the Apocalypse, seated in tiers around Christ's feet. They are separated by irregular lines like waves or clouds instead of the usual formal rectilinear frame, and the Greek key pattern round the semi-circle of the tympanum has become a dancing ribbon pattern. By contrast, the vaulting carries strictly regimented foliage, with a luxuriant pattern of flowers and eight-pointed leaf stars across the lintel, broken only by strange monsters at either end. There is a hint of Moorish influence here, as there is in the shaping of the central column and sides of the doorway: but it is no more than a memory of something seen, which has undergone a rich and strange transformation by the sculptor's own imagination. The central pillar is arguably the most powerful single piece at Moissac, with two of the sculptor's masterpieces, the prophet Jeremiah and St Paul, half-hidden on the right and left faces, while on the outer face a pride of lions echoes the theme of majesty above.

The scenes to the left and right of the porch have suffered badly from weathering, showing how fortunate it is that the depth of the vault has preserved the doorway itself. To the left St John records the vision of the Apocalypse in the top left-hand corner; the other scenes record the deeds of men and their punishment at the Last Judgment. Next to St John Lazarus rests in Abraham's bosom, while the story of how the rich man received him is shown at the right. Below, the dying miser's soul is snatched by demons from his guardian angel's grasp, and the sins of pride and luxury or sensual enjoyment are hideously punished. The right-hand side offers hope of escape from such a fate, recording the Annunciation, Visitation, Adoration of the Magi and flight into Egypt (reading from bottom to top). But only in the less worn figures – the Angel of the Annunciation and St John – do we recapture the masterly vision of the inner doorway.

Inside the doorway the narthex is unexpectedly large. Its capitals are of an earlier period than the porch, altogether simpler, with patterns of animals and leaves. The church itself is a disappointment; despite the laborious restoration of the original decoration during the last decade its Gothic style seems feeble. Even a wooden crucified Christ of the twelfth century pales into sentimentality beside the stone figures of the porch, though it would make its mark in any other context.

Walking round the west end of the church, we come to the remains of some of the abbey buildings, and to the cloister, nearly pulled down to make way for the railway in the 1840s. Fortunately the alarm was raised in time; the line runs through a tunnel behind it, and nothing disturbs its calm except the visitors. In the centre a huge cedar towers against the steep hillside behind, green against the lilacs and blue sky. The outer walls are plain: but the pillars and their capitals carry an immense wealth of sculpture. The page following gives a very abbreviated summary of the subjects: only after three or four leisurely circuits of the cloister can one begin to appreciate their variety and delightful detail. Besides ornamental and figured capitals, there is a series of Biblical scenes, whose sequence presents no apparent logic or meaning, though there may well be a missing key which would make sense of them. All three cycles are from the same studio, though there are immense differences of skill between the individual capitals: compare the vision of St John (15) with the resurrection of Lazarus (64). But it is composition and adroit use of decoration that makes the capitals miniature masterpieces. Only occasionally do the figures on them attain to the eloquence of the set of eight saints who appear on the corner pillars – solemn, archaic figures that might have come from some Babylonian royal procession immortalised in bas-relief. The most striking figure of all is that of Abbot Durand, evidently the work of someone who remembered this forceful personality well. Even though the pose is stylised in the extreme, we still sense the strength of character of the abbot-bishop, of whose work in the region the chronicler wrote, 'There are now churches where the boar used to have his lair in the woods.'

## *Capitals in the cloisters at Moissac: a summary of subjects*

S.E. corner (nearest entrance): bas-reliefs of St Matthew and St Bartholomew
1. (In gallery parallel with church) Story of John the Baptist
2. Birds in the Tree of Life
3. Babylon the Great
4. Exotic birds
5. Story of Nebuchadnezzar
6. Martyrdom of St Stephen
7. Acanthus leaves and wild animals
8. David and his musicians
9. The celestial Jerusalem
10. Visions of the Apocalypse
11. The four symbols of the Evangelists
12. The story of the woman of Canaan
13. The Good Samaritan
14. The temptation of Christ
15. The vision of St John
16. The Transfiguration
17. The deliverance of St Peter
18. The Baptism of Christ

N.E. corner pillar: bas-reliefs of St Peter and St Paul
19. Samson slaying the lion
20. Martyrdom of St Peter and St Paul
21. Moorish patterns
22. Fall of Adam and Eve
23. Double acanthus leaves
24. Martyrdom of St Lawrence
25. Jesus washing the feet of his disciples
26. Palm leaves
27. Lazarus and the rich man (cf doorway)
28. Fabulous animals

Central pillar: the Abbot Durand
29. Birds and human figures
30. The wedding at Cana
31. Foliage
32. Adoration of the Magi; Massacre of the Holy Innocents
33. Palms and wild animals
34. Acanthus leaves
35. Martyrdom of St Saturnin (Apostle of Toulouse)
36. Acanthus leaves
37. Martyrdom of St Fructueux (Bishop of Tarragona)
38. Annunciation and Visitation

N.W. corner pillar: St James (of Compostela) and St John
39. The angels triumph over two dragons
40. Birds and fishes
41. Fleurons and branches
42. Miracles of St Benedict
43. Fantastic birds
44. Miracle of St Peter
45. Branches
46. The court of heaven (angels)
47. The miraculous draught of fishes

Central pillar: marble facings
48. Daniel in the lions' den; Habakkuk and the angel
49. The Crusade: the Holy Sepulchre on the east face
50. Arabesque patterns
51. The Evangelists
52. Decorative birds
53. The three young men in the fiery furnace, rescued by an angel

**5. (right)** The old quarters of Sarlat, in the Dordogne

**6. (below)** Pau, on the edge of the Pyrenees

**7. (overleaf)** The masterpiece of Romanesque sculpture in the south-west: the tympanum over the south doorway at Moissac. The programme is explained on pages 230-1

38. **(above)** Capital in the church at Moirax, near Agen: a pride of most engaging lions

39. **(left)** The late Gothic splendours of the choir stalls in the cathedral at Auch

54. St Martin sharing his cloak
55. Arabesque patterns
56. The Samaritan woman at the well

S.W. pillar: St Andrew and St Philip
57. Abraham and Isaac
58. The worship of the Cross
59. Acanthus leaves
60. Decorative birds and lions
61. Daniel in the lions' den; the annunciation to the Shepherds
62. Acanthus leaves
63. Monsters blowing horns and drawing bows
64. The resurrection of Lazarus
65. Palms
66. Chimeras and figures

Central pillar: marble plaque with elegant and simple cross; the dedication reads: 'In the year after the Incarnation of the Eternal Prince, 1100, this cloister was finished, in the time of the Lord Abbot Ansquitil, amen.'
67. Samuel anointing David
68. Flowers and branches
69. Birds and beasts
70. Acanthus leaves
71. Figures symbolising the beatitudes
72. Beasts
73. The story of Cain and Abel
74. Branches
75. Men and eagles
76. David and Goliath

Very little has changed here since Ansquitil's workmen finished their task in AD 1100. In the thirteenth century the round arches were remodelled in the fashion of the day, but their relatively simple pointed form does not clash with the sculptures below. More serious was the loss of the great marble fountain and its portico, also Ansquitil's work, which stood in the north-west corner until the Revolution. But the cloister at Moissac still remains the most perfect of its kind in France and the key to much of the Romanesque art of the surrounding region.

Continuing east along the Tarn, which branches away from the Garonne just before Moissac, we come to the flat delta where the Aveyron joins the Tarn and then to **Montauban**. This is the limit of the area explored in the present book. Its architecture is almost entirely in brick, heralding the brick cathedral at Albi and the brick warmth of old Toulouse. Along the quays, high above the river, imposing seventeenth-century town houses bear witness to the prosperity of the town. It was founded as a new settlement in 1144, one of the earliest such enterprises in France, and a precursor of the *bastides*: its foundation charter of privileges pre-dates that of many far greater cities. The quays lead to the **Pont Vieux**, again brick-built, of 1303–16: the two architects who designed it adopted an unusual method of dealing with floods, by providing huge oval openings between the arches through which the river could flow when in full spate. Its fortifications have disappeared, victims of seventeenth-century sieges, when Montauban was a great Protestant stronghold. The churches, too, bear marks of the religious struggles: up the hill from the Pont Vieux the fortified brick tower of **St Jacques** has bullet marks on its tower. It was the cathedral until 1739, when the cathedral of Notre Dame, to the south-east, replaced it, a dull classical barn of a building.

Downhill from St Jacques, next to the Pont Vieux, stands the bishop's palace, built in 1664 on the foundations of a castle constructed on the Black Prince's orders. It now houses the **Musée Ingres**: Ingres was born in Montauban in 1780, and the main part of the collection is devoted to his work. The ground floor contains sculptures by another native of Montauban, Bourdelle, who was a pupil of Rodin. His work is less free of form and more romantic than his master's: the most ambitious piece is a plaster model for 'Heracles the archer', and there is a striking portrait bust of the anthropologist Sir James Frazer. But the most haunting is a bronze entitled 'Night', with a hint of the Michelangelo figure on the Sistine Tombs. Personally, I can arouse little enthusiasm for Ingres's own work, shown on the floor above; it seems pervaded by an arid academic classicism, and though it may be technically superb it seems as dull as ditchwater beside even his teacher David's work. The drawings are more subtle, but consist mostly of sketches or studies for the larger compositions. The basement includes one room of the medieval castle, the guardroom, with vaulting of the period: it houses a collection of Roman and medieval archaeological finds.

The gem of Montauban is in the very centre of the old town, the Place Nationale. A miniature Roman circus, it was built in the seventeenth century to replace a half-timbered market-place with covered arcades, linked at the corners by gateways. Its irregular oval shape and the warm rose-red of the double arcades and houses above give it an individuality which is enlivened by the markets which are still held there. It has a feeling of self-assurance and character which a grander scheme would have lacked.

Leaving the old town by crossing the Pont Vieux toward Castelsarrasin – there is little of interest here – we continue via Lavit to **Lectoure**, some forty miles west of Montauban. At first sight an ordinary market town, it has a good late Gothic and Renaissance cathedral, with an unusual gallery at the west end of the nave; its appearance is deceptive, because it was entirely reconstructed, to the original design, from 1659 onwards. We shall meet churches in this plain late Gothic style at Condom, Eauze and Auch: large Romanesque churches are almost unknown here. The choir had an even more chequered history: the Gothic choir of *circa* 1375 was rebuilt in 1540; but this rebuilding proved unsafe and was taken apart and reconstructed after 1743. In the course of operations in 1540 a re-markable collection of commemorative stones called *taurobolia* came to light, showing that this had been the site of a temple dedicated to Cybele. The initiation ceremony of Cybele's worshippers involved the slaughter of a bull above a pit in which the new member of the sect crouched. Bathed in the blood of the bull, he was considered to have been washed of his sins; and to mark the occasion a stone or *taurobolium* was set up, suitably inscribed. These are now the centre-piece of the excellent museum in the basement of the *mairie*, next to the cathedral. Arranged chronologically, the prehistoric finds are well laid out but not of great importance. There are interesting Gaulish burial chambers formed of flat tiles: those with a four-square hollow are early, the inverted 'V' later, just preceding the use of sarcophagi, of which there are a number here. Excavations in the area, which was evidently an important centre both in the Gaulish period and in Roman times, are continuing: to the *taurobolia* have been added a number of funerary altars (including statues which could be re-used by changing the heads!). There are also mosaics, coins, and items of jewellery, all arranged in 1972 and well displayed. To the north of the town, on the hillside below the old ramparts, is the Fontaine Diane; it was once a focal point of the town's life, but now, alas, its two slender Gothic arches are covered by a grille, and there is the familiar '*Eau non potable*' sign.

On the M 21 north of Lectoure is the fourteenth-century castle of Sainte-Mère, a massive building, which, like most Gascon castles, was both a residence and a military post: hence its size, because it had to accommodate the lord and his family as well as serving as a fortress. It has lost part of its upper works, but presents a handsome silhouette, perched on an outcrop beside the road which also houses a small fortified village.

West of Lectoure Terraube has a seventeenth-century castle and fortifications; Lectoure appears in the distance, beyond fertile hills and cypresses, in a richer version of a Tuscan landscape. The main road runs down the valley of the Gers to Fleurance, a *bastide* town with a good part of its original market-place, though the large central market hall is much later. The church is the original Gothic one, contemporary with the founding of the town; it has a sober, well-proportioned interior and sixteenth-century windows by Arnaut de Moles in the choir, not quite so rich as his masterpieces at Auch, but none the less outstanding compared with the windows usually to be found in such churches.

Echoes of a different world are to be found in the castle at Lavardens, six miles to the right of the main road to Auch. The huge
bulk of the castle seems to overwhelm the rocky hilltop on which it is
built. Its four-square lines suggest a medieval date, but documents
show that it is early seventeenth-century. A staircase cut in the rock
leads to the overgrown courtyard: massive repairs are in progress,
to save something of the crumbling structure. The interior is lofty,
with a well-lit arcaded and vaulted central passage; but all decoration, save for the elaborately patterned brickwork floors, has long
since vanished.

From Lavardens, we continue west to the N 130, and then turn
north toward Condom.

# Chapter 16

# The Gers and Pau

۶

The Gers is one of the most sparsely populated provinces of France; there are fewer inhabitants than there were during the Middle Ages, its people having drifted toward the cities during the years of agricultural depression. The attractive and little-known landscape of the Gers contains a large number of relics of its past, though none of them are major monuments. It was never a very rich area, as its churches show: they are often Romanesque, but very simple – there is rarely a bell-tower, the bell being hung in a little projection above a plain wall (*clocher-mur*). It is a countryside to be sampled at leisure, with many rewards in the way of unexpected Roman remains or medieval castles. What follows is necessarily only a selection, as the distances between sites are often considerable, and many of them are well away from main roads.

On the right of the N 130 as we head north for Condom is the square sixteenth-century keep of **Castéra-Verduzan**. Beyond Valence, also to the right, a byroad leads to the castle of **Tauzia,** another square keep, this time thirteenth-century with a sixteenth-century façade. It is now a ruin deep in the meadows, most appealing to the eye. If you return to the main road, a turning almost opposite on the other side leads to the abbey of **Flaran.**

Here the abbey church and some of the buildings stand deserted but more or less intact. If the door is open you will find a scene that could be straight out of an eighteenth-century engraving: a crumbling bare interior with barrels of Armagnac tucked away in the corners. It is a Cistercian church of the late twelfth century, and its present desolation makes it seem all the more severe in its grand simple lines. As with all true Cistercian architecture there is little decoration, and the architecture relies on proportion and balance for its effect. The spacious but dark nave is flanked by two high transepts, and roofed with Angevin vaults. In the half-light the arcading is massive, almost overwhelming. To the north is a little cloister, of the fourteenth century, much decayed; off it are a large chapterhouse and an elegant sacristy with a lovely central pillar of marble supporting the vault.

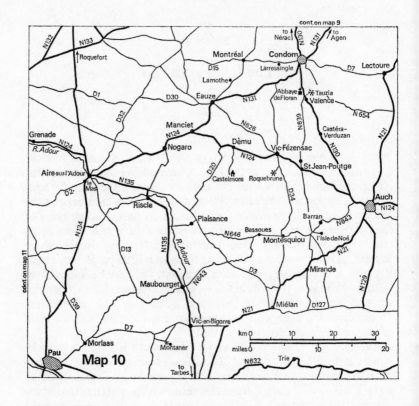

cont. on map 9

The exterior is equally severe; the adjacent seventeenth-century buildings are being restored, and it may be that the abbey too will gain a new lease of life. But it will also lose something in the process, because untended ruins of this kind are almost unknown now. It would be pleasing, but unpractical, to hope that it could be left as an example. When I last visited it in 1975, work had already started on the church itself.

**Condom**, once a decaying medieval town like Nérac, owes its prosperity to the trade in Armagnac. This type of brandy is less well known abroad than it deserves to be: long-standing English connections with Cognac have influenced taste in England, but some connoisseurs rate Armagnac as highly as the best products of the

Charente. The processes used to produce Armagnac are the same as for Cognac, the best being a local white wine of no interest at all as a table wine, exactly as at Cognac. Armagnac matures more quickly than Cognac, and tends to be softer and with more flavour. Given the choice between a run-of-the-mill Cognac and its equivalent from Armagnac, I would take the latter every time; but Armagnac does not produce anything to rival a really first-class Cognac.

There is far less evidence of the wine trade at Condom than at Cognac (though there is one excellent, expensive restaurant, the *Table des Cordeliers*, installed in an old house with Gothic vaults just off the Avenue de Gaulle). The cathedral is very late Gothic (built between 1506 and 1531), a single nave without a crossing which gives an effect of space and simplicity. Both in the church and the nearby cloister there are strikingly-coloured roof-bosses. In 1569 the Huguenots under Montgomery threatened its destruction, but the townspeople paid a ransom of 30,000 francs to save it. The cloisters are surprising: they are massive, with nothing like the usual fine web of tracery and carving to be found in Gothic cloisters. Instead a double arcade leads into a severe square, part of which acts as buttress to the north wall of the cathedral.

Three miles west of Condom is the village of **Larressingle**. This is so fortified that it is really a village inside a castle, the castle belonging to the bishops of Condom. Across the moat, where a bridge has replaced the drawbridge, a powerful western gateway leads into a small, shady square. A few inhabitants still live in the little cottages, while others have evidently become holiday houses without destroying the feeling of isolation in time and space which is the charm of Larressingle. The twelfth-century keep has only its four outer walls and a Renaissance staircase. There is a small church, little more than a chapel; and beyond it, to the east, the village blends into the countryside, the fortifications on this side having long since vanished. Many more such fortified villages must once have existed in this embattled part of the world; but, like the *bastides* further north, rebuilding and the re-use of outdated fortifications as a quarry have robbed them of their original defensive aspect. Only at Larressingle do we begin to get the feeling of these small communities, inward-looking and wary of a hostile outside world.

Beyond Larressingle, **Montréal** and the countryside around it have a number of interesting monuments, ranging from the site of a Roman villa to a variety of medieval churches and castles. In the town itself, a *bastide* founded by the English in 1289, there is the arcaded market-place and the original church, as well as some of the fortifications. Just south of the town is the site of a Gallo-Roman villa, at Séviac, with a geometrical mosaic floor. To the north of Montréal is another *bastide*, Fources, with the curious feature of a circular market-place. It also has a medieval bridge and remains of a castle.

Continuing south on the D 29 you will find a well-preserved square watch-tower, thirteenth-century, at Lamothe, typical of the plain medieval architecture of this area. We come to **Eauze,** which was once Elusa, the capital of a Roman province stretching south to the Pyrenees; now almost the only trace of its Roman past to be seen is in the rubble of Roman masonry used to build its late Gothic cathedral. It is unusual in that all the lighting is from the upper windows, and the side-chapels have no window-openings. Otherwise it is close to the style of the cathedral at Condom, though it is slightly earlier in date (1467–1521). There are some fine armorial roof-bosses with the arms of the patrons of the cathedral, particularly in the porch; and there are two windows in the style of Arnaut de Moles (see p. 241), to the east. In the Place d'Armagnac, beside the cathedral, is a fifteenth-century half-timbered house and an elegant seventeenth-century stone-built mansion.

The N 131 and N 124 toward Auch pass through Demu, where a turning to the right leads to Castelmore, the manor house where D'Artagnan, made famous in fiction by Dumas in *The Three Musketeers*, was said to have been born. Further along the main road is Vic-Fezensac, where bull-fights are held in the stadium each summer. To the south, at **Roquebrune,** an oddly-shaped ruin which looks like the apse of a chapel, and is known as 'La Monjoie', is in fact the remains of a third-century temple said to have been dedicated to the Eastern deities Cybele and Mithras. As the two cults were of different kinds, Cybele being the great Earth-Mother and Mithras the Persian God of Light who struggled against the forces of evil embodied in nature, the dedication seems improbable; but the ruins are genuine enough. At **St Jean Poutge**, back on the main road, the château of **Herrebouc** tucked away in the valley, down a side-road, is a twelfth-century watch-tower, adapted by later generations as a miniature castle. Its plain appearance is made attractive by the arrangement of the battlements and look-out points, and by the golden-yellow stone of which it is built.

**Auch,** the old capital of Gascony, stands on the banks of the river Gers. The older part of the town is on the west bank, grouped around the cathedral. This occupies a prominent site high above the river. It is late Gothic, being built between 1489 and 1562, but signs of its origins are concealed by a Renaissance façade, altered again in the eighteenth century. The architecture is similar to that of Condom, a high and spacious nave with chapels radiating off it. But it is the furnishings, not the building itself, that are remarkable. The choir stalls, an extraordinary blend of Renaissance figures with flamboyant Gothic tracery, were carved between 1515 and 1531, and form a complete enclosed section within the nave. The main figures are chiefly of characters from the Bible (with David in various different guises on the south side) while the misericords portray allegorical scenes. Unfortunately they can only be viewed in the presence of a guide, and there is rarely enough time to study all the intriguing details of these masterpieces.

The stained glass is the other glory of the cathedral. It is by Arnaut de Moles, a Gascon artist who was born *circa* 1465 at St Sever, fifty miles west of Auch. He seems to have worked in Toulouse, and the glass at Fleurance, fifteen miles north of Auch, is also signed by him; but there is nothing to show whether he travelled further afield. His style, like that of the stalls, stands at the border between Gothic and Renaissance, full of tenderness and realism. There are 360 figures in all in the series of windows, each of them individually characterised. Perhaps the finest window is that of the Crucifixion, in the east window, obviously intended as the focal point of the artist's work and his most carefully executed piece. Other noteworthy windows are to be found in the side-chapels, including scenes from the Creation and a touching Nativity with a beautiful kneeling Virgin. Above all it is the colours that mark out de Moles's work as extraordinary: these range from the traditional blues and reds of medieval glass to a glorious golden-yellow which is hardly ever seen elsewhere.

The square in front of the cathedral has some late medieval half-timbered houses, while to the south the Place Salmis (which in good weather offers a glimpse of the Pyrenees fifty miles away) leads to a monumental staircase down to the river's edge. To the right is a fourteenth-century defensive tower. On the Place de la République is a medieval chapel now used as a museum, with a collection of local art and archaeology, including a twelfth-century olifant or ivory horn.

From Auch the main road to Pau runs via Mirande, but a much more attractive route is the N 643, which branches off the N 124 three miles west of the town. Hilly and winding, it is not a road for fast driving, and often passes through narrow village streets. At **Barran**, once a fortified village, there are moats and ramparts outside the village and a well-preserved fourteenth-century gate on the road.

At L'Isle de Noe the old castle has been tamed into a jumble of red-tiled houses above the quiet waters of the river Baise, while Montesquiou still has one of its old gates and its ramparts, now a public garden. **Bassoues** offers a more dramatic sight, the keep of the castle, whose five storeys rise above the surrounding buildings to a height of 130 feet. This, the finest of the Gascon castles to survive, has buttresses on the corners and a projecting staircase tower. At the top are elaborate battlements. Despite its relatively simple four-square design it was completed in 1371 by Arnaud Aubert, Archbishop of Auch, whose arms appear on the roof-bosses. Parts of the outer defences, including a curtain wall and tower, also survive as buildings in the village.

The road runs on, becoming more and more twisting, until we reach the valley of the Adour at **Plaisance**, a much-rebuilt *bastide* with one or two old houses. The Ripa Alta, on the main square, is a comfortable hotel whose restaurant offers local dishes, including crayfish. Following the Adour valley we leave the level river-plain at Riscle, where the D 25 leads to **Nogaro**. The church here has a high Romanesque nave, with the original barrel-vaulting and elaborate foliage on the capitals; beside it is a charming cloister, with a traceried arcade against the side of the church, whose decoration shows clearly the same Moslem inspiration as the capitals inside. It dates from the late eleventh century, and is astonishingly sophisticated for such an early work.

**Aire-sur-l'Adour**, twelve miles south-west of Nogaro, is a busy commercial centre on the site of the Roman settlement of Atura. It was a bishopric until 1933, and the former cathedral is basically twelfth-century, though both façade and apse were rebuilt in the seventeenth and eighteenth centuries. It is spacious, but the main interest is its plan, with two chapels off the east wall of each transept, giving an impression of great breadth. This was originally the church of a Benedictine monastery, and the chapterhouse, with a graceful octagonal central pillar, is now the sacristy. The old bishop's palace is now the town hall, and houses the remains of a Gallo-Roman pavement.

Across the river, south-west of the town, is the church of Ste Quitterie at **Le Mas d'Aire**. Ste Quitterie was a Visigoth princess who was martyred here in 476, and her relics were a centre of pilgrimage from about 629 on. The present church, originally a Romanesque building finished in 1092, was remodelled in 1309, but fell into decay in the seventeenth century. It was restored in 1885, and the one remaining relic of Ste Quitterie (saved from a Huguenot pyre in 1569) was returned to the church from Toulouse.

The entrance is below a five-storey belfry; the tympanum of the main doorway has a mutilated but powerful Last Judgment. The choir has six Romanesque arches and capitals: to the right, in the south transept, is the entrance to the crypt, where the remarkable fifth-century sarcophagus which once housed the saint's remains is kept. What is particularly unusual is the appearance of Biblical scenes on it. The front shows, above, Abraham and Isaac, Jonah and the whale, Tobias and the fish, and, below, Lazarus, Daniel in the lions' den, the Good Shepherd, Adam and Eve, and a baptism scene. On the left side is Jonah and the whale, on the right a scene which is perhaps the drunkenness of Noah. Winged Medusa's heads stare out from each corner, and the traditional Roman togas of many of the figures are further reminders that this is one of the few surviving pieces of Christian art from the classical world.

The N 134 to Pau offers little; but it is worth turning off short of Pau down the D 39 to **Morlaas,** where the church has a much-restored doorway in the Byzantine manner of the twelfth century. (A longer detour to the east takes us to **Montaner,** twenty miles beyond Morlaas, where, isolated on a hilltop, a magnificent brick castle built for Gaston Phoebus, Count of Foix, by Sicard de Lordat in the 1360s, is being restored. The central brick keep is over a hundred feet high, and has his defaced arms over the doorway.) This is the limit of our explorations: Lourdes lies both beyond the chosen boundary of the present guide and outside the subjects on which I feel that I can be an adequate guide!

From Morlaas we reach **Pau** through its industrial suburbs. The old town lies to the south, on the edge of the Gave de Pau river. It is best to start at the west end, with the great fortress which has been the centre of Pau's history. This, like the castle at Montaner, was built by Gaston Phoebus's architect, Sicard de Lordat. Gaston Phoebus himself was one of the more flamboyant characters of the Middle Ages, who made Béarn virtually an independent kingdom. He moved the capital of his domains to Pau from Orthez (where Froissart had visited his court: see p. 249). There had been a small castle on this superb natural site from the twelfth century on, but most of this was swept away except for the 'Montauser' tower to the north. A new keep was built of brick, and this still stands to the left of the entrance arcade. Five generations later, in the 1460s, the castle was remodelled by Gaston Phoebus IV, and it was here, another

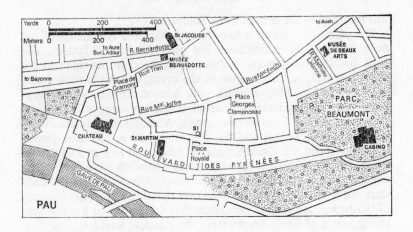

PAU

five generations on, that Henri of Navarre was born, later to become Henri IV. His remarkable career falls into two parts: his struggle to gain the throne and his reconstruction of the kingdom after his hard-won victory. The first part of his career belongs to the confused and violent history of the wars of religion in France. Brought up as a Protestant by his mother, Jeanne d'Albret, he assumed the leadership of the Protestant party in 1576. The murder of Henri III in 1589 left him king of France, but the Catholic league resolutely opposed his claim, and it took him a decade to overcome all opposition. However, he had had to become a Catholic himself in order to get Paris to open its gates to him, a purely political conversion which he himself summed up in the words '*Paris vaut bien une messe*' ('Paris is worth a mass'). After successfully removing his opponents he set about turning France into an authoritarian monarchy, with the aid of his friend the Duc de Sully, and he laid the foundations on which Louis XIII and Louis XIV were able to build. However, the legacy of hatred of the wars of religion was not yet at an end, and he was assassinated in 1610 by Ravaillac, a Catholic fanatic. Henri spent the last twenty-five years of his life away from Pau, but he remained deeply attached to Gascony. His easy Gascon manners made him one of the most popular kings of France, and tales about his affable way with the common people (and also about his amorous exploits) are legion. But the château at Pau reflects only the formal side of his life, during his youth and early manhood.

After Henri's death the castle was neglected, a little-used residence in the furthest corner of France. Only under Louis-Philippe, from

244

1837 on, was its restoration and refurnishing undertaken, a work continued under Napoleon III, which altered the appearance of the castle considerably as well as endowing it with a rich collection of tapestry and furniture.

To the right of the keep of Gaston Phoebus at the entrance is an arcade and tower built by Napoleon III in 1864. Inside the courtyard the north wing is largely as it was when Gaston IV's architect Bertrand de Bardelon built it in about 1465; the elaborate Renaissance façade of the west wing was built about 1530. The state rooms are on the first and second floors, reached by a spacious Renaissance staircase with a coffered ceiling. An exhibition of documents relating to Henri IV is usually shown here each summer. The decoration of the splendid rooms which follow is almost entirely the work of the Second Empire, influenced by the vogue of the time for things medieval; the effect is impressive and attractive even though not entirely authentic, the furniture in particular being the work of nineteenth-century designers. However, Henri IV's remarkable tortoise-shell cradle, in the room where he is said to have been born, and the fine series of tapestries are authentic. The latter include Gobelins tapestries of the months (seventeenth-century) and of Maximilian's hunting parties (*circa* 1720). Flemish weavers working in Paris were responsible for the series of the story of Psyche, an early-seventeenth-century set. The most impressive are the part-set of the 'Arabesque months', four of which hang in Henri IV's room and two in a specially-built exhibition room with the Psyche series. The last room to be shown contains Brussels tapestries of about 1510 showing the life of St John and medals and busts of Henri IV. Painted portraits of Henri IV have a room to themselves, next to the room where he was born.

West of the castle are the sixteenth-century gardens created by Marguerite d'Angoulême. The Boulevard des Pyrénées, to the south of the castle, runs along the edge of the town above the Gave de Pau. On a fine clear day there is a magnificent view of the Pyrenees from here (though I cannot claim to have seen it – mist and cloud are by no means uncommon). Near the Place Royale is an engraved table giving the names of the various peaks, with the Pic du Midi d'Ossau in the centre. At the east end of the Boulevard des Pyrénées is the attractive Parc Beaumont and the casino, a reminder of Pau's heyday as a spa in the nineteenth century, when it was particularly popular with English travellers as a wintering place 'on account of the stillness of the air'. One of the legacies of the English colony here is a pack of hounds, started in 1840, which still meets regularly north of Pau on

Saturdays in winter.

North of the park, in the rue Mathieu-Lalaune, is the modern building which houses the **Musée des Beaux Arts**. Although there are no major masterpieces it is a wide-ranging collection with some excellent pictures ranging from Rubens, El Greco and Romney to the Impressionists. Degas's 'The Cotton Exchange at New Orleans' and Berthe Morisot's delicate 'Girl Sewing' stand out, but there are pleasing pieces by minor Impressionists such as Boudin and Guillaumin.

To the north-west of the town, off the Place de Gramont at 8 rue de Trau, is a small collection of mementoes of Bernadotte, Napoleon's marshal who became the founder of the present ruling house of Sweden as Charles XIV.

# Chapter 17

# Bayonne to Bordeaux: the Landes

❧

From Pau, we head east to **Lescar,** just outside the town off the N 117. It is older than the former, and has preserved the ancient cathedral which Pau so conspicuously lacks. It stands inside a little fortified enclave with a red granite gateway, on a hill a mile north of the main road. Originally a Roman colony (Beneharnum) it later became the capital of Béarn until it was sacked by the Saracens in about 850. It was rebuilt on the hilltop, and became the chief bishopric of Béarn; the kings of Navarre were buried here. The cathedral dates from 1115–41, but was damaged and rebuilt at the end of the fourteenth century and in the sixteenth century. The nave collapsed in 1600 and the belfry in 1608, leading to yet another building from 1609 to 1633. Surprisingly, a good deal of the late Romanesque building survives, though the capitals are a mixture of originals and copies by the nineteenth-century architect Boeswillwald. In the choir is a mosaic with secular subjects, hunting scenes and wild beasts, a twelfth-century work showing Spanish or Eastern influence. The royal tombs have disappeared, crushed by the falling roof in 1600, and the furnishings are mostly excellent seventeenth-century woodwork.

Beyond Lescar the valley of the Gave de Pau is dotted with the chimneys and rigs of the huge natural gas field at Lacq, discovered in 1949, which produces over 5,000 million cubic metres of gas a year. Small quantities of petrol and a number of chemical by-products are also obtained, and an industrial area has grown up on the far bank. Toward Orthez the countryside gradually reverts to agriculture, and **Orthez** itself is a quiet town which seems scarcely to have emerged from the nineteenth century. This was the capital of Béarn from 1194 to 1464, during the years when the counts of Foix were transforming it from a small lordship to a powerful state. Their castle was built in 1242 and remodelled by Sicard de Lordat in the fourteenth century; now all that remains is the Tour Moncade, off the N 133 on the northern edge of the town. Here in 1388 Jean Froissart, the chronicler of the Hundred Years' War, visited Gaston Phoebus of

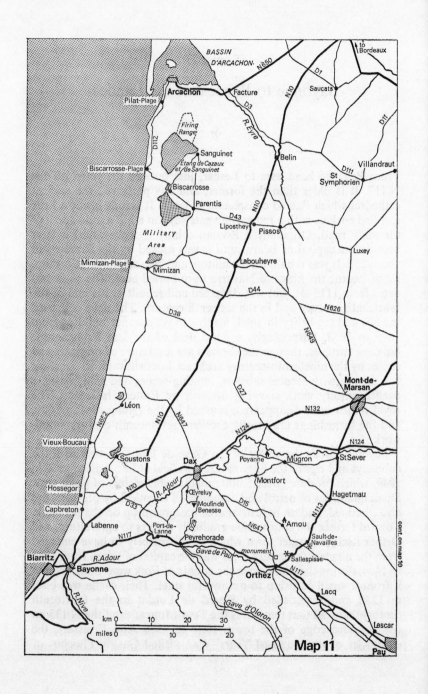

BASSIN D'ARCACHON

to Bordeaux

N650

D1

N10

Saucats

Facture

Arcachon

Pilat-Plage

D3

R. Eyre

D17

Firing Range

Belin

D111

Villandraut

St Symphorien

Sanguinet

Étang de Cazaux et de Sanguinet

Biscarrosse-Plage

Biscarrosse

Parentis

D43

Liposthey

Pissos

N10

Luxey

Military Area

Labouheyre

D44

Mimizan-Plage

Mimizan

N626

D38

N649

Mont-de-Marsan

D27

Léon

N10

N647

N132

N124

St Sever

N124

Vieux-Boucau

N124

Poyanne

Mugron

Soustons

Dax

Montfort

Hagetmau

Hossegor

N10

R. Adour

Œyreluy

D15

Moulin de Benesse

N647

Amou

N113

Capbreton

D33

D29

Sault-de-Navailles

Labenne

Port-de-Lanne

N117

Peyrehorade

monument

Sallespisse

Biarritz

R. Adour

Gave de Pau

Orthez

N117

Bayonne

Lacq

R. Nive

Gave d'Oloron

Lescar

km 0   10   20   30

miles 0   10   20

Pau

**Map 11**

cont. on map 10

Foix. Gaston Phoebus, whose nickname came from his bright yellow hair, was one of the most flamboyant characters of the day, maintaining a splendid and autocratic court. This is how Froissart depicts him at dinner:

> When he quitted his chamber at midnight for supper twelve servants bore each a large lighted torch before him, which were placed near his table and gave a brilliant light to the apartment. The hall was full of knights and squires; and there were plenty of tables laid out for any person who chose to sup. No one spoke to him at his table, unless he first began a conversation. He commonly ate heartily of poultry, but only the wings and thighs; for in the day-time he neither ate nor drank much. He had great pleasure in hearing minstrels, as he himself was a proficient in the science, and made his secretaries sing songs, ballads and roundelays. He remained at table about two hours; and was pleased when fanciful dishes were served up to him, which having seen, he immediately sent them to the tables of his knights and squires.
>
> In short, everything considered, though I had before been in several courts of kings, dukes, princes, counts, and noble ladies, I was never at one which pleased me more, nor was I ever more delighted with feats of arms, than at this of the Count de Foix. There were knights and squires to be seen in every chamber, hall and court, going backward and forward, and conversing on arms and amours. Everything honourable was there to be found. All intelligence from distant countries was there to be learnt; for the gallantry of the count had brought visitors from all parts of the world.

But there was also a darker side to his character: he killed his only son, on the suspicion that he was plotting to poison him, and had his brother assassinated.

With the removal of the court to Pau in 1464 the prosperity of Orthez declined, although a university continued there; and its sack by the Huguenots in 1569 was followed by plague. The university closed, and Orthez became a small provincial town. Only a few medieval houses survive, in the centre of the town and on the riverbank. The most notable are the house of Jeanne d'Albret at 39 rue Bourg Vieux, and the Hôtel de la Lune at 15 rue de l'Horloge, where Froissart is said to have stayed in 1388. Orthez's most striking monument is the fortified bridge, dating from the thirteenth century. It originally had two towers (like the Pont Valentré at Cahors), one of which remains intact, and outer defences on the southern side. The scene is only marred by the presence along the bank of the Gave de Pau of the railway, which runs between the bridge and the old houses to the north.

Two miles north of Orthez, on the N 647, a monument marks the site of the battle of Orthez in 1814, when Wellington defeated Marshal Soult in the penultimate engagement before the fall of Napoleon. The N 117 continues along the north bank of the Gave de Pau to **Peyrehorade**, where the sixteenth-century castle of Montréal, with four round towers at the corners of its keep, houses a good collection of furniture. But we turn north along the N 133, to St Sever. Ruined castles at Sallespisse and Sault de Navailles bear witness to the former prosperity of this country. Off the road, at Amon, is a little seventeenth-century château, said to have been designed by the architect Mansart. At **Hagetmau,** to the west of the town, is the crypt of St Girons, a place of pilgrimage since the ninth century. St Girons converted this part of Gascony in the fourth century; the abbey which bore his name was ruined in 1569, and the last traces disappeared in the nineteenth century, except for the crypt. This is now sheltered by a nondescript building; but it contains three powerful mid-twelfth-century capitals, showing an unknown saint being martyred, the story of Lazarus, and a frieze of men and birds. The central columns, which once surrounded the tomb of St Girons, were re-used from a classical building. In the town is the house where Wellington stayed after the battle of Orthez and before his final victory over Soult at Toulouse.

**St Sever,** on a hilltop overlooking the Adour valley, was once known as Cap-de-Gascogne, 'chief of Gascony', from its splendid position. Its abbey was vast and wealthy; and the present town seems to be built entirely around it, many of the seventeenth-century abbey buildings still being in use, such as the town hall and a number of private houses. The market hall is a disused church, not part of the abbey. But the focal point is the abbey church, despite its poor state of repair and the many vicissitudes it has undergone.

St Sever, like St Girons, was one of the apostles of Gascony, and his shrine became a monastery at some time in the seventh or eighth century. It was ruined in the ninth century and rebuilt in the eleventh, under a remarkable abbot, Gregory of Montaner, who held office for forty years, and was also Bishop of Lescar and Dax. His great church was damaged in the fifteenth and sixteenth centuries, and the apse and choir had to be extensively rebuilt in the seventeenth century. As at Aire sur l'Adour, the plan is typically Benedictine, with three apse chapels on the east side of each transept: the scale is very large, and the already elaborate row of arched openings that appears from the crossing is enriched by the tribunes at the end of each transept. Further, the apses increase in depth toward the centre. This profusion of vistas and pillars is studded with capitals, whose decoration alone would be enough to make the church remarkable. Most of them are ornamental; but the ornament is strikingly like that of Moslem Spain, and indicates that there was a lively exchange of ideas between the very different communities north and south of the Pyrenees. To the south of the west door is a striking figured capital, showing Salome dancing before Herod and receiving the head of John the Baptist. St Sever, too, was supposed to have been executed, which may explain the choice of subject.

From St Sever take the D 32 toward Dax. At Mugron a byroad leads to the château of **Poyanne**, once the home of Bernard de Poyanne, one of Henri IV's captains. It was rebuilt in the seventeenth century, and the laurels in the park, planted by Henri IV, cannot be seen from the road; it is now a monastery, and visitors are not admitted. Turn north along the D 7 to Tartas, and then toward Dax again on the N 124, and you come to the hamlet of **Lesgor,** on the edge of the Landes. It has a well-preserved defensive church, whose massive exterior is dotted with arrow-slits. A precarious staircase leads up to the defensive chamber below the roof, with its openings for archers to fire through; it is unchanged since it was built in the late thirteenth or early fourteenth century.

On the outskirts of Dax the first turning to the right after the junction with the N 647 leads to the little eleventh-century church of St Paul les Dax, on the hillside overlooking the town. On the outside of the apse are a series of simple but appealing bas-reliefs above a blind arcade. Starting to the south, the subjects are: the women at the Sepulchre, the Holy Trinity, three monsters, the Last Supper, the betrayal of Christ, the Crucifixion, Samson astride a lion, St Veronica, a dragon, and an allegory of heaven. They date from the eleventh century and from about 1120, the older pieces being taken from another building, and are among the earliest examples of the Romanesque style.

**Dax** itself has been famous for its hot springs since Roman times, when it was known as *Aquae Tarbellicae*, after the Tarbelli, an obscure Gaulish tribe who lived in this area. Of its Roman section only a part of the ramparts remains, set in a park on the south bank of the Adour, near the main source of the waters or *Fontaine Chaude*. It was an English stronghold in the Middle Ages, and was one of the last places to fall into French hands, in 1451. The Gothic cathedral built during the English rule was demolished as unsafe in the seventeenth century and replaced by a pleasant but unremarkable classical building. However, the fine north doorway of the old cathedral was built into the north transept. Its style is that of the northern cathedrals, and only at Bordeaux and Bayonne is there anything similar in the south-west. It shows Christ and the apostles, with a very mutilated Last Judgment on the tympanum. The contrast of Gothic and classical is surprising, and enhances the richness of the sculpture.

On the D 6 south-west of the town is the church of St Vincent de Xaintes, a nineteenth-century building which incorporates a Gallo-Roman mosaic of geometric pattern taken from a villa or temple which was on the same site. A byroad to Oeyreluy, where the church has a rustic Romanesque portal, leads to the **Moulin de Benesse,** on a hilltop outside Benesse-les-Dax. From the ruins of the mill the foothills of the Pyrenees unfold in the sun, a fertile landscape very different from either the wastes of the forests of the Landes to the north or the mountains to the south. The D 24 brings us back to the Pau-Bayonne road at Peyrehorade, the confluence of the two rivers that run along the northern edge of the Pyrenees, the Gave de Pau and Gave d'Oloron. At Port de Lanne we cross the Adour, which in turn joins the two Gaves near this point; but the road swings north of the river and we only rejoin it at Bayonne.

**Bayonne** lies on the south bank of the river, which is here only five miles from the sea and is nearly quarter of a mile wide. It has been an important town since Roman days, because it commands the main road along the western edge of the Pyrenees, and is also a useful port. It was used as a port by the Romans, who called it 'Lapardum'. Its history is obscure until the twelfth century, when it reappears under the name of Baiona; it was part of the lands of Eleanor of Aquitaine in 1152 when she married Henry II of England, and it remained in English hands until 1451; as a trading centre, it did much business with England, and the town also enjoyed considerable freedom, having its own elected government from 1215 on. It ranked with Bordeaux as a base for the English administration, and prospered under English rule. But in 1451 the town was besieged by the Count of Foix and by Dunois, Joan of Arc's companion-in-arms. The resistance was brief, and after a fortnight terms were agreed: the citizens of Bayonne clearly realised that the English cause was

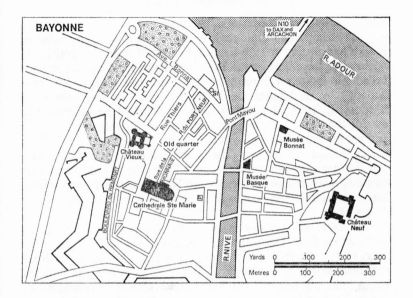

failing, and as if political realism was not enough to convince them
local legend has it that a miracle occurred after the terms had been
arranged. A white cross appeared in the sky, clearly seen by all for
half an hour. A contemporary chronicler recorded: 'And then the
townsmen who had surrendered and made terms the previous day,
whose banners and pennants bore red crosses, said that it was God's
pleasure that they should be French, and that they should bear white
crosses.'

Under the French Bayonne was transformed into a fortress.
Vauban built the citadel on the east bank between 1674–9, while in
the old town the old castle had been rebuilt in the late fifteenth
century, and to the south-east the Château Neuf was completed in
1489. This triangle of fortresses bears eloquent witness to Bayonne's
new strategic importance, on the frontier between the two great
powers of seventeenth-century Europe. It has withstood fourteen
sieges, all unsuccessful, since 1451. Wellington failed to take it in
1813, and the garrison only surrendered in 1814 at the fall of Paris.
But this military golden age was not always matched by commercial
prosperity. After 1451, with the loss of the English market, the
town's trade declined, and did not revive for two centuries. Its
modern resurgence dates from the 1720s; in 1784 it became a free
port; much of its eighteenth-century income came from the privateers

253

fitted out by local merchants. Bayonne was also the scene of a number of important diplomatic events in the long rivalry between France and Spain; in 1526 Francis I returned from his captivity in Spain after the defeat of the French at Pavia in 1525, and at once belied his famous comment on the battlefield ('All is lost save honour') by repudiating the treaty by which he had gained his freedom. In 1808, at the now vanished Château de Marracq just outside the town, Napoleon deposed the Bourbon dynasty of Spain and put his brother Joseph on the Spanish throne instead, an action which, instead of containing the opposition to the French in Spain and Portugal, brought resistance into the open, and led to the first serious French military reverses since Napoleon's campaigns began. Six years later Joseph was back in Bayonne with the English army on his heels.

The centre of Bayonne is relatively small, and can easily be explored on foot. The cathedral and the Château Vieux mark the heart of the medieval town, though the latter has been much re-modelled, and is now a block of flats. The cathedral was founded about 1140, but this original Romanesque church was damaged by fire in 1258 and struck by lightning in 1310. The rebuilding was carried out in the Gothic style from 1258 on, beginning with the cloisters and the chapels round the apse. By the end of the sixteenth century the new cathedral was complete except for the north tower. This was added, and the towers crowned with steeples, by Boeswillwald, Viollet-le-Duc's pupil, in the 1880s. The overall effect is re-strained; proportion is more important here than decoration, though some of the windows have elegant tracery. The clerestory is particularly deep, and the apse has an unusual double line of windows. One good window, dated 1531, is to be found in the chapel dedicated to St Jerome. The roof bosses are interesting: that of the south transept shows a fourteenth-century ship, while in the aisles the English leopards appear several times. The former doorway into the cloister, now leading into the sacristy, is the only one to retain its sculpture; this depicts the Last Judgment. The cloister itself, much restored, has a striking tracery design.

North of the cathedral is the sixteenth-century quarter of the town: the rue de la Monnaie leads to the rue de Port Neuf, whose low arcades are busy with shoppers. Here, too, are expensive cafés and salons-de-thé, where one of Bayonne's specialities is served: chocolate. Chocolate was at first a Spanish monopoly, imported from the New World, and Bayonne was the first town in France to become a centre for trading in it. The early spiced chocolate, scarcely a sweet drink at all, has given way to the more familiar blend; the art of making it is said to have been brought by Jewish refugees from Spain.

West of the cathedral the boulevard de Rimpart runs inside the ring of fortifications to the Porte d'Espagne, the remains of an eighteenth-century gate, and then round to the banks of the river Nive. On the far bank, opposite the old quarter, is the **Musée Basque**. Most of the inhabitants of Bayonne today are of Basque blood, and Bayonne is the centre of the French Basque territory, stretching away to the south and east. Most of this lies outside the scope of the present book, and the Basques and their culture are indeed too complex a subject to compress into a paragraph, with their mysterious non-Indo-European language (of which it is said that the Devil tried to learn it, and after seven years had mastered only three words). Their fierce independence is a serious and often tragic political force in Spain today. For a traveller going further south the Musée Basque is a good introduction to their customs and traditions: its displays are often unselective and rambling; some of the material is intriguing – especially the early tombstones, with their distinctive shapes and Basque inscriptions, and the display on the manufacture of walking sticks – while other parts, such as the section devoted to the Basque national game, pelota, are strictly for the connoisseur.

Round the corner, facing on to the Adour, is the **Musée Bonnat**, Bayonne's art gallery. It is principally the private collection of Léon Bonnat, the painter, who left it to the town. It is not particularly well-displayed, and the labelling is very poor. Bonnat himself was a portrait painter, and the collection reflects his interest, from the Egyptian and classical collection on the ground floor, which is almost entirely statues or busts, to the examples of his own work on the second floor. The best items are on the first floor: an Ingres of a girl bathing, a sketch of Napoleon by David, a crayon by Leonardo da Vinci, a Goya self-portrait and two portraits by Sir Thomas Lawrence, of Henry Fuseli and Carl Maria von Weber. There are also Van Dyck, Rubens and Rembrandt sketches. Bonnat's own portraits are mostly 'society' pieces, a French equivalent to John Singer Sargent. The collection of drawings, of which there are over 2,000, is displayed in rotation, and the catalogue of the museum covers only the paintings, sculpture and *objets d'art*.

From Bayonne we turn north, away from Biarritz and the different world of the Basque country. The N 10, through the heart of the

Landes, is our quickest route to Bordeaux, but the coast road, which branches off at Labenne, is much more varied. The first two towns are now a continuous resort, **Capbreton** and **Hosségor**; at Hosségor the Côte d'Argent restaurant overlooking the lake is a good place for lunch, but these are not resorts with much to offer the passing traveller. It is better to turn inland – unless you must have a beach – and go to **Soustons**, where the Pavillon Landais on the edge of the lake, or La Bergerie, a villa in its own grounds, are both attractive.

Soustons is on the south-western edge of the Landes, which stretch east to Nérac, a hundred miles away, and north to Bordeaux, sixty miles away. Its soil is poor and sandy, and until the nineteenth century the lakes along the sea-coast were salt-water lagoons, infested by malaria mosquitoes, while the countryside became a huge marsh in winter, because of a layer of tufa just below the surface through which water could not drain. The inhabitants used to take to stilts during this time of year, as the only means of crossing this half-submerged landscape. Along the shore the sand dunes defied any attempts at settlement or agriculture; the scale on which they moved can be realised by looking at a map and tracing the course of the Adour river over the centuries. In the early Middle Ages it flowed out at Capbreton; but in AD 907 the mouth moved north to Vieux Boucau. In the twelfth century it began to turn south, but two hundred years later it was flowing out at Vieux Boucau again. Its course was finally fixed by a man-made canal cutting through the dunes west of Bayonne in 1578.

In the late eighteenth century the engineer Nicholas Brémontier succeeded in devising a system of plantation which fixed the dunes along the shore, by planting marram grass and pines. From 1801 on he found a system for stabilising the inland dunes by planting broom, reeds and pines under a protective screen of brushwood. From 1855 François Chambrelent succeeded in draining the marshes, and despite opposition from the shepherds the pine forests took over the Landes almost completely. Now the province is a very rich one, its economy based on the products of the pine forest: timber, resin, paper, turpentine. Its landscape is monotonous, the roads often straight strips of tarmac vanishing into the distance beneath a slit of blue sky in the dark grey-green of the forest. Here and there the traditional half-timbered, single-storeyed Landais houses still appear, but it is one of the least populated areas of France.

The coastal strip, once the least attractive of all, now has a relatively high population. Its scenery, too, is more varied, with the lakes, such as those at Soustons and Léon, and the high coastal dunes. It is slowly being developed for holiday-makers, though the prevailing Atlantic winds and strong currents close inshore are not ideal for sunbathers and swimmers. Indeed, you are unlikely to see such vast spaces of empty sand – over a hundred miles of it – anywhere else in Europe. The occasional beach resorts are usually ramshackle affairs, open in July and August only. Inland, the little village of Léon offers a little variety, but otherwise there is nothing of interest until we reach Mimizan and Mimizan Plage. **Mimizan** has the ruins of a Benedictine abbey; a thirteenth-century tower emerges from the dunes, which overwhelmed the town in the eighteenth century. This was one of the few shelters for pilgrims who fought their way through this inhospitable country en route for Compostela in Spain. Beyond Mimizan the coast becomes an army testing centre for short-range missiles, while inland the derricks of the Parentis oilfield appear on the Étang de Biscarrosse.

**Arcachon** presents a very different aspect. After Pyla-Plage, with the highest sand dune on the coast, we are no longer on the edge of the Atlantic, but on the shore of the relatively sheltered lagoon of the Bassin d'Arcachon, fed by the river Leyre (whose current prevents the silting-up of the mouth). Like the forests of the Landes, Arcachon is a creation of the nineteenth century. Before then the bay had been famous (and still is) for its oysters, which Rabelais praised in the sixteenth century. In the 1850s a railway was built to Arcachon, which was developed by the railway owners as a popular summer resort; the next decade it was also developed as a wintering place, the villas sheltering behind the high dunes south-west of the town. Connoisseurs of seaside architecture will have a field-day here, starting with the Moorish casino in the centre of the town; there is something in almost every conceivable manner, from Louis XIV châteaux to Edwardian fantasy. The harbour, to the east, is now filled with yachts rather than fishing boats, while the promenade with tamarisk trees runs along the main beach. If you are feeling affluent Chez Boron will give you an excellent choice of the local sea-food.

# Chapter 18

# Western Guyenne

✤

When in the thirteenth century the English lands in France began to dwindle, the vast province of Aquitaine was quickly reduced to a narrow strip of territory stretching east from Bordeaux to the edge of the Massif Central. This area became known as 'Guyenne', and there was a province of that name until the Revolution in 1789. It was a diverse area, with no particular unity, and lacking the almost nationalist feeling of the Gascons for Gascony. Its heart was the region just east of Bordeaux, from Libourne to the edge of the Landes and west to Bergerac, the land lying between the Dordogne and the Garonne before they meet near Bourg.

From Arcachon we skirt the Bassin d'Arcachon and come to Facture, where a left turn down the D 3 to Belin, and the D 111 east beyond Belin, brings us thirty miles east across the Landes to **Villandraut**. It is dominated by its castle, one of the most splendid ruins in the region. It was built by Pope Clement V, who was born at Villandraut in about 1264. He was one of the few popes to be elected to the Holy See without first becoming a cardinal, as he was only Archbishop of Bordeaux when he was chosen in 1305. Two years later the papal court moved to Avignon, and Clement, willingly or unwillingly, became almost entirely dependent on the French king, at whose behest he suppressed the order of the Templars in 1312, despite the fact that no ecclesiastical court had found them guilty of heresy. He died two years later, having secured his family's fortune by giving his relations many church offices; but the Church itself he left much weakened by the move to Avignon and his own extravagant spending. Villandraut is a residence for a secular prince, not a ruler of the Church, and Clement V was the forerunner of the Medici prince-popes of the fifteenth and sixteenth centuries. It is rectangular, with a moat (now dry) and outer curtain walls; its six towers give it a formal silhouette, because it is built in open country. Here a four-square plan can be used without any modification to fit the difficulties of the site, and the result is very different from the castles of the Dordogne perched on their cliff sites.

South of Villandraut is **Uzeste**, whose church was endowed by Clement V, and it is where he is buried. The impressive Gothic building is nearer to a cathedral than a parish church, but this is the result of papal patronage. His mutilated effigy in white marble is behind the high altar. The plan is that of the cathedrals at Auch and Condom, nave and side-aisles ending in a choir with an ambulatory and chapels radiating from the apse, but without a crossing. This scheme preserves the effect of height and length beloved of Gothic architects, while the Romanesque ground-plans emphasise space and volume and the transepts are often as broad as the nave. There is a fine Coronation of the Virgin over the south porch.

By way of contrast to Uzeste, go to the little church at **Préchac**. On the edge of a vast open grassy square, its nave is encased in sixteenth-century aisles; but the outside of the east side has survived untouched. It is very simple, with tall engaged columns reaching up to simple capitals and narrow arches; in the centre the east window is marked by two columns set in the window frame. All this is eleventh-century, its restrained mass and curving lines nearly complemented by two flanking twelfth-century additions. In its simple harmony it is almost a match for Uzeste's much more contrived effects.

South-east of Préchac a road off the D 9 leads to the Moulin de Caussarien, on the river Ciron, which flows through a wooded canyon at this point; there are walks for some distance along the riverbank.

**Bazas**, on the D 11 from Villandraut, is a town of Roman origin. The father of Ausonius (see p. 97) came from Bazas, and it remained until the fourteenth century an important place, ruled by its bishops. Not surprisingly, the cathedral is the focal point of the town, which is set in a broad irregular square sloping up to the great Gothic portal. This was the first part to be completed of a new cathedral begun in 1233 by the then bishop; but the rest of the plan was too ambitious and work had to be suspended. In 1306 Guillaume de la Mothe (Clement V's nephew, builder of Roquetaillade) became bishop, and work was resumed, completing the nave, apse and chapels in a style related to that of the Gothic cathedrals of the north. Severely damaged by the Huguenots in 1576, it was saved from total destruction (for a ransom of 10,000 crowns) and rebuilt by Arnaud de Pontac, his nephew and grand-nephew between 1576 and 1635; the same plan and style were retained. During the Revolution damage was confined to the monuments and furnishings, so that the cathedral appears today much as it was in the seventeenth century. The interior, lacking its original glass and darker than the

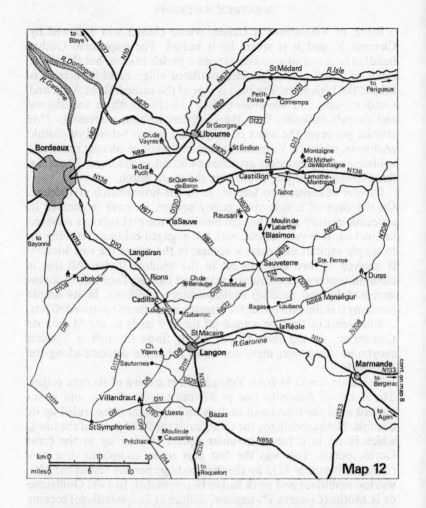

cont. on map 8

Map 12

cathedral at Auch, to which it is otherwise similar, leaves only an impression of cavernous space after the bright light of the square outside. The portal, with its wealth of statues – there were originally 286 – is by far the most accomplished part of the cathedral: below a façade of periods ranging from the late fifteenth to early eighteenth centuries the three doorways unfold their riches. To the left, the outer vault shows the story of the Temptation and expulsion from Eden, followed by five wise and five foolish virgins (instead of the usual seven) and, on the third vault, the story of Cain and Abel.

A line of angels and a line of popes complete the vaulting, while the tympanum depicts the life of St Peter.

The central portal represents the Last Judgment, with rows of the different ranks of heaven on the vaults: confessors, martyrs, prophets, angels. The bands of the tympanum show Christ in Majesty flanked by the Virgin and St John (to whom the church is dedicated); below, souls are weighed and sent to paradise or hell, with Leviathan ready to swallow the damned on the right; below this is the resurrection of the dead, and on the lintel the story of John the Baptist, marred by a sixteenth-century statue of him cut into the line of figures.

The right-hand doorway, like that on the left, was altered in 1537 to allow for a buttress. The outer vaults, with the signs of the zodiac, were cut into at both ends, and the third vault, the tree of Jesse, was also damaged. The next vault and the tympanum show the life of the Virgin, ending with her death and coronation. All this is carried out in a style which has much of the manner of Romanesque. The figures are upright and formal, and there is little of the individuality of northern Gothic: perhaps the most important concession to the new style is the elongation of some figures.

On the other side of the square, the rue Fondespan, with late medieval houses, leads to the Porte du Gisquet, the one remaining gateway of the ring of ramparts which surrounded the town until the late eighteenth century. In the rue Fondespan the Hôtel du Lion d'Or serves two famous local dishes which are not always easy to find: lampreys and frogs' legs. Lampreys, which figure in so many accounts of medieval banquets, have a meaty rather than fishy flavour, and make an excellent stew; though it is hard to imagine anyone becoming so enamoured of them as to die of a surfeit of them, as Henry I is supposed to have done.


We take the N 132 northwards, and turn left for the castle of **Roquetaillade**, built by Clement V's nephew in 1306 beside the ruins of an earlier castle, which still survive; these include a battlemented gateway tower. Roquetaillade's style is similar to that of Villandraut, but it is on a smaller scale. Instead of a massive outer curtain wall the main strength of the building is its central keep. Far from being a ruin it was extensively rebuilt by Viollet-le-Duc in the mid-nineteenth century, and is still inhabited. If you are lucky 'Mlle la propriétaire' herself may show you round. Viollet-le-Duc left the basic shape of the château unchanged, but completely redecorated it and provided much of the furniture. Very little has been altered since then, and as a result it is a superb example of his work, from the remodelled battlements to the wall and ceiling paintings and the 'Gothic' furniture. One of the beds has a canopy supported on two croziers, an allusion to Cardinal de la Mothe as the original builder; another bedroom, once a coal-cellar, has a reminder of this, a rat carved below the statue of the Virgin and Child on the chimneypiece. There is a miniature drawbridge, complete with counter-weights, which one person can work; and there is a perfect Victorian kitchen, full of gleaming copper stoves, iron ranges and stoneware sinks. Set in open parkland, Roquetaillade is welcoming and hospitable compared with Villandraut's grandiose decay.

From Roquetaillade the D 125 takes us to **Sauternes,** whose vineyards grow on gently rolling chalky hills facing north. Somehow it does not look as though it was the home of the most famous sweet white wines of France; but the names on the signposts reassure us. Château Yquem itself is marked by a simple stone pillar carved with a coat of arms and the one word, 'YQUEM'. This golden, liqueurlike wine continues to fetch the dramatic prices that it first began to sell for in the mid-nineteenth century, and is now, alas, beyond the pockets of all but the very few; but at a more reasonable price there is still Rieussec, Climens or Suduiraut to be had which can almost equal Yquem itself. The secret of the production of Sauternes is that the grapes are left on the vines after they have ripened, and the leaves are removed. The sunlight falls on the grapes and a mould forms on them, the *pourriture noble* or *Botrytis cinerea,* which also produces the finest German hocks. (The Germans, being more down-to-earth in such matters, describe such wines as '*Trockenbeerenauslese*', 'made from selected dried grapes', which is a very fair summary of the process.) The skill lies in the picking and sorting of the grapes according to their degree of over-ripeness, and in handling the very concentrated must after it has been pressed. The whole 'over-ripening' process takes only a few days, and is even more susceptible to bad weather than ordinary vintage operations; and the quantity produced is naturally reduced by the shrivelling of the grapes – hence the relative rarity of these wines.

While on the subject of wine, the two other wine districts of this part of the world must be mentioned. Graves, stretching from north of Bordeaux, where the Médoc ends, to east of Langon, produces more white wine than red, but for quality its red wines are superior. Ordinary white Graves tends to be insipid, though the wines made only from Sauvignon grapes – 'cépage Sauvignon' – can be as pleasing as those from the Loire for everyday drinking. At the head of the red wines is Château Haut-Brion, 'associated with' the five *premiers grands crus* of the Médoc. It was known in England in the seventeenth century: both John Locke, the philosopher, and Samuel Pepys mention it in their diaries – Pepys records on 10 April 1663 how at the Royal Oak in Lombard Street he drank 'a sort of French wine called Ho Bryan, that hath a good and most perticular taste that I never met with'. Its position, in the suburbs of Bordeaux, and a succession of indifferent owners, led to part of the estate being sold off for building in the 1930s; but the recent vintages have reputedly done much to restore it to its old pre-eminence. The other Graves châteaux are of lesser standing: some, such as Domaine de Chevalier, make very fine examples of both red and white wine. Entre-Deux-Mers, across the river, stretches from just east of Bordeaux to Langon, and has no particularly distinguished names; this is from where the bulk of the wine sold under a simple 'Bordeaux' label comes.

From Yquem, the D 8 brings us west to Langon, a commercial centre for the wine trade, where we cross the Garonne. The north bank of the Garonne toward Bordeaux offers a number of castles and churches. At Gabarnac, on the hills above the river, there is a west door on an otherwise plain church, which, despite considerable weathering, has some unusual details, particularly of soldiers and knights. Loupiac has a Romanesque church, severely restored by Abadie, but which retains its striking design of a projecting doorway with an arcade and pediment above. Just below this pediment is a group of figures, Christ and the eleven apostles. The façade as a whole has a strongly classical flavour, perhaps inspired by some Roman building which had survived nearby. Cadillac is grouped round the huge barrack-like château of the dukes of Epernon; the interior is being restored, but contains a magnificent series of monumental chimneypieces dating from the early seventeenth century. Rions, on the riverbank, has a late-fourteenth-century gate-way in very good condition, and part of its ramparts, including a square corner-tower; and Langoiran has a thirteenth-century castle, ruined in the civil wars of the mid-seventeenth century. At Benauges, north of Cadillac, is another ruined castle, which has a long curtain wall and two massive fourteenth-century towers. It was taken from a rebellious baron by Henry III in 1253, and later belonged to the dukes of Épernon, who rebuilt it in the seventeenth century; the balustrades and living quarters are of this period.

At Cadillac cross the Garonne and take the N 113 toward Bordeaux, turning left after ten miles to **Labrède**. The château (open in summer 10–12, 14.00–18.00, except on Tuesdays; in winter only at weekends and on holidays) is to the left of the road, set in an eighteenth-century park in the English style, with an avenue of trees leading up to the medieval buildings within the moat. Montesquieu, famous as an essayist, lived here; he was a great lover of things English, a friend and travelling companion of Lord Chesterfield, and the park was avowedly based on English models. Trained as a lawyer, he preferred the solitude of his estates to the busy life of Bordeaux, and spent most of his life here. The château had been built by his ancestors in the fifteenth century, and indeed still belongs to his descendants. Montesquieu's room is kept as it was in his lifetime, and the library, on a suitably vast scale, is filled with his books; he claimed that he had never suffered from any depression which an hour's reading had not cured. His magnum opus was the *Esprit des Lois*, published in 1748, an examination of laws and their relationship to society which led him to suggest widespread reforms in the French State and contributed to the thinking of the leaders of the Revolution forty years later. It had considerable success in England, and Montesquieu, who also sold wines from his estate to England, wrote to a friend that the fame of his book was helping sales of his wine!

Retracing our steps through Cadillac and Loupiac we come to the *bastide* of **St Macaire**. The main road runs past the old town, which is enclosed by its thirteenth-century battlements and by the river, an island in time and space. Its stone-built houses are almost all sixteenth-century or earlier, and until recently the town was quietly decaying. Now some discreet restoration is in progress, but by and large there are corners as magical in their remoteness from the twentieth century as the streets of Collonges la Rouge (see p. 178). Even the river has moved away from the town, and the cliff to the south ends in meadows. The old market-place survives with its arcades, but the market has vanished, and there are no longer even shops around it. The church, St Sauveur, is to the south of the town. Once a priory, it had a troubled history of internal disputes, its monks between 1120 and 1163 being 'rebellious and disobedient'. The present church is late twelfth-century despite the survival of an earlier inscription recording the dedication of a previous church in 1040. The most important part is the east end, with its remarkable plan of three equal openings off the crossing, each describing a semi-circle. Those to north and south have only a blind arcade below and a single window; the western opening is appropriately more elaborate. The Gothic frescoes (lighting available) on the vaults were ineptly overpainted in 1825, but something of their original splendour comes through to show that they were of exceptional quality. The east end is also laden with *badigeon*, wall paintings in the worst nineteenth-century style. Properly restored, this could be a rival to any church in the area. Some of the capitals, difficult to read in the half-light, have striking scenes, notably a Daniel in the lions' den.

From St Macaire the road winds up and down the hills on the north bank of the Garonne to **La Réole**, a much-disputed stronghold in the Hundred Years' War, which still has a number of seventeenth- and eighteenth-century houses in its narrow streets. The Hôtel du Centre is a good, fairly basic place to stay: some of the bedrooms have a lovely view to the south, and the food is excellent at the price. In the middle of the old town is the market hall, a rare survival from the twelfth century, when it was built as the town hall, and formed part of the town's defences. A lively market has been held here for seven hundred years, below the battlements and arrow-slits of the upper storey.

The abbey, around which the town grew up (as at St Sever in Gascony), had many misfortunes in the Middle Ages: as a result, the abbey church, planned about 1200, was only completed (with a vault to the original plan) in the eighteenth century, at the same time that the abbey buildings (now offices) were put up. These contain some superb ironwork and two grand staircases, behind an austere exterior. From the square there is a view across the Garonne to the plains beyond. The same skill in ironwork, an echo of that at Bordeaux, is to be found in the balconies of the town's houses.

From La Réole the N 668 runs through attractive hilly country to **Monségur** and **Duras**, both former *bastides*. Duras has its arcaded market-place, and, on the end of the spur of hill on which the town is built, a castle which belonged to the niece of Clement V. It dates back to the twelfth century, but was partly transformed in the sixteenth and seventeenth centuries into a classical château. Restoration is in progress, and the result should be interesting, because the Renaissance parts look as though they are of excellent quality.

Returning to Monségur, we take the D 15 and D 127 to **Ste Ferme**, a surprisingly complete abandoned abbey in the middle of the countryside, with a small cluster of houses around it. The courtyard of the monastery, paved with huge flagstones, still stands beside the church, and the plan of the village still follows the medieval grouping. The church itself is spacious but gloomy, with a high, aisleless nave, rebuilt in the seventeenth century. The east end, with a choir and two chapels opening off the transepts, has a remarkable group of capitals; they are high up and difficult to see without binoculars, but repay the effort needed to make them out. In the north chapel the subjects are Daniel in the lions' den, Habakkuk and the angel, and David and Goliath. These are the finest of the group, the work of a master whose hand can also be seen at Rimons and Esclottes nearby. His individual style is decorated and simple at once, balancing the small upright figure of Daniel against the two lions, dancing with rage and impotence, or creating the mass of Goliath by spreading him round two sides of the pillar while David crouches in wait on the other. The other sculptures, by different hands, include a Christ washing the feet of the poor, and two figures in carnival masks in the south transept, also of high quality.

Between Ste Ferme and the road from La Réole to Castillon are three small churches which have imitations of the capitals at Ste Ferme, those at **Rimons** being the best, perhaps even from the same hand as the originals. At **Loubens** and **Bagas** David and Goliath reappear, but the figures are clumsy shadows of the original. Bagas also has a vivid fresco of the seven deadly sins, in a church which appears to be abandoned. In the valley below there is a fourteenth-century fortified mill.

North of Bagas **Sauveterre de Guyenne**, a *bastide* founded in 1281, has its four original gates and much of the market-place. A road to the west (the D 139) brings us to **Castelvieil**, whose humble church has a sumptuous doorway set in the south wall. Five broad arches springing from pillars carry – beginning with the outer arch – the signs of the zodiac, the combat of the vices and virtues, two teams of men apparently engaged in a tug of war who in fact represent the faithful united by faith, and, on the innermost arch, interwoven foliage. The signs of the zodiac are interspersed by the 'labours of the months', and in spite of the weathering caused by their exposed position the strong character of these scenes is still apparent: from left to right, January (Capricorn) sits at table; February (Aquarius) warms himself at a fire; March (Aries) prunes a vine; April (Taurus) seems to be a young girl; May (Gemini) is damaged, though for June (Cancer) the reaper has survived. July and August have been defaced, and only the presser of grapes can be made out for September. October, the fruit-picker, has a damaged Scorpio next to him. November (Sagittarius) is slaughtering a pig for the last scene, December's feast. Elsewhere on the doorway, between the main carvings on the arches and on the capitals, you will find stag-hunts, musicians, monsters and elaborate foliage. The capital in the middle of the right-hand group, showing a king ordering the death of a man, has sometimes been taken to refer to Henry II's part in the death of

Thomas à Becket; but as it appears next to a scene which is clearly
Salome with the head of John the Baptist it is much more likely to
be connected with that, and to show Herod ordering John the
Baptist's execution.

We return to the main road at Sauveterre, and continue north to
the abbey church of **Blasimon**. It is set in a group of cypresses by the
little river Gamage. The shadows of the trees screen the doorway
from the morning light, so this façade is best seen in the afternoon.
As the broken arch suggests, this dates from the last flowering of
Romanesque art: vigorous, well-rounded forms whose exuberance
almost overflows the framework in which they are set. The convoluted
foliage in particular seems to be shaped from wax rather than stone.
On the inner arch four angels adore a mandorla, from which the
figure of the Lamb is missing. Two bands of foliage separate this
from the combat of the vices and virtues: even though the virtues
are now headless, their long svelte figures with immaculate draperies
– particularly the figure at bottom right – are images not easily
forgotten, with a warmth and eloquence that Gothic sculpture only
rarely captured. On the outer edge of the arch hunters pursue their
quarry. The capitals below are weathered; one outstanding scene
depicts a dancer accompanied by two musicians. The two blind
arcades and the cornice above continue the richness of the decoration,
with the same suppleness in the handling of the ornaments which
distinguishes the work on the doorway.

A mile to the north is the ruined **Moulin de Labarthe,** built by the
monks of the abbey at Blasimon in the fourteenth century and later
fortified; when I was last there in 1974 there were signs that it was
at last being repaired. Although there were traces of the millpond and
sluices, and the wheel was still in place, it would be a major under-
taking to put it into anything resembling working order. A more
dramatic ruin, also being restored, is that of the castle at **Rauzan,**
four miles to the west. Built by Guilhem-Raimond de Gensac, one
of Edward I's captains in Aquitaine, in the early fourteenth century,
the round keep was rebuilt later in the century. Originally over a
hundred feet high, it lacks its upper storey. Although it is now
difficult to make out there is a similarity with Villandraut: the
irregular plan of Rauzan is due to the terrain on which it is built,
but details show that the same approach has been used. Just outside
the castle one of the houses has a remarkable doorway with Renaissance mermaids which looks as if it had come from the castle,
though there is no Renaissance work apparent there now.

Yet another ruin is that of the abbey of **La Sauve Majeure,** ten miles to the west on the N 671. This rich and famous foundation, patronised by the English kings, stood on the junction of two of the pilgrim roads to Compostela. Its history is obscure, but the evidence for its riches is in the buildings themselves, even in their ruinous state. The funds for the abbey church were raised in the second half of the twelfth century, and it was dedicated in 1231. Largely in the late Romanesque style, it had a Gothic roof-vault in the nave: there is no trace of Gothic in what we see today, save for the octagonal bell-tower which crowns the whole group and the bases of the vaults at the top of the pillars. The choir is severe by comparison with the rest of the building: here lay the body of St Gerard, founder of this abbey, who died at the abbey in 1095. To either side of the choir proper are deep chapels, with arcades opening on to the choir. The rotund pillars of these and their figured capitals seem almost voluptuous beside the puritan lines of the latter. To the north a little book of beasts has been compiled on the capitals: basilisks, griffins and sirens. The south side contains scenes from the Bible, notably the three Temptations of Christ in the wilderness, the work of a sculptor who knew the great masterpieces of Burgundy. Samson's story takes up three capitals, including a scene in which Delilah cuts off his hair with a formidable pair of shears; and the theme of Daniel in the lions' den, evidently popular in this region, produces two fierce toy lions and an inscrutable prophet. All this is carried out in a stiff and stilted style, deliberately old-fashioned. It is hard to believe that it is contemporary with or even possibly later than the free-flowing forms of Blasimon.

La Sauve's prosperity was brief, from the end of the twelfth century to the beginning of the fourteenth. When repairs were undertaken early in the sixteenth century they marked only a temporary halt to the decline in the abbey's fortunes, since its far-flung priories in England and Aquitaine had been lost. By the seventeenth century it was said that 'you went into most churches to receive the sacraments, but you needed to receive them before going to La Sauve'. In 1809 the vaults fell in, and only in recent years have the ruins been cleared and restored.

At the opposite end of the scale from La Sauve's grandeur is the little church at St Quentin de Baron, on the D 120 two miles to the north, with a single nave and no more than touches of decoration. The apse has pilasters which run to the height of the original roof, broken only by a cornice, below which is a mutilated bas-relief of the martyrdom of St Quentin. Inside, on the frieze, there is a striking figure of a monk holding a book inscribed *'Canta debe debe'*, roughly translated as 'You must sing' – perhaps a reminder to idle choristers!

A detour to the left along the N 136, and then along the D 20 toward Libourne, leads to the castle of **Le Grand Puch,** just to the left of the road. This square, early-fourteenth-century fortress has been extensively rebuilt and only the main mass of the walls is original. All the openings, except two little windows to the north, have been remodelled, and the roofline is now a nondescript mixture. Again, this is the work of allies of the English; one of the family was an important administrator under Edward III.

North of Le Grand Puch, on the bank of the Dordogne, is the **Château de Vayres,** rebuilt in the sixteenth century by Louis de Foix (designer of the Phare de Cordouan) on a site fortified since Roman times. Parts of the medieval castle survive, but the general appearance is Renaissance, with an arcaded *cour d'honneur.* More work was done at the end of the seventeenth century on the river front.

From St Quentin take the road to **Castillon,** known as 'Castillon-la-Bataille' because it was the site of the battle which marked the end of the Hundred Years' War in July 1453. Sir John Talbot, Earl of Shrewsbury, the veteran English commander, who had first been in action in France in 1419, was attempting to raise the siege of Castillon by making a foray from Bordeaux. The French forces were well-equipped and in particular had three hundred pieces of artillery. Talbot rashly attempted to take their camp, to the east of the town, on the riverbank.

> Talbot and his men now marched right up to the barrier, expecting to make an entry into the field; but they found themselves courageously opposed by a body of valiant men, well tried in war, which was surprising after the information they had received. Talbot was riding a small hackney, and remained in the saddle because of his age, but he ordered all the other riders to dismount. As they arrived the English marched under eight banners, those of England, Saint George, the Trinity, Lord Talbot and four others skilfully executed . . .
>
> The attack then began, with great show of valour and hard fighting on each side, and lasted for a full hour. At this point the Duke of Brittany's men, who had been sent to the King under the chief command of the Comte d'Étampes, were sent for to relieve the French who had laboured to defend the barriers. When they arrived with the Seigneur de Montauban and the Seigneur de la Hunodaie in command, the French, who had fought all day and

with renewed courage at the sight of these reinforcements, were able with the help of God and their own skill to turn the English back, and the Bretons fell upon them and trampled all their banners underfoot. In the camp there was such a noise of culverins and ribaudekins being loaded that the English were forced to flee. Many, however, were killed in the field, and Lord Talbot's hackney was struck down by a shot from a culverin and he was killed where he lay beneath the horse.

The English held out at Bordeaux until October, but without strong leadership and little support from home their cause was hopeless. But the English claim to French territory remained even after the loss of Calais in 1558; the English royal arms bore the fleur-de-lis of France, and English coinage the legend 'King of Great Britain, France and Ireland' until 1801.

The spot where Talbot was killed is marked by a small monument on the riverbank south-east of Castillon.

Continuing from there to Lamothe-Montravel, cross the N136 and take a side-road to St Michel-de-Montaigne and the castle of **Montaigne**. This was the home in the sixteenth century of Michel de Montaigne, whose *Essays* are the spiritual autobiography of a man of the Renaissance. The very word '*essai*', as the name of a short piece of prose, was his invention; it means literally a trial or attempt, and in them Montaigne tries to weigh up philosophical and moral topics which occur to him in the course of his reading. His motto was *Que sais-je?*, and this inquiring spirit is evident throughout. But he is not a sceptic: his conclusions are often optimistic, and there is an underlying belief in the value of human reason. Montaigne's home was a manor house rather than a castle; the wars of religion largely passed by this particular corner of France, though Montaigne himself was unwillingly involved in them in the 1560s at Bordeaux and elsewhere. Like Montesquieu a century later, Montaigne was a lawyer by profession, at Bordeaux, where he met Étienne de la Boëtie of Sarlat (see p. 197) who became his close friend and inspired the famous essay on friendship. But even when he had prospects of a career at court he hankered after the peace of his country home. If you visit it today, only the library tower remains of the original building. The rest decayed in the early nineteenth century, was rebuilt in imitation feudal style, but was then burnt down in 1885. Only the general plan remains the same.

The tower and the gardens are open to visitors. Inside the tower, the ground floor is occupied by a little chapel, placed next to the gateway as in many other châteaux. Above is Montaigne's bedroom, furnished only with a bed of the period brought from elsewhere. The famous library, too, is almost bare: a chair and table similar to those used by Montaigne, pictures and engravings, and a statue of Montaigne himself. But there is no trace of the thousand volumes that once stood, row upon row, around the walls: they were dispersed by Montaigne's daughter, and are now to be found scattered in libraries throughout the world, identifiable only by their owner's signature on the title page. The only real traces from Montaigne's day are the fifty or so inscriptions on the beams, now difficult to read, consisting of Greek and Latin quotations which had some special appeal for him. His own description is the only way to evoke what this room must once have been:

When at home I turn a little more often to my library, from which I can easily overlook my whole household. There I am above the gateway, and can see below me my garden, my farmyard, my courtyard, and most parts of my house. There I turn the pages now of one book, now of another, without order and without plan, reading by snatches. Sometimes I reflect, and sometimes I compose and dictate my reflections, walking up and down, as at present.

My library is in the third storey of a tower. On the first is my chapel, on the second a bedroom with ante-chambers, where I often lie to be alone; and above it there is a great wardrobe. Formerly this was the most useless part of the house, but now I spend most of the days of my life there, and most of the hours of the day. I am never there at night. Adjoining my library is a very neat little room, in which a fire can be laid in winter, and which is pleasantly lighted by a window. And if I were not more afraid of the trouble than of the cost – trouble which deters me from every kind of business – I could easily join to each side a gallery a hundred paces long and twelve paces wide on the same level. For I have found the necessary walls built for another purpose to the requisite height. Every place of retirement requires a room for walking. My thoughts go to sleep if I sit still. My mind does not work if my legs do not shake it up. Those who study without books are all in this plight.

My library is circular in shape, with no flat wall except that taken up by my table and chair; and, being rounded, it presents

271

me with all my books at once, arranged about me on five tiers of shelves. From this room I have three open views, and its free space is sixteen paces across. In winter I am there less continually, for my house is perched on a hill, as its name implies, and there is no room more exposed to the winds than this. It is a little difficult of access and out of the way, but this I like, both for the benefit of the exercise and for its keeping people away from me. It is my throne, and I try to rule here absolutely, reserving this one corner from all society, conjugal, filial, and social.

A small study opens off the library, decorated with scenes from Ovid's *Metamorphoses*, classical legends of the loves of gods and goddesses, by the same painter who worked in the chapel and elsewhere. Making your way down again, a path round the outside of the château leads to a viewpoint over the Forêt du Landais to the north, little changed in aspect since the days when it was one of Montaigne's 'three open views'.

To the north of Castillon the D 17 to St Médard brings us to two contrasting country churches. Cornemps is a casualty of the wars of religion, ruined by the Protestants in 1587 and never rebuilt. Only the choir was re-roofed, and has remained as an example of an untouched eleventh-century interior, simple yet with pleasing lines. **Petit-Palais** is also simple enough inside, but has a dazzling façade which looks like an Oriental jewel-casket. Nowhere is there a single, simple pillar: they are all grouped in pairs or threes, the arches are polylobed, and the window above the door even has a triple polylobed arch of which the ends are animals' heads. So often with these 'screen façades' the upper part has crumbled or some other alteration has been made; but Petit-Palais is intact, right to the cornice on the roofline. The village must surely owe its name to this extraordinary church, which does indeed look like a little palace.

On the road from Petit-Palais to St Émilion, the church of St **Georges de Montagne** is equally well preserved, but its plain late-eleventh-century lines are a world away from the exotic art of Petit-Palais: a sober bell-tower dominates the building, its succeeding storeys pierced by windows which decrease in size. The nave has a simple timber roof, and is built of rubble; only the bell-tower and apse are of dressed stone. There is a minimum of decoration: a bas-relief near the south door which is in a debased classical style, details here and there of cornices or friezes with a hint of ornament.

St Émilion has a striking and attractive site. It is built on the slope overlooking the Dordogne, which curves away in the distance, leaving a wide plain between the edge of the valley and the river. It is worth making a detour to approach it from the south, so that the road brings you up through the town. Whether there was a Roman settlement here seems uncertain: the town's real prosperity dates from the twelfth century, when the settlement which had grown up round a monastery (founded in the eighth century) was granted a charter of privileges by King John, in 1199. Loyal to the English cause until the last, it was taken immediately after the battle of Castillon, and its privileges removed. The town never regained its old stature, though it is now world-famous as the centre of one of the great wine-producing areas of Bordeaux.

The town walls survive more or less intact, sometimes built into later houses (except to the south). Then, just outside the walls, are the ruins of a Dominican convent; nearby, inside the walls is a twelfth-century house, said to have been a cardinal's palace. Only one of the gates and a watch-tower remain, both to the east of the town: the best-preserved part of the walls themselves is to the west. Inside the walls the atmosphere of a medieval town remains. Though there is little in the way of really well-preserved buildings or details, the older houses are built of silver-grey limestone or a pale orange stone, and recent new buildings have used the same materials, so the town remains a visual unity. To the west of the town is the collegiate church, with a twelfth-century nave and an impressive Gothic choir and transept. The main doorway and cloister are also good fourteenth-century work. South of this church is the bell-tower of the subterranean church, which rises high above the town and gives it a distinctive silhouette from the distance. From it there is a panorama as far as the abbey of La Sauve-Majeure to the south, Libourne to the west and the forest beyond Montaigne to the east. The square beside it offers a good roofscape of the town, its red-tiled houses clustered on the hillside.

To reach the **subterranean church** take the street leading out of the eastern side of the square and then turn right down a very steep lane, past the Logis de la Cadène (where you can lunch on a peaceful wistaria-shaded terrace). The entrance to the church is in the little square below. This was a natural cave, perhaps used as a temple in pagan times, which was enlarged and turned into a church from the ninth century on. The modern entrance is to one side of the original Gothic doorway, and passes through what may have been a funeral chapel, with a curious cupola: a false lantern opens above, and three bearded men holding hands are carved round the aperture. The low entrance gallery leads into the church itself, now very austere, with nothing but rows of rectangular pillars and a sixteenth-century altar. It was once painted in vivid colours, like the rock-churches of Greece and Turkey, but damp has destroyed the frescoes, leaving only a depressing green mould. Only a few bas-reliefs survive, notably two very Byzantine angels on the roof. With the original decoration, it must have been a most impressive and haunting shrine: now it seems forlorn and barn-like. The visit also includes the so-called hermitage of St Émilion himself, founder of the monastery here, and an early cemetery.

Returning up the hill and turning right, the street curves round to the Place du Cap-du-Pont. Here is the cloister and chapel of the Franciscan convent, ruined and overgrown; but one side of the cloister is more or less complete, though roofless, with simple yet attractive arcading. Equally ruinous is the royal castle, on the other side of the town. What remains has now been made safe, and there is a good view from the top. This is the keep built about 1237 by Henry III, four-square and old-fashioned for the period. The whole castle was little more than this simple tower, and a few outer defence works, designed to hold a garrison rather than to resist a siege.

From the castle, each year, the opening of the vintage is proclaimed with due ceremony by the *jurade* or town council of St Émilion. St Émilion's wines are slightly fuller than those of the Médoc: its two foremost vineyards, Ausone and Cheval Blanc, are ranked among the foremost clarets, and Cheval Blanc commands prices almost as astronomical as those paid for the *premiers grands crus* of the Médoc. (Château Ausone, incidentally, seems to have no real connection with Ausonius, whose vineyard was probably on the Gironde.) St Émilion has its own separate classification, which until recently caused not a little confusion to the amateur wine-buyer, since practically everything was labelled '*premier grand cru*'. These have now been reduced to eleven, though even the most distinguished, Ausone and Cheval Blanc, would have difficulty in ranking higher than 'deuxième' in the Médoc. The next area to St Émilion is that of Pomerol, which again produces full-bodied wines: of the Pomerol vineyards Château Pétrus has always enjoyed a high reputation, and in recent years has vied in price with the most expensive clarets.

**Libourne**, once on the main Paris–Bordeaux road, is one of the largest of the *bastide* towns, though only a tower of the old ramparts and the main square keep anything of their medieval appearance. It was founded by an English seneschal of Aquitaine, Roger de Leyburn, in 1265, and named Libournia after him. The fifteenth-century town hall was badly restored in the last century. Beyond Libourne is the minor wine-growing area of Fronsac, and just before St André de Cubzac, where the Paris–Bordeaux road now runs, is the church of **Lalande de Fronsac.** Beneath a timber porch, this has a most remarkable tympanum above the south doorway. This shows the first vision of St John in the Book of Revelation, the Son of Man amid the seven golden candlesticks. The outer vault carries a procession of the twelve apostles, hurrying toward the figure of Christ on the keystone with exaggerated, clumsy movements. This is the least polished piece of work in the whole of the Romanesque sculpture we have seen; but it has a rough vigour and simplicity which marks it as the work of a real artist.

# Appendix 1

# Food

❧

There is so much variety within the region – and so much good cooking to be found – that what follows is only a brief list of some of the particular specialities, arranged by area.

**Poitou** has no outstanding dishes, though the local goats' cheese (*chabichou*) made in the shape of small pyramids, is excellent.

**Saintonge** and the Atlantic coast down to Arcachon are famous for sea-food, chiefly shell-fish and some flat fish. The mussels and oysters of Marennes and the coast east of Saintes are outstanding: *mouclade*, mussels cooked in white wine and cream, is very rich and delicious. The *fruits de mer* on many menus are liable to arrive at your table live – oysters, limpets and winkles as well as some more exotic creatures – so be warned!

**Bordeaux** offers lampreys (an eel-like creature which preys on other fish); these are often cooked in red wine sauce and have an unexpected rich meaty flavour. Sturgeon and shad (*alose*) are caught in the Gironde. Steaks roasted over vine shoots have a delicate, almost scented flavour – much more interesting than the overworked 'entrecôte à la bordelaise' adopted by international hotels.

**Perigord** has truffles, rooted up by pigs in the January woods (well out of sight of tourists – or anyone else, for that matter). They are expensive luxuries, to be met with occasionally in an omelette, a chicken dish or a *sauce périgueux*. *Foie gras* is also in the luxury class, and even the delicious salad oil made from walnuts, *huile de noix*, is very expensive. (Do not confuse the latter with *crème de noix*, a quite unspeakably revolting liqueur.) *Confit d'oie*, a kind of potted goosemeat, I personally find rather dry and unexciting. *Terrine de marcassin*, made from wild boar, is justly famous.

**Limousin**, with a rich variety of local produce, has only one item to be singled out, *clafoutis*, a pudding made of a light batter with fruit such as cherries or gooseberries in it. Further south, **Agen** specialises in prunes of remarkable sweetness and flavour, **Bayonne** in chocolate in all its different forms.

It is always worth asking about particular local specialities – and remembering that in France, in the country districts at least, chickens have not yet lost their flavour, and that even a simple apple tart (*tarte aux pommes*), properly prepared, can be a great delicacy.

# APPENDIX 1

It may seem sacrilege to suggest any other wine than claret in an area centred on Bordeaux; but good claret is if anything even more expensive in France than in England, and the local regional wines usually offer better value. For white wine, apart from that brought down from the Loire, the wines marketed under the label **Sauvignon** (a type of grape, not a vineyard or region) are usually consistently pleasant to drink. **Cahors** produces a heavy red wine, often sold after being aged in cask as Vieux Cahors. The red wine of **Bergerac** is rather lighter, while **Monbazillac** (see p. 201) is a sweet white dessert wine. Further south, in the Landes, **Tursan** produces a good dry white wine of character.

## Appendix 2

# Hotels and Restaurants

❧

The list below is not intended to be a balanced or representative survey: those listed are simply places that I have eaten at or stayed at and have found pleasant. But standards can change quickly, and it is as well to check their standing in a current guide.

For planning a tour – because the list below is not complete in the sense of recommending somewhere in each major area – the red Michelin and the Guide Kléber-Colombes are the two basic reference books. None of those named are in the luxury class, but nor will they be particularly cheap! For outstanding expensive restaurants, see the Michelin guide: for cheap hotels, the *Guide des Relais Routiers* is probably the best. The *Logis de France* guide covers medium priced hotels and several of those which follow belong to this association. Michelin also publish a guide to camping and caravan sites.

(r = restaurant, or restaurant only recommended)

Agen: La Rigalette (to north of town, off Marmande road)
Arcachon: Chez Boron (r)
Barbezieux: Boule d'Or
Bazas: Lion d'Or
Cierzac: Moulin de Cierzac
Cognac: Logis de Beaulieu (to west of town)
Collonges la Rouge: Relais St Jacques de Compostelle
Durance: La Palombière (r)
Les Eyzies du Tayac: Les Glycines
Gourdon: Hostellerie de la Bouriane
Ile d'Oleron: Trois Chapons at St Georges d'Oleron (r)
Ile de Ré: St Hubert at St Martin de Ré (r)
Layrac: La Terasse (r)
Limoges: Jeandillou (to south of town on N 21 at Isle)
Montmorillon: Hôtel de France
Niort: Cloche d'Or (r)
Queyssac: Au Vin Paillé
Plaisance: La Ripa Alta
Poitiers: Le Chalet de Venise (2m south of town, at St Benoit on D 88)
Pons: Auberge Pontoise
Périgueux: Léon (r)
La Réole: Hôtel du Centre

Rocamadour: Sainte Marie
La Rochelle: Trianon et Plage
                    Bar André (r)
La Rochefoucauld: Vieille Auberge
La Roque-Gageac: Belle Étoile
St Émilion: Logis de la Cadène (r)
                    Thélème            (r)
St Saud Lacoussiere (nr Chalus) Auberge Vieux Moulin (r)
St Savin: Hôtel du Midi
Saintes: Brasserie Louis (r)
Sarlat: Hostellerie Meysset (to north of town)
Siorac: Scholly (r)
Soustons: La Bergerie
Surgères: Trois Piliers
Tremolat: Hôtel du Perigord (r)
Vivonne: La Treille (r)
Villeneuve de Marsan: Hôtel d'Europe (r)

## Appendix 3

# Bibliography

꙰

The best general history of the region, by a team of specialists, is *Histoire de l'Aquitaine*, ed. Ch. Higounet, Toulouse 1971.[1] Two good small books in the *Que sais-je?* paperback series are *Histoire de Poitou* by the distinguished scholar René Crozet (1970), and *Histoire de la Guyenne* by Charles Dartigue (1950).

The *Horizons de France* series, consisting of articles on the geography, history and culture of different provinces, are well-illustrated introductions to their subjects. The relevant volumes are *Visages de Poitou* (1965), *Visages de Aunis Saintonge Angoumois* (1967), *Visages de Limousin* (1966), *Visages de Gascogne* (1968), and *Visages de Guyenne* (1966).

On Romanesque architecture the series published by Zodiaque at the monastery press of La Pierre-qui-vire is outstanding, despite variations in the level of different volumes. The following volumes cover the area (though there is nothing on the area between the Garonne and the Pyrenees): Yvonne Labande-Maillefert, *Poitou Roman*, 1962 (recently replaced by Raymond Oursel, *Haut-Poitou Roman*, 1975, which appeared too late for me to use); François Eygun, *Saintonge Romane*, 1970; Charles Duras, *Angoumois Roman*, 1961; Pierre Dubourg-Noves, *Guyenne Romane*, 1969; Jean Maury, *Limousin Roman*, 1960; Jean Secret, *Périgord Roman*, 1968; Marguerite Vidal, *Quercy Roman*, 1969.

The rather less satisfactory *Dictionnaire des Églises de France* has a volume (III A) on Pyrenees, Gascogne (1967), which covers part of the area not yet described in the Zodiaque series. There are also, on a more technical level, two masterly works by René Crozet: *L'art roman en Poitou* (1948) and *L'art roman en Saintonge* (1971).

For castles and manor houses there is a useful little series of pamphlets, cheap and simply produced, published by *Nouvelles Editions Latines*, some on individual places such as the Château de Biron; the list is too long to give in full, but local booksellers will be able to help. Jean Secret's two pamphlets in this series on *Châteaux de Périgord*, and Henri Polge's *Châteaux du Gers* are particularly useful.

Other local histories include:

Colle, J. R. *Petite histoire de la Rochelle* (La Rochelle, 1971)

Delafosse, M. *Petite histoire de l'Ile de Ré* (La Rochelle, 1965)

Daras, Charles. *Anciens châteaux, manoirs et logis de la Charente* (Angoulême, 1968)

[1] Place of publication is Paris unless otherwise indicated.

Botillac, M. *Le pays d'Albret* (Vianne, 1972).

For 'impressions' of the region there are Freda White's books *Three Rivers of France* (London, 1952) and *Ways of Aquitaine* (London, 1968); Henry Myhill's *North of the Pyrenees* (London, 1973) is in a similar vein. On the Dordogne, there is Philip Oyler's *The Generous Earth* (London, 1950), a portrait of the region before it became a popular tourist area.

Some French guidebooks to the area should be mentioned. The Michelin green guides *Côte de l'Atlantique*, *Périgord* and *Pyrénées* cover most of the area, though there is nothing on the area between the Garonne and Pau. They are the best available guides to the region, and the present book could not have been written without them. The *Guides Bleus* are rather out of date, but for those who want facts they are indispensable. The two relevant volumes are *Poitou, Guyenne* and *Pyrénées, Gascogne*.

On special topics there is a useful if rather general book on *Roman France* by Paul Mackendrick (London, 1971).

On the prehistoric art of the Dordogne there is a general introduction by the Abbé Breuil, one of the pioneers of the subject: *Four Hundred Centuries of Cave Art* (Montignac, 1952).

On claret the best single book seems to me to be – and writing on wine is very much a matter of taste – E. Penning Rowsell, *The Wines of Bordeaux* (London, 1973). C. Cocks and E. Feret's classic handbook *Bordeaux et ses vins* (many editions) is interesting, though I have not seen an edition later than 1962; it describes and illustrates (in steel engravings) almost all the individual châteaux.

Finally, fiction: there are a number of candidates for inclusion here, from dialect novels to early Gide and Malraux, but I prefer to quote just two works. One is by a writer more revered by the French than by his own countrymen: Charles Morgan's *The Voyage* (London, 1939) set in the countryside near Cognac. The other is Eugène Fromentin's *Dominique*, a romantic novel whose scene is the coast near La Rochelle.

# Index

282

# INDEX